T0329970

The OECD and European Welfare States

GLOBALIZATION AND WELFARE

Series Editors: Denis Bouget, *MSH Ange Guépin, France*, Jane Lewis, *Barnett Professor of Social Policy, University of Oxford, UK* and Peter Taylor-Gooby, *Darwin College, University of Kent, Canterbury, UK*

This important series is designed to make a significant contribution to the principles and practice of comparative social policy. It includes both theoretical and empirical work. International in scope, it addresses issues of current and future concern in both East and West, and in developed and developing countries.

The main purpose of this series is to create a forum for the publication of high quality work to help understand the impact of globalization on the provision of social welfare. It offers state-of-the-art thinking and research on important areas such as privatisation, employment, work, finance, gender, and poverty. It will include some of the best theoretical and empirical work from both well established researchers and the new generation of scholars.

Titles in the series include:

Social Exclusion and European Policy
Edited by David G. Mayes, Jos Berghman and Robert Salais

Social Exclusion and European Welfare States
Edited by Ruud J.A. Muffels, Panos Tsakloglou and David G. Mayes

Restructuring the Welfare State
Globalization and Social Policy Reform in Finland and Sweden
Virpi Timonen

The Young, the Old and the State
Social Care Systems in Five Industrial Nations
Edited by Anneli Anttonen, John Baldock and Jorma Sipilä

The OECD and European Welfare States
Edited by Klaus Armingeon and Michelle Beyeler

The OECD and European Welfare States

Edited by

Klaus Armingeon

Chair of Political Science and Director, Institute of Policial Science, University of Berne, Switzerland

and

Michelle Beyeler

Research Assistant, Institute of Political Science, University of Zurich, Switzerland

GLOBALIZATION AND WELFARE

Edward Elgar

Cheltenham, UK • Northampton, MA, USA

Published by
Edward Elgar Publishing Limited
Glensanda House
Montpellier Parade
Cheltenham
Glos GL50 1UA
UK

Edward Elgar Publishing, Inc.
136 West Street
Suite 202
Northampton
Massachusetts 01060
USA

A catalogue record for this book
is available from the British Library

Library of Congress Cataloguing in Publication Data
The OECD and European welfare states/edited by Klaus Armingeon and Michelle Beyeler.
  p. cm.—(Globalization and welfare)
  1. Welfare state—Europe. 2. Public welfare—Europe. 3. Europe—Social policy. 4. Organisation for Economic Co-operation and Development. I. Armingeon, K. (Klaus) II. Beyeler, Michelle, 1974– III. Series.

JC479.O36 2004
361.6'5'094—dc22

2003056457

ISBN 978 1 84376 321 5

Typeset by Cambrian Typesetters, Frimley, Surrey
Printed and bound by CPI Group (UK) Ltd, Croydon, CR0 4YY

Contents

Contributors

Santiago Álvarez, Professor at the Economics Department, University of Oviedo.

Blanca Ananiadis, Associate Professor at the Department of Social Sciences, University of La Verne, Athens.

Klaus Armingeon, Professor and Director at the Institute of Political Science, University of Berne.

Fabio Bertozzi, Research Assistant at the Institute of Political Science, University of Berne.

Michelle Beyeler, Research Assistant at the Institute of Political Science, University of Zurich.

Harmen Binnema, Research Assistant at the Department of Political Science, Vrije Universiteit Amsterdam.

Eero Carroll, Researcher at the Swedish Institute for Social Research, Stockholm University.

Paolo Graziano, Research Assistant, Bocconi University.

Ana M. Guillén, Professor in Sociology at the University of Oviedo.

Lars Bo Kaspersen, Associate Professor at the Department of Sociology, University of Copenhagen.

Nanna Kildal, Research Director, Stein Rokkan Centre for Social Studies, University of Bergen.

Pekka Kosonen, Senior Researcher Fellow at the Department of Sociology of Law, University of Helsinki.

Stein Kuhnle, Professor at the Department of Comparative Politics, University of Bergen.

Nick Manning, Professor at the School of Sociology and Social Policy, University of Nottingham.

Martin Marcussen, Associate Professor at the Department of Political Science, Copenhagen University.

Séamus Ó Cinnéide, Jean Monnet Professor at the Centre for Applied Social Studies, National University of Ireland, Maynooth.

Bruno Palier, 'chercheur CNRS' at CEVIPOF, Sciences po Paris.

Philippe Pochet, Director of the Observatoire social européen, Belgium.

Paul Ryan, Lecturer at the Department of Social Sciences, Dublin Institute of Technology.

Marina Serré, PhD in Political Science from the Université Paris 1.

Maria Svaneborg, Research Assistant at the Graduate School of Political Science, University of Copenhagen.

Reimut Zohlnhöfer, Assistant Professor at the Institute of Political Science, University of Heidelberg, Germany.

Jan Zutavern, Research Assistant at the Institute of Political Science, University of Berne, Switzerland.

Abbreviations

ALMP	Active labour market policy
AOW	General Pensions Act (Netherlands)
ATA	Automatic Inflation-Indexation Wage System (Greece)
ATP	Public occupational superannuation (Sweden)
CDU/CSU	Christian Democratic Party (Germany)
CSC/ACV	Christian trade unions in Belgium
EC	European Community
ECU	European Currency Unit
EDRC	Economic and Development Review Committee (OECD)
EEA	European Economic Area
EES	European Employment Strategy
EMU	European Monetary Union
ESRI	Economic and Social Research Institute (Ireland)
EU	European Union
FDP	Liberal Party (Germany)
FGTB/ABVV	Socialist trade unions in Belgium
GATT	General Agreement on Tariffs and Trade
GDP	Gross Domestic Product
GNP	Gross National Product
HRG	*Hochschulrahmengesetz* (legal frame for higher education) (Germany)
IKA	Social Insurance Organisation (Greece)
IGO	Intergovernmental Organisation
ILO	International Labour Organization
IMF	International Monetary Fund
NAPs	National Action Plans
ND	New Democracy Party (Greece)
NEC	National Employment Commission (Norway)
NESC	National Economic and Social Council (Ireland)
NGO	Non-governmental organisation
NHS	National Health Service (UK)
OECD/OEEC	Organisation for Economic Co-operation and Development
OGA	Farmers' Social Insurance Organisation (Greece)
OLIS	Online Information Service

PASOK	Panhellenic Socialist Movement (Greece)
PISA	Programme for International Student Assessment
PSBR	Public Sector Borrowing Requirement
PvdA	Labour Party (Netherlands)
R&D	Research and Development
RMI	Revenu Minimum d'Insertion (Minimum Insertion Income)
SDP	Social Democratic Party (Germany)
SEV	Federation of Greek Industries
SPD	Social Democratic Party (Sweden)
UK	United Kingdom
VVD	People's Party for Freedom and Democracy (Netherlands)
WTO	World Trade Organization

Acknowledgements

The idea for this study developed during the regular meetings of Working Group 1 of the COST Action 15 'Reforming Social Protection Systems in Europe'. The task of this working group is to explore the linkages between globalisation, European integration, and social protection systems changes. In this book we focus on the link between national policies and ideas promoted by international organisations. Our aim is to describe and analyse the development of OECD ideas concerning national social policies, and to assess their possible impact on national welfare reforms in 14 countries. Such a goal would have been difficult to achieve by a national research team. Accordingly, this research benefits greatly from an international network, bringing together social policy experts from different countries. COST stands for 'European Co-operation in the field of Scientific and Technical Research' and is supported by the European Union. We have benefited from the co-operation network established by this research platform – and are grateful for the financial support. We also thank the Swiss National Science Foundation (SNF), which provided additional financial support for a meeting of the research group held in Berne. In addition the editors are grateful to the SNF, which funded their research project on the interplay of national and supranational institutions ('Critical Junctures'). This project is closely linked to the research question of this book and it provided us with resources and opportunities to contribute to the analysis of the OECD.

Many thanks go to Daniel Kselman, Merike Blåfield, and Carina Blåfield for copy-editing the contributions of non-native English speakers, to Edward Elgar for editorial support, and especially to Beatrice Leisibach for preparing the manuscript for publication. Our greatest thanks go to the contributors to this volume. Without their commitment and considerable investment of time and resources, this joint research project would not have been possible.

Klaus Armingeon and Michelle Beyeler
Berne and Zurich, July 2003

1. Introduction: a comparative study of the OECD and European welfare states

Michelle Beyeler

This book is about the internationalisation of ideas concerning the design of national welfare systems. How do ideas develop in international organisations and to what extent and under what conditions are they translated into national policies? We focus on the Organisation for Economic Co-operation and Development (OECD). This international organisation is well suited for our purpose, because it can neither exert regulatory nor financial pressure to influence the behaviour of national actors. If the OECD wants to influence national policies, it has to persuade national actors of the solutions it provides to cope with domestic economic problems. One method by which the OECD presents these solutions to national actors is the regular country surveys issued for all member states. The organisation uses the surveys as a means of pushing their agenda for policy debates and reforms in member countries (cf. Marcussen in this volume).

Two major questions about the interaction of the OECD and domestic systems guide this research. First, we are interested in the consistency of OECD recommendations. Do the ideas and suggestions about welfare state development vary according to the national contexts, or is the OECD promoting uniform best practices for all countries? Second, we analyse the effectiveness of the recommendations. To what extent are actual policy developments in a country in concordance with the OECD policy recommendations? When and why does concordance not occur? Rather than expecting OECD ideas to have a direct and uniform impact on national welfare states, we hypothesise that the impact depends on the fit of national institutions, policies and politics as well as other external pressures – for instance, Europeanisation.

Our aim is to describe and analyse the development of OECD ideas concerning national social policies, and to assess their possible impact on national welfare reforms. This is done by highlighting the problems, criticisms and recommendations the organisation puts forward in its periodical country surveys and contrasting them with the reforms actually realised in 14 Western European welfare states. This procedure allows for systematic descriptive longitudinal and comparative analyses. We are aware of the difficulties in measuring ideational impact. Thus, our objective in this respect is modest: we want to give an impression of the extent to which ideas put forward by the OECD could have been received and accepted by national governments.

This introduction is divided into five sections. The first two sections briefly introduce the literature on globalisation and welfare state change, as well as touching on the different conceptualisations of the relationship between ideas and public policy. Based on these accounts, we have developed a framework of analysis which acts as a guide for our study. This framework of analysis is discussed in the third section. Our principal research methods are presented in the fourth section. The introductory chapter concludes by describing the plan of this book.

GLOBALISATION AND WELFARE STATE CHANGE

According to Schmidt (2001), globalisation can be defined as a set of international economic, institutional and ideational forces for change affecting national policies, practices and politics. Systematic comparative research on welfare state reform, so far, has often focused on the first two types of external forces which result in change: increasing economic integration, and international regulation. A large body of literature discusses the effect of economic integration (both global and European) on welfare states (e.g. Esping-Andersen 1996; Huber and Stephens 2001; Rhodes 1995; Scharpf and Schmidt 2000).

Originally the argument was that high levels of capital mobility, and an international coordinated deregulation of markets (negative integration) both increase competition between welfare regimes and trigger a 'race to the bottom', leading to welfare retrenchment in countries with high levels of social security spending (Strange 1988). Positive integration – i.e. common international regulation – is seen as the recipe for preventing such competitive deregulation. However, positive integration because of the intergovernmental mode of decision making at the international level needs a high level of consensus, which is hardly achievable if governments disagree on the level of social regulation (Scharpf 1996). Jensen (2000) identifies a trend toward increasing integration in the fields of labour market and social policies in the European Union. Still, common European regulation in the field of social policies – except in regard to gender equality and working conditions – remains restricted (Liebfried and Pierson 2000).

The Role of the National Political and Institutional Context

Two sorts of arguments were put forward to explain why empirical studies found limited direct impact when analysing the effects of international economic and political transformation on domestic welfare states. One points to the role of domestic institutional and political reform capabilities as mediating factors between international developments and domestic change, whereas the second argument is based on the concept of path dependency and institutional lock-in.

According to the first argument, the impact of economic globalisation is mediated by the domestic political and institutional context. Political institutions are seen as constraints (veto-points or veto-players), impeding governments from undertaking large reforms, and producing policy stability (Immergut 1992; Schmidt 1996; Tsebelis 2002). The pressures stemming from global transformations are filtered by domestic political institutions and power structures (Garrett and Lange 1995; Huber and Stephens 2001; Keohane and Milner 1996; Scharpf 2000; Schmidt 2001). Furthermore, Europeanisation research holds that the effects of European integration on domestic systems are differential. They are contingent on the domestic institutional, political and economic particularities, as well as on the degree of 'fit' between the required policies and institutions and those already in existence (Börzel and Risse 2000; Cowles et al. 2001).

The institutional lock-in argument is put forward by a tradition of comparative welfare state research treating different national systems of social provision as the products of long periods of institutionalisation (Pierson 2000a). From this perspective, welfare states are seen as stable institutions which develop in a contingent, path-dependent manner. They are not just the outcome of functional demands or power struggles; rather, their development can be traced to a particular series of historical conjunctures. Power distribution can, but does not necessarily have to, correspond systematically to the evolution of institutions. Relatively small events, if they occur at the right moment, may have long and enduring consequences, whereas an event that happened 'too late' may have no impact at all (Pierson 2000a, p. 263).

Esping-Andersen (1990, 1999) identifies three welfare regimes which can be traced back to different political configurations. Central to this regime-typology are the different underlying values and ideologies. Liberal welfare states, for instance, emerged in relation to the liberal ideology of market sovereignty and minimal states, while the ideological roots of social democratic welfare states consist of values such as egalitarianism, and those of conservative welfare states are based on Christian values of family and solidarity. These underlying policy paradigms not only explain why welfare states developed in quite distinctive ways, they also contribute to their reform resistance.

IDEAS AND POLICY CHANGE

Besides the objective, material constraints which are put on welfare states through international economic and political integration, there is a third, 'soft' channel through which globalisation may affect national welfare systems: the policy models and ideas promoted by international actors. '[G]lobalization . . . can also be thought of as a provider of specific solutions for the problems met by welfare states' (Palier and Sykes 2001, p. 10). It is this facet of globalisation that we are interested in discussing in the remainder of this volume.

Why should we expect ideas to have an impact on welfare reform? The technical answer to this question is that due to the extremely high complexity of the issue and the great uncertainty about future developments, human beings are only capable of calculating limited models of possible policy effects on different social groups. They need simplifications, in the form of models or theories, in order to be able to sufficiently grasp the range of problems and possible solutions (Simon 1955, p. 100). These theories which individuals or communities employ to explain the world around them are subjective perceptions, coloured by normative views of how the world should be organised (North 1990, p. 23). New ideas may trigger policy changes, because they provide alternative 'theories' that are seen to be more appropriate. Most likely, social actors will adjust their perceptions when they believe that their previous views and models have yielded poor policy outcomes. This means that it is the experience of failure which triggers the search for new solutions (or policy models) (Marcussen 1999, p. 388). One could also say that, by means of policy experimentation, ideas bring about welfare reform (Hall 1993; Hemerijck and Schludi 2000).[1]

Epistemic Communities

The question this book seeks to answer is not *whether* ideas matter. We are interested in the *how*. How do international actors shape causal social policy models and when and under what conditions do these ideas affect domestic policies? One way to conceptualise the link between international ideas and domestic policies is to point out the role of policy experts. Take, for example, the role of analysts of epistemic communities (Haas 1992). 'An epistemic community is a network of professionals with recognised expertise and competence in a particular domain and an authoritative claim to policy-relevant knowledge within that domain' (Haas 1992, p. 3). Epistemic communities gain political influence in two ways. First, they affect policy making by diffusing ideas and thereby influencing the positions of a wide range of actors, such as bureaucrats and decision makers, as well as the general public. Second, epistemic community members may acquire bureaucratic positions and exert a direct influence on policy design.

The legitimacy and power of epistemic communities stems from their capacity to process more information, and their ability to present more realistic models of the world. But why should policy makers rely on the expertise of the epistemic community? Yee (1996, p. 88) raises this question and points out that politicians often shape the scientific agenda and also use science selectively to legitimate policies chosen by means of other criteria. The strength of the epistemic community approach is the way in which it exposes us to the role of international scientific communities as promoters of common policy models. Its weakness is that it offers little insight into the dynamics of how ideas are translated into domestic policy making.

New Institutionalist Approaches to Ideas and Policy Effects

New institutional analysis conceptualises such effects in more detail. This approach especially points to the role of political institutions in implementing and consolidating policies based on new ideas. 'Powerful individuals are important for the adoption of ideas, but if these ideas do not find institutional homes, they will not be able to sustain themselves over the long term' (Sikkink 1991, p. 248). Or, to put it even more directly: '[I]deas acquire force, when they find organizational means of expression' (Hall 1986, p. 141). The conceptualisation of institutions in this approach is a key factor in understanding this claim. Institutions are defined as systems of rules that can be both formal, like written norms and procedures, law and contracts, and informal, like norms of behaviour, codes of conduct and conventions (Hall 1986, p. 19; North 1990, p. 30). Institutions embody supra-individual abstract devices and guiding ideas of what the institution does and what can legitimately be expected of it (Edeling 1998, p. 730). Therefore, once policy ideas are institutionalised as guidelines in a system of rules, they become powerful motors of future policy development.

The same mechanism, on the other hand, explains why many policy ideas do not find their way into the actual policy-making process. Implementing a policy based on a new idea means that one has to change one or several aspects of the system of rules constituting an institution. The more the new policy idea challenges the current modes of operation, based on prevailing formal and informal rules, the more difficult it becomes to implement. Institutionalists hold that decisions taken within this system of rules are often not consequential in the sense of a rational calculated reaction to the problem; rather, actors make decisions in a way which is appropriate within their institutionally defined roles (Finnemore and Sikkink 1998; March and Olsen 1989, 1998). Accordingly, the more the new policy ideas fit in with the existing ideas and ideologies, the more chance they have of becoming influential (Hall 1989; Sikkink 1991).

Discourse theories are the most explicit on the mechanisms of ideational transfer to policy action (Yee 1996). Discourse and communicative action are seen as important mediators, explaining why certain ideas gain importance in the policy-making process (Risse 2000; Schmidt 2000, 2002).

ANALYSING OECD IDEAS AND EUROPEAN WELFARE STATES

In this study we are interested in the relationship between ideas stemming from an international organisation – the OECD – and their possible impact on national welfare states in Western Europe in the period from 1970 to 2000. By 'policy ideas' we mean the OECD's perceptions about the deficiencies, virtues and improvements of welfare institutions and policy instruments. Our focal point is the possible ideational effects on the welfare functions concerning employment, old age, health, education, poverty and social transfers in general.

The analysis is further restricted to 14 OECD member countries in Western Europe. There are two substantial and one practical reason for this selection. On one hand, European welfare states have often been regarded as an identifiable group forming a 'European social model' (Palier and Sykes 2001, p. 2). Therefore the comparability between the different systems is given. On the other hand, variation within this 'social model' allows for the study of different contexts in a controlled setting. The more practical reason for the country sample is that the project originates from a European research initiative and the selection was partly defined by the availability to participate of national social policy experts. Still, we are able to present analyses from countries covering all important welfare varieties in Western Europe: the four Scandinavian countries exemplify different aspects of the Nordic model, which in the Esping-Andersen (1990) typology is classified as social-democratic, characterised by an egalitarian and universalistic approach to social welfare. From the continental welfare states (often classified as conservative or Christian-democratic), we cover France, Belgium, Germany, the Netherlands, Switzerland and the southern European countries of Greece, Italy and Spain. In these welfare systems, the emphasis lies on the social security contributions of employers and employees, rather than on universalistic social provisions. Ireland and the United Kingdom represent the liberal approach, which relies more on private welfare and means-tested state provisions.

How does the OECD address the problems each of these welfare states is confronted with? What aspects of the system are criticised? What recommendations and solutions does the organisation present to different countries? Drawing on the theoretical conceptualisations discussed above regarding the link between ideas and public policy, it is possible to derive two competing hypotheses concerning the kind of ideas we can expect to be addressed towards domestic welfare states. The epistemic communities approach tells us that a policy idea becomes powerful if the diffusers are conceived of as actors with expertise and policy-relevant knowledge. This implies that the OECD's analyses, criticisms and subsequent recommendations for problems must follow the criteria of clean, scientific analysis. In addition, there should be coherence in the way the OECD reports on different countries and welfare systems. On the other hand, new institutionalist approaches to the impact of ideas hold that the more compatible an idea is with prevailing values, the more chance it has of becoming influential. The implication of this claim is that the OECD can improve its influence by taking specific national policy cultures and values into account. We should thus be able to see differences in the way in which the OECD interacts with different member countries. For instance, we should be able to observe differences in when, how and why the OECD offers criticism – as well as noting differences in the recommendations given. Our first question guiding the empirical analysis therefore concerns the consistency of the OECD's ideas: are the ideas the same across the board, or do they vary according to the national context?

Our second guiding question refers to the possible impact of OECD ideas on policy development. Are the ideas promoted by the OECD effective in changing domestic policy? Based on the globalisation and Europeanisation literature, as well as on ideational new institutionalist accounts, we can assume that the OECD's ideas will be more effective provided the politico-institutional structure in a country is favourable for the adoption of the recommendations. We expect that the 'fit' of the politico-institutional structure is an important mediating factor on ideational 'pressures'. In addition, the possibility of ideas changing policies also varies with the actual policy design. A necessary condition, for observing a policy change is that the prevailing policy differs from that advocated by the OECD. Ideas will only produce an actual change in policies if they do not 'fit' with the current national policy solution. Based on institutional lock-in arguments and new institutionalist views on ideational impact, we expect that policy development remains within the path that is possible given prevailing institutional legacies and values. Both national varieties of welfare state design, as well as the broader domestic political and institutional context, are thus likely to matter for the effectiveness of OECD ideas.

METHODOLOGICAL ISSUES

Our research method is qualitative and comparative over time and between countries. For each country we gathered comparative data on the OECD's analyses, criticisms and recommendations in a standardised manner. The sources for this content analysis are the summarising chapters of the OECD's *Economic Surveys* in the period from 1970 to 2000. We extracted the OECD's statements on social expenditure in general or on specific social policies (related to employment, old age, health, education or poverty) according to three criteria: What are considered the major problems in the respective policy fields? What are the major criticisms? What are the major policy recommendations issued? The question of whether the OECD has been consistent over time and between countries can be answered based on these descriptive data.

Assessing the effectiveness of the OECD in changing domestic policies is more complicated. Yee (1996) distinguishes three methodological procedures to measure the effects of ideas on policy: co-variational analysis, the congruence procedure and process tracing. According to proponents of co-variational analysis, ideational effects can be tested if the development of ideas correlates with the development of policies. However, this type of analysis is problematic as soon as we expect the relationship between ideas and policies to be non-linear, highly contingent on other factors, and differential in relation to the time lags between ideational and policy change. In this case the absence of co-variation cannot be interpreted as proof for the absence of a relationship. Process tracing, on the other hand, is a method particularly attentive to the sequences as well as the complex relationships between policies (Hall, forthcoming). The drawback of this method is that it requires the gathering of a large amount of information and is thus quite costly and time-intensive.

Therefore, in this study, we apply the congruence procedure (Yee 1996, pp. 76–77). This research method essentially entails establishing 'congruence' (or concordance) between ideas and the content of policy decisions. If the policy development is consistent with the policy recommendations raised by the OECD, this can be taken as an indication of a possible OECD influence. However, concordance in policy changes and recommendations does not establish 'proof' of the OECD's impact. Perhaps the idea of policy change has been developed on the national level, and was later incorporated into and published as part of the *Economic Survey*. Or the need for reform has been felt on the national level and the solution to the problem has been developed by national actors like politicians or administrative elites quite independently of the arguments of the international organisation. If there is discordance, i.e., the national policy development does not follow the OECD's recommendations, or even goes in the opposite direction, we can consider this an example of a situation where the OECD lacks efficacy in influencing national policy. Still, it is not proof of a complete absence of impact, since the national policy might have been even more radical had it not been for the tempering influence of the OECD's proposal.

One major problem with the method employed is that the ideas promoted by the OECD are not exclusive to the organisation. The same or largely similar ideas can also stem from other international or domestic sources. By searching for instances where actors make a clear reference to the OECD during a discourse on reform, we attempt to further validate our assessment of the organisation's impact. In most countries, as well as in the different policy fields under study, a limited number of significant policy changes occurred. If during such reform debates national actors explicitly refer to OECD recommendations, we consider this an indicator of influence. Of course, national actors can adopt these arguments on purely strategic reasons or actors may adopt the OECD ideas without quoting the OECD. Thus, these cases do not produce unequivocal evidence. They hint, however, at the direct impact the OECD can have on national policy discourse.

Although we are sensitive to the criticism that with this frame of analysis we cannot establish conclusive proof of the OECD's relevance or non-relevance, we still consider our study a valid means of assessing the effectiveness of the organisation. Even if we had conducted in-depth case analyses, for instance with semi-structured interviews, it would be difficult to pin down the effective impact of the ideas. Our frame of analysis has the advantage over other research strategies that it generates comparable data based on clear criteria.

PLAN OF THE BOOK

In the next chapter Martin Marcussen presents the view from within the OECD. He argues that the organisation has established a form of multilateral surveillance based on moral pressure and soft regulation. The contribution contains both a description of how this type of multilateral surveillance works, as well as a conceptual framework to characterise the various roles the OECD plays in this process.

Chapters 3 to 16 are devoted to the country studies. Each chapter starts with a short description of the political institutional context and the historical roots of the respective welfare system. In the second part, the authors present a table covering the main social policy issues (recognition of problems, criticisms and recommendations) raised in the OECD country surveys. Then they contrast the recommendations given by the OECD with the actual policy development. The country experts assess whether there had been concordance or discordance between recommendations and policy reforms, and whether the OECD's ideas had been explicitly addressed in the national policy discourse.

The book concludes with a comparative account. Klaus Armingeon systematically compiles the findings from the country chapters in order to evaluate the two guiding questions regarding the consistency and effectiveness of OECD ideas. He comes to the conclusion that OECD recommendations have been highly consistent between countries and also over time – if one takes into account a clearly visible shift from demand-oriented policies in the early 1970s to supply-oriented ones thereafter. It is, however, this consistency in policy ideas which often inhibits the reflection of OECD recommendations in concrete policy developments at the national level. Only when the OECD comes up with proposals that correspond with national policies, institutions and broadly held values is there likely to be meaningful policy development. Otherwise, national political opposition and institutional inertia inhibit a clear and direct effect.

NOTE

1. Note that social learning in this definition does not contain a normative judgement on the quality of the theories before and after the 'learning' process. Social learning can be a means of adding new information and thus of introducing more complexity into one's perception of the world, but it does not always have that effect. There is also the possibility that the old perceptions are given up entirely, and that the new model is seen as the appropriate one in the future – if the amount of information processed in each model remains the same, then there is no guarantee that the second model is more realistic than the first.

REFERENCES

Börzel, Tanja A. and Thomas Risse (2000), 'When Europe hits home: Europeanization and domestic change', *European Integration Online Papers* **4** (15), <http://eiop.or.at/eiop/texte/2000-015a.htm>.

Cowles, Maria Green, James Caporaso and Thomas Risse (eds) (2001), *Transforming Europe. Europeanization and Domestic Change*, Ithaca, NY and London: Cornell University Press.

Edeling, Thomas (1998), 'Economic and sociological institutionalism in organization theory: two sides of the same coin?' *Journal of Institutional and Theoretical Economics* **154** (4), 728–734.

Esping-Andersen, Gøsta (1990), *The Three Worlds of Welfare Capitalism*, Princeton: Princeton University Press.

Esping-Andersen, Gøsta (ed.) (1996), *Welfare States in Transition. National Adaptations to Global Economies*, London: Sage.

Esping-Andersen, Gøsta (1999), *Social Foundations of Postindustrial Economies*, New York: Oxford University Press.

Finnemore, Martha and Kathryn Sikkink (1998), 'International norm dynamics and political change', *International Organization* **52** (4), 887–917.

Garrett, Geoffrey and Peter Lange (1995), 'Internationalization, institutions, and political change', *International Organization* **49** (4), 627–655.

Haas, Peter M. (1992), 'Introduction: epistemic communities and international policy coordination', *International Organization* **46** (1), 1–35.

Hall, Peter A. (1986), *Governing the Economy. The Politics of State Intervention in Britain and France*, New York and Oxford: Oxford University Press.

Hall, Peter A. (1989), 'Conclusion: the politics of Keynesian ideas', in Peter A. Hall (ed.), *The Political Power of Economic Ideas. Keynesianism across Nations*, Princeton, NJ: Princeton University Press, pp. 361–391.

Hall, Peter A. (1993), 'Policy paradigms, social learning, and the state, the case of economic policymaking in Britain', *Comparative Politics* **25** (3), 275–296.

Hall, Peter A. (forthcoming), 'Aligning ontology and methodology in comparative research', in James Mahoney and Dietrich Rueschemeyer (eds), *Comparative Historical Analysis in the Social Sciences*, Cambridge: Cambridge University Press.

Hemerijck, Anton and Martin Schludi (2000), 'Sequences of policy failures and effective policy responses', in Fritz W. Scharpf and Vivien A. Schmidt (eds), *Welfare and Work in the Open Economy, Volume I, From Vulnerability to Competitiveness*, Oxford: Oxford University Press, pp. 125–228.

Huber, Evelyne and John D. Stephens (2001), *Development and Crisis of the Welfare State. Parties and Policies in Global Markets*, Chicago and London: University of Chicago Press.

Immergut, Ellen M. (1992), *Health Policies. Interests and Institutions in Western Europe*, Cambridge: Cambridge University Press.

Jensen, Carsten S. (2000), 'Neofunctionalist theories and the development of European social and labour market policy', *Journal of Common Market Studies* **38** (1), 71–92.

Keohane, Robert O. and Helen V. Milner (eds) (1996), *Internationalization and Domestic Politics*, Cambridge: Cambridge University Press.

Liebfried, Stephan and Paul Pierson (2000), 'Social policy. Left to courts and markets?' in Helen Wallace and W. Wallace (eds), *Policy-Making in the European Union*, Oxford: Oxford University Press, pp. 267–292.

March, James G. and Johan P. Olsen (1989), *Rediscovering Institutions. The Organizational Basis of Politics*, London: Macmillan.

March, James G. and Johan P. Olsen (1998), 'The institutional dynamics of international political orders', *International Organization* **52** (4), 943–969.

Marcussen, Martin (1999), 'The dynamics of EMU-ideas', *Cooperation and Conflict* **34** (4), 383–411.

North, Douglass C. (1990), *Institutions, Institutional Change and Economic Performance*, Cambridge: Cambridge University Press.

Palier, Bruno and Robert Sykes (2001), 'Challenges and change: issues and perspectives in the analysis of globalization and the European welfare states', in Robert Sykes, Bruno Palier and Pauline M. Prior (eds), *Globalization and European Welfare States*, Basingstoke: Palgrave, pp. 1–16.

Pierson, Paul (2000a), 'Three worlds of welfare state research', *Comparative Political Studies* **33** (6/7), 791–821.

Pierson, Paul (2000b), 'Increasing returns, path dependence, and the study of politics', *American Political Science Review* **94** (2), 251–267.

Rhodes, Martin (1995), 'Subversive liberalism: market integration, globalization and the European welfare state', *Journal of European Public Policy* **2** (3), 384–406.

Risse, Thomas (2000), 'Let's argue!: communicative action in world politics', *International Organization* **54** (1), 1–39.

Scharpf, Fritz W. (1996), 'Negative and positive integration in the political economy of European welfare states', in Gary Marks, Fritz W. Scharpf et al. (eds) *Governance of the European Union*, Thousand Oaks, CA and New Delhi: Sage, pp. 15–39.

Scharpf, Fritz W. (2000), 'Economic changes, vulnerabilities, and institutional capabilities', in Fritz W. Scharpf and Vivien A. Schmidt (eds) *Welfare and Work in the Open Economy, Volume I, From Vulnerability to Competitiveness*, Oxford: Oxford University Press, pp. 21–124.

Scharpf, Fritz W. and Vivien A. Schmidt (eds) (2000), *Welfare and Work in the Open Economy, Volume I and II*, Oxford: Oxford University Press.

Schmidt, Manfred G. (1996), 'When parties matter: a review of the possibilities and limits of partisan influence on public policy', *European Journal of Political Research* **30** (2), 155–183.

Schmidt, Vivien A. (2000), 'Values and discourse in the politics of adjustment', in Fritz W. Scharpf and Vivien A. Schmidt (eds), *Welfare and Work in the Open Economy, Volume I, From Vulnerability to Competitiveness*, Oxford: Oxford University Press, pp. 229–309.

Schmidt, Vivien A. (2001), 'Europeanization and the mechanics of economic policy adjustment', *European Integration online Papers* (EIoP) **5**(6), <http://eiop.or.at/eiop/texte/2001-006.htm>.

Schmidt, Vivien A. (2002), *The Futures of European Capitalism*, Oxford and New York: Oxford University Press.

Sikkink, Kathryn (1991), *Ideas and Institutions. Developmentalism in Brazil and Argentina*, Ithaca, NY and London: Cornell University Press.

Simon, Herbert A. (1955), 'A behavioral model of rational choice', *Quarterly Journal of Economics* **69** (1), 99–118.

Strange, Susan (1988), *States and Markets*, London: Pinter.

Tsebelis, Georg (2002), *Veto Players. How Political Institutions Work*, Princeton, NJ: Princeton University Press.

Yee, Albert S. (1996), 'The causal effects of ideas on policies', *International Organization* **50** (1), 69–108.

2. Multilateral surveillance and the OECD: playing the idea game

Martin Marcussen

Multilateral surveillance implies that a multitude of state authorities, working together, have agreed to formulate a set of 'rules of the game', best practices and norms for appropriate behaviour. It also implies that they have established mechanisms which they can use to ensure that these rules of the game, best practices and norms are actually regulating, constraining or enabling the behaviour of state authorities. To that effect, state authorities have most typically established a formalised institutional structure that by itself, or with the assistance of concerned state authorities, helps enforce the agreed-upon rules. So 'rules', 'enforcement mechanisms' and 'enforcement institutions' all constitute parts of a system of multilateral surveillance (Chayes and Chayes 1993; Raustiala 2000).

In terms of content and form, international rules can exist anywhere on a continuum: they could be very simple, formalised, easy-to-understand and unambiguous guidelines for action, or they could be general principles, informal, interpretable and ambiguous discursive codes. The quintessence of multilateral surveillance is that these rules, however their form and content might be defined, have to be enacted. Surveillance does not take place by itself. A sort of compliance 'pressure' is always involved to ensure that the individual state authorities deliberately adjust their behaviour in rule-conforming ways (Hurd 1999). The pressure exerted upon state authorities can be based either on a fear of being punished or on a wish to be rewarded. Regulative pressure exists when there are clear and written rules to conform with. In these cases an international enforcement institution has most typically been installed that evaluates whether the written-down rules have been violated or not. In a similar vein, a direct financial pressure can be involved in multilateral surveillance. In these latter cases international organisations have been authorised to reward norm-conforming behaviour through the allocation of finances.

However, multilateral surveillance does not always function through regulatory or financial pressure. Sometimes moral pressure does the trick (Bomberg and Peterson 2000; Drezner 2000). Shaming, ridiculing and exclusion are all part of the arsenal of moral pressure. In an interdependent world, all state authorities need to, from time to time, intermingle with fellow colleagues in other countries, if not for any other reason than to solve common problems through common means. Because many political problems are international in scope, and because a multitude of international organisations have been founded with a view to deal with these international problems, national state authorities are playing a so-called legitimacy game at the international level (Hurd 1999; Marcussen 2000). The game is complicated and a number of factors can influence the terms and the outcome of the game. However, all state authorities are critically aware of the existence and importance of the international legitimacy game. If state authorities are not legitimate members of the many policy-specific international communities, they are highly unlikely to be able to live up to their domestic obligations. If they are unable to live up to their domestic obligations, they cannot take for granted that they will get re-elected. Thus, the international legitimacy game is closely related to the national legitimacy game. Sometimes the two games are mutually in conflict with each other. Legitimate discourse and behaviour in one game need not constitute appropriate behaviour in the other. In these cases decoupling between the two games is most likely to take place (Marcussen 2000, 2002a; Schimmelfennig 2000).

In general, very few state authorities in liberal democracies can afford to be exposed to international shaming. Shaming takes place if the state authorities in question have not, for some reason, been willing to live up to international standards for appropriate behaviour. In these cases, a series of best practices has been established and the state in question is being shamed for behaviour that directly interferes with these international norms of appropriateness. The shaming mechanism consists of exposing and thereby uncovering the norm-violating behaviour for the wider international policy community, as a result of which the blameworthy state authorities can expect a series of more or less explicit reactions from other state authorities that all serve to, temporarily, socially exclude the guilty party. Social exclusion in international fora can mean anything from being directly expelled from the international policy community to just being ignored in international talks and negotiations (Checkel 2001).

Ridiculing also plays a role in moral pressure. Ridiculing takes place if state authorities have failed to live up to international norms either through passivity or through incompetent behaviour. The ridiculing mechanism consists of exposing and uncovering the failed and far from sufficient actions that a set of authorities has undertaken to comply with international standards for appropriate behaviour. Like shaming, the ridiculing of incompetence can lead to social exclusion, although expulsion from a policy community very seldom takes place only on these grounds. However, for the state authorities in question, ridiculing can be just as serious as shaming because it means that the state authorities can look forward to serious difficulties when trying to work together with other national authorities in order to solve problems that are international in scope.

It is in terms of moral pressure and the consequent soft regulation that the OECD exerts multilateral surveillance among its member states. Unlike many other international organisations, the OECD does not produce formal legislation to any significant extent, nor does it posses financial resources to allocate and distribute as it wishes. The OECD is bound to play the so-called idea game (Marcussen 2002b).

In the first section below, I will describe in more detail how the OECD and its various roles in the idea game can be conceptualised. A distinction will be made between OECD as an ideational artist, an ideational arbitrator and an ideational authority. These roles are not mutually exclusive and they can best be described as ideals for the founding fathers when OEEC was reinvented as OECD in 1961. In the second section, I will describe the two parties involved in OECD multilateral surveillance within the area of macro-economic policy making. First, I will chart the part of the OECD secretariat that formally overviews and analyses the economic situations in the various OECD member states and writes the final OECD country surveys. In later chapters, it will be these OECD country surveys that constitute the main indicators of OECD multilateral surveillance within the area of social and welfare state policies. Second, I will outline the main characteristics and procedures of the Economic and Development Review Committee (EDRC). This is where country representatives meet on a very frequent basis and, through deliberation and peer pressure, define problems and formulate recommendations.

OECD'S VARIOUS ROLES IN THE IDEA GAME

At some point, the first Secretary-General of the OECD, the former Danish Minister of Finance Thorkil Kristensen, argued that the core of OECD's work is the continuing process of 'consultation'. Consultation comprises 'regular discussion between officials coming from capitals, regular examinations of the policies of each individual member country, studies undertaken by expert groups on problems of special interest, [and] formal or informal recommendations to countries' (Kristensen 1967b, p. 106). The overall objective of this consultation activity was, according to Thorkil Kristensen, to develop a common value system at the level of civil servants in the OECD countries that should form the basis for consensually shared definitions of problems and solutions in economic policy making. A common worldview could be developed, according to Kristensen's philosophy, through intensive interaction on specific policy areas between the concerned parties. With the assistance of the skilled OECD secretariat, a common ideational base would eventually lead to increased policy coordination and the development of common political programmes for the entire OECD area. This testifies to the importance of a few of the roles that the OECD is playing in the idea game – the idea game being a question of formulating, transferring and authorising principled or causal beliefs with a view to constraining or enabling certain types of social behaviour within the OECD area. Principled beliefs can be anything from visions and good practices to norms for appropriate behaviour, and causal beliefs can range from theories on the one hand, to facts and data on the other.

According to Thorkil Kristensen, the OECD, first, plays the role of an *ideational artist*, which formulates, tests and diffuses new policy ideas. In so doing, the OECD achieves credibility among its member states because it actively steps in with a view to help them learn in situations in which they have gone through a painful process of unlearning. Playing that particular role, the OECD can be depicted as an enormous think-tank which continuously attracts the very best academics from its member countries and offers them considerable room to manoeuvre when inventing new ideas on old policy areas. In accordance with the fundamental principles of the ideal-typical bureaucracy, OECD employees are well paid and independent of their home countries. As a result of this, their loyalty should ideally be directed at the overall purpose and function of the OECD, rather than at narrow selfish considerations. This is the kind of institution Thorkil Kristensen had in mind when describing the OECD as a consultation forum (Kristensen 1962a, 1962b, 1963, 1966, 1967a, 1967b, 1989). As a financially and politically independent body, the OECD would be able to distance itself from national controversies and dedicate itself completely to science. According to this point of view, the OECD exists in a political vacuum that allows it to formulate, refine and diffuse new policy ideas. This it can do most effectively if it possesses a high degree of scientific authority and a reputation of political neutrality.

Second, in order to be an efficient player in the idea game, the OECD plays the role of an *ideational arbitrator* that helps national civil servants meet each other in supportive surroundings, thereby teaching them to develop their personal and technical skills, and even sometimes develop their personalities and feelings of belonging. Such learning processes can take various forms – such as socialisation, imitation and coercion – and the concrete meeting can be characterised by social interaction ranging from tough bargaining to amiable deliberation (Risse 2000).

The OECD itself estimates that on an annual basis some 40,000 civil servants enter the meeting rooms of Château de la Muette in Paris. The set up of a meeting, of course, differs considerably from one context to the next. On one extreme, some meetings can be characterised as hard-nosed negotiation fora in which the success of participants can easily be deduced by comparing their national mandates with the final negotiation compromise (Putnam 1988). On the other extreme, a large group of meetings can be characterised by a deliberative social logic in which the participating civil servants do not posses a clear mandate and do not even really grasp what role they ought to play, what the problem at hand is, and what possible solutions there might be for these problems (Lerdell and Sahlin-Andersson 1997). Through deliberation, however, the civil servants in question slowly learn more about these matters (Risse 2000). Between these two extremes, a variety of different types of social interaction may characterise the various meetings. On some occasions, as a result of an issue being politicised, an element of bargaining and negotiation is injected into the room. On other occasions, the sessions become increasingly routinised, as a result of which a set of group norms will start regulating appropriate social behaviour.

In full accordance with such a picture of the organisation, the OECD has since a very early stage been characterised as a 'talking shop' in which participants go through a process of simple learning:

> Meetings . . . also provide informal contacts in the corridors and over meals and serve as two-way channels of communication. They afford opportunities for testing the climate for some future policy alternatives, entirely off the record and with even less publicity than that usually accorded to consultative meetings in a 'talking shop'. (Aubrey 1967, p. 29)

Aubrey speaks about 'mutual education', 'important formative roles' and 'mutual appreciation and trust' resulting from the many direct confrontations between national civil servants in the many OECD fora (ibid, pp. 143–145). According to an observer, such a description of simple learning processes apparently still holds strong:

> [O]ften, there is no formal agreement, but officials return to their capitals with an enhanced understanding of their colleagues' thinking and with ideas that will find their way into national legislation or regulations. An innocent-sounding device, but the fact is that OECD committees do serve as a crucible for its members' future actions. In the relative privacy of the Organization's committee rooms, tough issues can be 'pre-negotiated,' advanced ideas floated, difficulties ironed out. In the corridors and coffee bars between sessions, officials with similar interests but very different backgrounds meet, argue, forge friendships. (Sullivan 1997, p. 98)

Furthermore, qualitative research has indicated that socialisation processes have resulted in complex learning as a result of which not only the behaviour but also the self-perception and role-conceptions of the involved actors are transformed. In this regard, it has been illustrated that national civil servants in the OECD tend to go through various stages of learning in the socialisation process (Sjöstedt 1973, pp. 322–323). First of all, national civil servants who regularly interact in OECD fora seem to develop a common language so that they are able to communicate effectively. Then they start to employ the same technical instruments and tools when analysing problems of common concern. And finally, they start using the same kind of causal reasoning when discussing these issues. Furthermore, and on a much deeper level, the national civil servants, according to Sjöstedt's research, seem to develop a common selective perception of the world and they start to employ a common frame of reference and a common world view. The latter helps them to define what can be considered as a relevant problem in the first place and which instruments can legitimately be employed to solve this problem.

Learning also sometimes involves elements of indirect coercion or peer pressure. It can be argued that indirect coercion through powerful and regular peer-review processes is the only means that the OECD has at its disposal in its attempt to execute multilateral surveillance. Some of the many publications produced by the OECD secretariat can maybe best be understood as constituting criteria for correct and moral behaviour. Take booklets such as:

- *A Caring World* and *The Battle Against Exclusion* about global social policy;
- *Transition to Responsible Fisheries* about future fishery policies;
- *The Digital Divide: Bridging the Learning Gap* about education policy;
- *Preparing Youth for the 21st Century* about labour market policy;
- *Automotive Fuels for the Future* about energy policy;
- *Trust in Government* and *Fighting Bribery and Corruption* about public administration; and
- *Towards Sustainable Development* about the integration of environmental and economic issues.

These are reports and analyses that on the surface cannot possibly be contested by anybody since their titles per definition signal a 'correct' and 'good' opinion about a complex set of problems. This type of report consolidates what is at any point in time considered by the OECD and its committees to be politically correct behaviour, and it indirectly compels member states into promoting a certain legitimate discourse and sometimes even a certain concrete behaviour.

Another category of reports has a sort of review process attached to it. Examples are many, but the best-known reports are *OECD Economic Outlook* and *OECD Employment Outlook*, which allow all member countries to evaluate the efforts that the individual countries have undertaken within a certain area of interest. Although the member countries cannot be formally sanctioned for not respecting the benchmark criteria for 'responsible' behaviour, these scrutiny processes are extremely powerful mechanisms because they warn the individual member countries that they run the risk of social exclusion from 'good company' if they fail to conform. A prominent example of a peer-review process is the annual *OECD Economic Survey* (the focus of this book's research), which specifically deal with single countries, and can sometimes be very critical in that regard. In describing that latter mechanism, Aubrey wrote about 'moral suasion' and 'collective pressure':

> Participation by high-level national officials who have significant responsibility for the formation of policy in their own countries [is] a vital condition for the success of efforts that depend on the exchange of information, better understanding, and influence by 'moral suasion' or collective pressure. The annual confrontation of each country's policies in the OECD's Economic and Development Review Committee supplements this work. (Aubrey 1967, p. 39)

Unsurprisingly, Aubrey concluded that this indirect coercive learning mechanism is most effective in regard to the laggards among the OECD countries:

> In short, the work of the OECD has exercised a significant, if intangible, influence through a number of channels from the Paris meetings back to the capitals. Confrontation, critical review, and 'appeals to conscience' can have powerful effects in bringing the laggards along in a collective endeavour. (Aubrey 1967, p. 113)

Today, these mechanisms are reported to still be going strong:

> A complex process called 'peer pressure' occurs. Subtly but powerfully, ideas and standards advocated by a majority of committee members gain the agreement of all or nearly all and are shaped to account for the views of dissenters. No country likes to feel itself on an entirely different wave length from all its partners. Ultimately peer pressure makes international co-operation among [30] countries possible. (Sullivan 1997, p. 99)

In summary, the vision that Thorkil Kristensen developed on behalf of the OECD was of an autonomous and innovative organisation elevated above the political quarrels of everyday politics and therefore potentially in a position to play around with new and provoking policy ideas. Kristensen was of the opinion that no other organisations – national think-tanks, national universities or national bureaucracies – were in a position to 'think the unthinkable', as a result of which the OECD ought to play the roles of ideational artist and arbitrator in order to bring the ordinary policy processes out of their essentially dysfunctional direction.

If these two supplementary roles in the idea game are being played by the OECD, it is indispensable at this point to direct our attention towards the OECD member states in order to consider the ways in which these various roles actually make a difference. Does OECD multilateral surveillance matter?

The issue at this stage is to investigate whether the OECD, through its efforts in the idea game, is considered to be an *ideational authority* in the OECD member countries. One indication of the extent to which the OECD is actually performing the role of ideational authority in the member states is that the organisation at a general level is considered to be a mythical, neutral, scientific and objective soothsayer that one cannot afford to ignore. An initial way to evaluate whether this is the case would be to investigate the extent to which the OECD, through its ideational roles, is raising a specific form of consciousness among the many and varied actors in the national polity, be it national parliamentarians, the media, national civil servants, national economic experts or the broader population. In other words, does the effect of OECD multilateral surveillance manifest itself in the fact that OECD ideas over the years have become internalised in the world views and cognitive frames of citizens from OECD member states?

A second way of evaluating whether the OECD functions as an ideational authority in the member states consists of studying the policy effects of OECD multilateral surveillance. The question at this point is whether the OECD, through the idea game, has been able to influence policy discourse in the member states and even the content and timing of policy reform? Whereas the consciousness-raising effects of OECD surveillance are part of a long-term, ongoing process, a study of the policy effects of OECD surveillance focuses on the direct and short-term consequences to member states of the OECD idea game.

Third, an indication of OECD ideational authority might be that the organisation is being explicitly referred to in national political processes such as national referenda, national elections and in regular national decision-making processes, such as the adoption of the annual Finance Act. If, in a national political context, it seems to be the case that a simple reference to OECD data, OECD ideas and OECD theories strengthens one's legitimacy and argument, it might well be concluded that the OECD, apart from having consciousness-raising effects and policy effects, also has some degree of political effect in OECD member countries. Clearly, the simple act of referring to OECD ideas does not mean that anything has been learned (consciousness-raising effects) or that policy is being changed (policy effects) but it does illustrate a belief that an organisation such as the OECD has a fundamental *raison d'être*. If, on the other hand, it is impossible to trace any of the above-mentioned effects, it becomes necessary to critically ask whether the OECD has any future in the idea game and, indeed, whether the game itself is over (Marcussen 2002a).

In the next section I will step into the organisational and procedural structure of the OECD, with a view to taking a closer look at the routines and practices that define OECD multilateral surveillance within the area of macroeconomic policy making. I will make an analytical distinction between the 'political' layer of the OECD surveillance procedure and the more 'administrative' layer.

THE EDRC IN THE OECD LABYRINTH

The present book systematically describes and explains the ways in which the content and style of the regular OECD country surveys have developed over the years. To be able to better grasp the mechanisms and effects of OECD multilateral surveillance, it is necessary to gain a better understanding of both the processes through which these country surveys are developed, and of the institutional framework upon which OECD multilateral surveillance rests. In this section, I will sketch the relevant parts of the OECD structure that encapsulate OECD surveillance and in the next section, I will take a closer look at the procedure currently in practice through which multilateral surveillance is taking place, as an interplay between national central administrations, the EDRC and the Economics Department of the OECD secretariat.

The Basic Organisational Structure of the OECD

At the most general and simplified level, it makes sense to distinguish between two layers of the OECD organisational structure. The first layer is political, deliberative and consultative, where national civil servants and, to a much lesser extent, national politicians meet each other in committees, working groups, expert groups and council meetings. Another layer is administrative, analytical and data-processing, also known as the OECD secretariat.

The secretariat of the present organisational structure is constituted by some 800 A-grade officials, some 300 temporary consultants and trainees and some 1 100 employees in other functions (OECD 2001) (see Figure 2.1).

It is this organisational level that Thorkil Kristensen had in mind when describing the OECD as an ideational artist. Some parts of the secretariat collect data, monitor trends, and analyse and forecast economic developments, while others research social changes or evolving patterns in trade, the environment, agriculture, technology, taxation and many other areas.

The second level of the OECD organisational structure more closely relates to the OECD's role of ideational arbitrator. This is where we can locate 42 committees and no less than 98 working parties and working groups. Over the course of a year, national experts and civil servants gather in these committees and working groups in order to discuss matters of common interest, most typically on the basis of data and analysis elaborated by the OECD secretariat or by the member states themselves. The OECD has itself described this level of its organisation as a permanent intergovernmental conference (OECD 1998a,

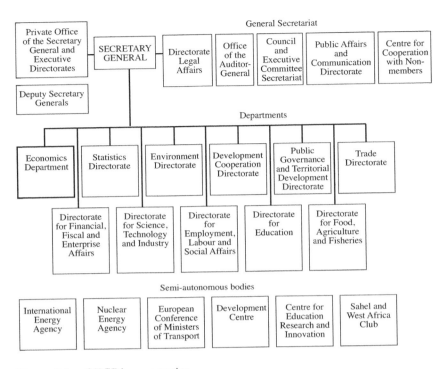

Figure 2.1   OECD's secretariat

p. 12). Year by year since the foundation of the organisation in 1961, the committee structure has become increasingly complex. New layers of groups, parties and committees have been added to the original core.

In order to better grasp OECD multilateral surveillance we will need to identify the relevant organisational elements from both of the above-mentioned levels.

The Heart of the OECD Structure: The Economics Department and its Committees

At the level of the secretariat, it becomes necessary to take a closer look at the Economics Department that constitutes the very essence of the OECD staff's self-definition. At a first glance, one notices that the OECD secretariat has five layers of leadership. At the top, of course, we find the Secretary-General, who has the overall administrative, financial and political responsibility for the OECD secretariat. He or she delegates some responsibility to four Deputy

Secretary-Generals. Below the Secretary-General we find the Heads of Department, who take responsibility for the individual Directorates and Departments of the OECD secretariat. In the Economics Department's case, this person is referred to as the Chief Economist of the OECD.

The Economics Department is functionally split into two branches: the Policy Studies Branch, which deals with general macro-economic and structural issues, and the Country Studies Branch, which deals with macro-economic and structural issues relating to individual member and non-member countries. A Director and a Deputy Director head each branch. At the fourth level of management we find the Heads of Division who, in the case of the Country Studies Branch, overview a group of countries, normally six. Finally, at the lowest level of management we find the Heads of Teams and Units (in the Policy Studies Branch) and Heads of Desks (in the Country Studies Branch). This person is normally a senior economist who is working together with one or two administrators or economists. Each desk in the Country Studies Branch has responsibility for writing country surveys for at least two countries once every one or two years. The EDRC has responsibility for the reports published by the 15 desks in the Country Studies Branch that cover the 30 OECD member countries on a regular basis (see below), whereas the three desks that deal on an ad-hoc basis with non-member countries (the Baltic States, Brazil, South America, Russia and other Newly Independent Countries, Asia and China) do not need the approval of the EDRC. Surveys of these countries fall under the responsibility of the Secretary-General.

There are some interesting observations to be made at the political level of the OECD's organisation diagram in Figure 2.2. It is here that one can find the Economic and Development Review Committee (EDRC), which is central to studying the country-specific surveillance of the OECD. The EDRC is one of the OECD committees that convenes most frequently in Paris. Thirty delegates, who in many cases are the Economic Counsellors from the member states' permanent OECD delegations in Paris, constitute the committee members. They convene four to six times a year in special sessions to discuss strategic, organisational and administrative issues among themselves and 20–24 times a year to examine a draft survey produced by the country desks of the OECD secretariat. On the latter occasion, as we will see in the next section, the permanent members of the committee, the chair, the two vice-chairs and a few OECD staff members are joined by a national delegation which has travelled to Paris to explain/defend the problematic issues raised by the draft country survey. The number of participants in these regular meetings can vary from around 45 to well over 100. Since the year 2000, a Danish economics professor from Copenhagen University, Niels Thygesen, has presided over the EDRC meetings.

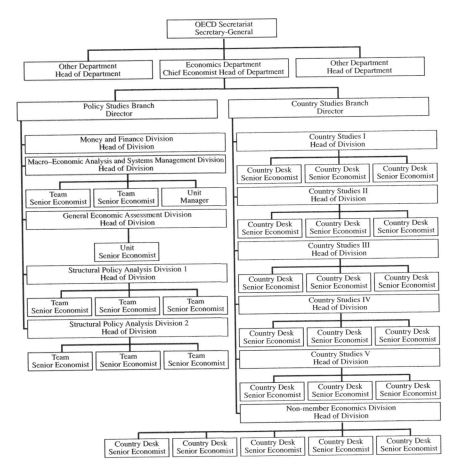

Figure 2.2   The structure of the Economics Department of the OECD

THE EDRC AT WORK

The EDRC multilateral surveillance process can be roughly split into five consecutive stages (see Figure 2.3). In the first stage, the country desk economists will start to collect impressions, ideas and plans from their immediate institutional environment. This they will do by investigating the degree to which political developments in the country in question make certain macroeconomic and structural aspects topical. They will also need to look at the following: requests from EDRC members for certain topics to be dealt with in

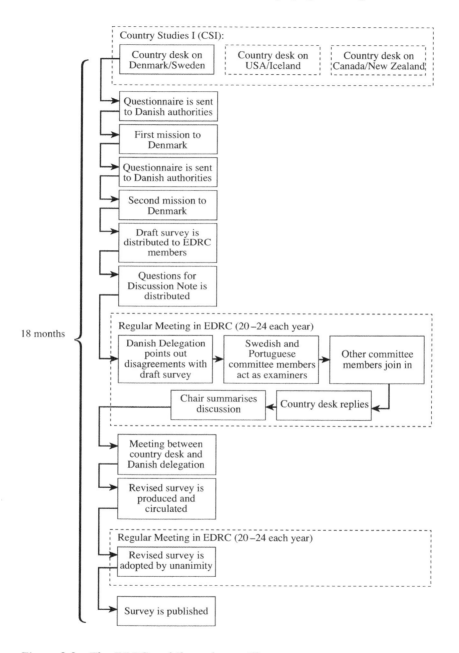

Figure 2.3   The EDRC multilateral surveillance process

the survey; which kinds of issues are being worked on in other parts of the Economics Department; and what prior surveys have focused on in greater detail. In other words, the two economists in the relevant country desk do not start to write a report in a political vacuum – on the contrary. They pay attention to the political, organisational and functional conditions in the OECD as well as in the country to be studied. For instance, the EDRC members discuss among themselves on a regular basis which special structural themes should be dealt with in detail by the country desks. They typically end up with a plan which lists a series of topics they would like to see under investigation in as many country reports as possible in order to allow for cross-country comparison. Also, if other parts of the Economics Department have already made cross-country comparisons on selected areas of research, it does not make much sense for the country desk to reiterate such an endeavour.

Once the initial idea stage has ended, it is time to enter the second stage, during which updated data are collected in the surveyed country. This is the stage when a vast number of national civil servants are directly involved in the survey process. Initially the country desk formulates a rather long list of detailed questions, which are sent to the relevant national authorities, asking them to respond, preferably in writing, within a quite short deadline. To draw an example from the preparations for the 2002 annual survey of Denmark, the Danish/Swedish country desk sent a questionnaire with 44 questions concerning the structural part of the survey to the relevant public authorities in Denmark. Having responded to these questions one by one, the Danish authorities could then wait for the first of two so-called OECD missions. The first mission (from 2–4 April 2001) only concerned the selected in-depth structural theme (on this occasion: 'expenditure policy') and involved in-depth interviews with numerous Danish civil servants, economic experts and societal groups throughout the three days of the mission. Having already read the written answers to the many detailed questions on the questionnaire, the OECD delegation (the economists from the country desk and the Head of Division) concentrated on policy issues in their interviews. Thus loaded with information, the OECD delegation then returned to Paris to draft the first version of the survey's structural chapter.

Some four months later, the country desk formulated yet another questionnaire to be sent to the Danish authorities. This time they included no less than 92 detailed questions about general macro-economic issues that they sought written replies to within a short deadline. Again, having received the answers from the Danish civil service, the country desk next organised the so-called main mission (5–7 September 2001) to Denmark, which entailed the participation of the economists from the country desk, the Head of Division and also the Deputy Director of the Country Studies Branch. As with the previous mission, the purpose of the mission was to talk with a variety of different people. In practice, the OECD delegation managed to have in-depth discussions with no less than 15 different authorities in the Danish polity.

This ended the second stage of the survey process and launched the third stage, in which the country desk finalised the first complete draft of the survey. The first draft, with its four parts (assessment and recommendations; recent trends and prospects, and macro-economic policy requirement; an overview of structural policy developments, key challenges, priorities and progress in implementing structural reforms; and an in-depth structural chapter), could now be published on the Online Information Service (the OLIS database) to which all permanent members of the EDRC have access. They, as well as the Danish public authorities concerned, now had a chance to read the survey and consider their own interventions. This was also the stage in which the country desk formulated a so-called 'Questions for Discussion Note' that is normally no longer than two pages. These questions are supposed to help structure the debate during the forthcoming EDRC meeting; thereby making the encounter more output-oriented and dynamic.

The fourth stage constitutes the regular EDRC meeting itself. The working procedures of the committee meetings have been formulated in writing so that any new member and participant can prepare for the meeting in advance in the best possible way (OECD 1998b). In the case of the Danish example, the morning immediately prior to the meeting itself (on 7 January 2002), the chair of the committee met briefly with the OECD secretariat and with the so-called examining countries (in this case the economics or financial counsellors from the Swedish and Portuguese OECD delegations in Paris) to discuss the day's meeting. Having planned the strategy to follow in the examination procedure, the EDRC meeting started at 9:30 and lasted all day until 18:00.

The chair opened the meeting and then gave the floor to the head of the Danish delegation to make some introductory notes on the macro-economic part of the survey. Normally eight (and sometimes up to 15) high-ranking Danish civil servants from the Danish civil service show up for the examination. Included are two to three people who are especially concerned with the structural chapter of the survey as well as a representative from the Danish central bank and four to six representatives from the Danish ministries of finance and economics. The economic counsellor and the ambassador from the permanent Danish OECD delegation in Paris second the Danish delegation. For 20 minutes, the head of the Danish delegation had a chance to underline the issues with regard to the Danish macro-economy that he wanted to see at the centre of the first part of the day-long meeting.

Following these introductory statements, the examination started. Two selected examining countries, in this case Sweden and Portugal, sent delegates to the meeting with a view to asking critical questions of the Danish delegation. These examining countries are normally represented by two delegates each, who both spend a maximum of 10 minutes underlining the critical points of the survey. Having listened to the examiners, the Danish delegation had an opportunity to respond before the permanent members of the committee started to ask questions. These questions can be based on the circulated Question for Discussion Note or they can be on entirely new topics. The floor is normally reasonably open for debate although this depends on the chair and his or her time-management skills.

At this point, a break normally separates the macro-economic discussion from the structural discussion which takes place after lunch. The structural discussions are organised in exactly the same way as before, with the head of the delegation introducing the session and then passing the floor to the examining countries and the permanent committee members. At the end of the meeting, the chair summarises the discussion and underlines the consensus that has arisen during the meeting, which he or she expects the OECD secretariat to have in mind when redrafting the survey for adoption and publication. This ends the regular EDRC meeting.

The day following the EDRC meeting, the OECD secretariat (the country desk economists) and the country delegation meet again in order to settle the last outstanding issues that were not dealt with in detail. Importantly, during this meeting no further changes in the survey can be introduced, only matters of technical character can be handled at this stage. The chair has already defined the bottom line conclusions of the EDRC meeting itself and has written the message to appear in the introductory Assessment and Recommendations part of the survey, and these cannot be altered. Under normal circumstances, therefore, the fifth and final stage of the survey process now starts. However, sometimes the examined country refuses to accept the chair's conclusions and requires that the bureau (the chair and the two vice-chairs) are convened for another meeting. This happens on relatively rare occasions, but when it happens the ensuing adaptations to the report are spelled out in extra detail before the final draft is circulated among the permanent members of the committee.

In the fifth and final stage, the permanent members have a few weeks to comment on the revised report before the next regular meeting of the EDRC. If no comments have been made, the survey is adopted as the first point on the agenda. If comments have been made, it can take a few extra meetings before the committee unanimously adopts the report for publication. This ends the formal part of the survey procedure, concluding a process that has been going on not only during the day of the EDRC examination, but on a regular basis during the preceding 18 months, with the involvement of a great number of national civil servants. When evaluating the impact of OECD surveillance, various permanent members of the committee have pointed to the importance of the lengthy survey formulation process, rather than the EDRC meeting itself. In their view, it is the ongoing process that is important, rather than the punctual examination in Paris or the debates – of varying degrees of intensity – which follow the distribution of the final report in the national political communities. Some national authorities take the initiative to invite representatives from the OECD secretariat to their country in order to present the new OECD survey to the broader public. In other countries the survey does not manage to get one single headline in the national newspapers.

In summary, three points are worth emphasising with regard to the EDRC surveillance procedure. First, the choice of structural themes dealt with in the respective reports is based on political as well as practical considerations related to the financial and skill-based capacities of the OECD. There are political considerations because the choice of structural themes to be dealt with in the surveys reflects the priorities of the Ministerial Council as expressed in the annual communiqués as well as the priorities of the Secretary-General and the Economics Department. There are practical considerations because the individual surveys are written by two OECD economists who do not have infinite resources at their disposal when planning the individual surveys.

Second, the survey process is quite long and not limited to the meeting of the EDRC itself. During the data-gathering stage, a great number of national civil servants are involved in answering questionnaires and in receiving various OECD missions. This is a lengthy learning process which in itself might have longer-lasting consciousness-raising effects among national civil servants than the political messages resulting from the final survey. The survey itself might not play a role in the national policy processes, but the surveillance procedure might help raise important questions and ideas in the minds of the political and administrative actors in the national polity.

Finally, the reception of the survey varies considerably from one country to the next. To theorise about the factors that impact on the different ways in which the survey is received in different countries is the object of the last chapter of this book.

CONCLUSIONS

The OECD does not play a primarily regulatory game when surveying its member countries, nor does it play a financial game. This is quite natural, since the OECD does not produce formal laws to any significant extent and does not possess resources that can be applied as incitements for norm-conforming behaviour. Thus, the OECD is bound to play the so-called idea game through which it collects, manipulates and diffuses data, knowledge, visions and ideas to its member countries and, to a still larger extent, to a series of non-member countries.

One significant and important way in which the OECD engages in multi-lateral surveillance by playing the idea game is through its regular country surveys, produced in the Economics Department and finally adopted by the Economic and Development Review Committee. Through the lengthy procedure by which these country surveys are produced, a great number of national civil servants are involved in gathering data and answering questions posed by the OECD secretariat. One significant factor that characterises this part of the surveillance process is that it is the OECD secretariat that decides *what* data and *which* questions the national civil servants should focus on. At a later point in the process, a national delegation travels to Paris to defend the national macro-economic and structural strategies of the government in power. Again, it is the OECD secretariat which, through a 'Questions for Discussion Note' and through its presence during the committee meeting, tries to influence the agenda of the examination. Finally, when the survey is published, it is the EDR Committee and its chair who take full responsibility for the assessments and recommendations resulting from the survey; on various occasions, these have been rather straightforward and critical in their tone. Therefore, it can be concluded that the OECD is really trying to set the agenda for policy debate and reform in its member countries. But is it succeeding? Various intervening and country-specific variables can come in the way of using the idea game to undertake effective surveillance. Some of these will become obvious in the following country-specific chapters. These variables will also be addressed in the final and concluding chapter of the present book.

ACKNOWLEDGEMENT

1. Thanks for many helpful comments and suggestions from the many interviewees who have read the first version of this chapter and to the two editors of the present book, Klaus Armingeon and Michelle Beyeler. Of course, none of these people carry the responsibility for the final product.

REFERENCES

Aubrey, Henry G. (1967), *Atlantic Economic Cooperation – the Case of the OECD*, New York: Frederick A. Praeger Publishers.
Bomberg, Elisabeth and John Peterson (2000), 'Policy transfer and Europeanization: passing the Heineken test?', *Queen's Papers on Europeanization*, no. 2/2000.
Chayes, Abram and Antonia Handler Chayes (1993), 'On compliance', *International Organization* **47** (2), 175–205.
Checkel, Jeffrey (2001), 'Why comply? Social learning and European identity change', *International Organization* **55** (3), 553–588.
Drezner, Daniel W. (2000), 'Bargaining, enforcement, and sanctions: when is cooperation counterproductive?', *International Organization* **54** (1), 73–102.

Hurd, Ian (1999), 'Legitimacy and authority in international politics', *International Organization* **53** (2), 379–408.

Kristensen, Thorkil (1962a), 'L'Organisation de Coopération et de Développement Économique, ses origines, ses buts, sa structure', *European Yearbook*, vol. IX, 88–101.

Kristensen, Thorkil (1962b), 'Introduction' in *OECD Annual Report 1962*, 10 November, Paris: OECD.

Kristensen, Thorkil (1963), 'OECD efter to års arbejde', *Ekonomisk Revy* **7** (September), 417–423.

Kristensen, Thorkil (1966), 'OECD in the years to come', *OECD Observer* **29**, 3–7.

Kristensen, Thorkil (1967a), 'Tyve år efter', *Udenrigsministeriets Tidsskrift* **21**, 402–404.

Kristensen, Thorkil (1967b), 'Five years of O.E.C.D.', *European Yearbook*, vol. XIII, 100–113.

Kristensen, Thorkil (1989), *Erindringer*, Odense: Odense Universitetsforlag.

Lerdell, David and Kerstin Sahlin-Andersson (1997), *Att lära över gränser – En studie av OECD's förvaltningspolitiska samarbete. Rapport till förvaltningspolitiska kommissionen*, Stockholm: Finansdepartementet.

Marcussen, Martin (2000), 'Uafhængigheden hærger i Europa: Reform af central-bankerne i Frankrig, Sverige og England', *Politica* **32** (3), 300–320.

Marcussen, Martin (2002a), 'EMU: a Danish delight and dilemma', in K. Dyson (ed.), *European States and the Euro – Europeanization, Variation, and Convergence*, Oxford: Oxford University Press, pp. 120–144.

Marcussen, Martin (2002b), *OECD og idéspillet – Game Over?*, Copenhagen: Hans Reitzels Forlag.

OECD (1998a), *The OECD Committee Structure – A Review (The Vinde Report)*, Paris: Organisation for Economic Co-operation and Development.

OECD (1998b), *EDRC Agreed Principles and Practices*, Paris: Organisation for Economic Co-operation and Development.

OECD (2001), *OECD Staff Profile Statistics, 2000*, Paris: Organisation for Economic Co-operation and Development.

Putnam, Robert D. (1988), 'Diplomacy and domestic politics', *International Organization* **42** (3), 427–460.

Raustiala, Kal (2000), 'Compliance and effectiveness in international regulatory coop-eration', *Case Western Reserve Journal of International Law* **32** (2), 453–508.

Risse, Thomas (2000), 'Let's argue!: communicative action in world politics', *International Organization* **54** (1), 1–39.

Schimmelfennig, Frank (2000), 'International socialization in the New Europe: ratio-nal action in an institutional environment', *European Journal of International Relations* **6** (1), 109–139.

Sjöstedt, Gunnar (1973), *OECD-Samarbetet: funktioner och effekter*, Stockholm Political Studies 3, Stockholm: SU, Statsvetenskapliga institutionen.

Sullivan, Scott (1997), *From War to Wealth – Fifty Years of Innovation*, Paris: Organisation for Economic Co-operation and Development.

3. The OECD as a scientific authority? The OECD's influence on Danish welfare policies

Lars Bo Kaspersen and Maria Svaneborg

DEVELOPMENT OF THE DANISH WELFARE STATE

From the late nineteenth century onward, we can detect the emergence of a welfare state in Denmark. The country became a liberal-democratic nation-state with the introduction of the Constitution in 1849. That was the year that Denmark became a *Rechtsstaat*, with the separation of the state and the market/civil society based on constitutional law. From the 1860s onward we see the first tentative steps towards state intervention in society. The first and very modest attempt to regulate the market was in the arena of housing and planning regulation. The major breakpoint, however, came in the year 1891/92, when the Conservative Prime Minister Jacob S. Estrup introduced a set of social security schemes, although these were still very limited in their scope (old age assistance in 1891, sickness insurance in 1892). These were later followed by, among others, accident insurance (1898), an occupational safety and health act (1901) and an unemployment act (1907). All these acts demonstrate clear state intervention in the market to meet basic needs among various segments of the population. These acts were all passed when bourgeois parties dominated both chambers in the parliament (Nørgaard 2000). Although the Social Democrats were gaining ground rapidly, the timing of the acts demonstrates that at least the foundation of the Danish welfare state was not laid out by the Social Democrats, as Esping-Andersen seems to suggest (1990). What is crucial about these first welfare acts is their common institutional features. They all involved a decentralised administration. The decentralised character of the Danish welfare state is its most significant feature, and still dominates the structure of the welfare state in the country today.

The next step in the development of the Danish welfare state took place during World War I, when an intensive and extensive state intervention occurred. After World War I the state was rolled back and society returned to 'normal'. A new set of social acts was passed in the 1930s during the crisis years, but these did not change the character of the welfare state. Two other events must also be mentioned. The first concerns Denmark's acceptance of Marshall Plan aid in 1947. Thus Denmark was a member of the OEEC from its very beginning. In any analysis of the impact of the OECD on Denmark it is important to remember that membership in the OECD and the acceptance of the Marshall aid resulted in a major transformation of Danish society. Liberalisation of trade and industry in Denmark had to take place as a consequence of the aid (Schmidt 1993). In other words, OEEC had an enormous impact on the restructuring of the Danish welfare state.

The other important event to take place was the social reforms of 1972–74, which can be said to have constituted a development and consolidation of the welfare state based on more universalistic principles – in other words, the creation of a social citizenship state (Nørgaard 1999). In this instance, as before, the bourgeois parties supported most of the reform acts. This act can in some respects be seen as the peak of the universalistic Danish welfare state.

The reform had only just been implemented when Denmark was hit by two oil crises and the economy went into a deep recession. This was reinforced by a failed macroeconomic policy, first put in place by a right-wing coalition government and later continued by a Social Democratic minority government. In 1982 a new bourgeois government took over and began a number of reforms, but by 1986 it had lost its focus. From 1993 onward a new Social Democratic majority government replaced the only partially successful centre-right coalition. Despite the fact that they lost their majority in 1994, the Social Democrats governed with support from the Social Liberals and did not have any problems in passing their policies in the parliament. They managed to quite successfully bring more coherence to governing the economy, and did so with support from both the left and the right. In the 1990s, the Social Democrat-led government passed several acts which had been discussed but never passed in the 1980s by the centre-right government, especially in the field of social security. Interest groups, particularly the trade unions, became more 'government friendly' once the Social Democrats were in power. Among other things, a more active labour market policy was introduced.

In order to understand the Danish version of the welfare state, one must first study the Danish party system and the basic structure of the political system. The party system proved to be a key to understanding why Denmark – after more than a decade of major economic problems – suddenly surprised everyone by responding to new international challenges with coherence and strong policies which strengthened the economy and the welfare state (Green-Pedersen 2001). In addition, it is important to mention that the Danish political system is a combined associative and representative democracy, in which interest groups and voluntary associations play an important role in policy making. These two factors contribute to a higher level of political consensus (Kaspersen and Ottesen 2001).

Measured in terms of GDP, Denmark is one of the richest countries in the world. At the moment, the state's finances are in good shape and in the year 2002 unemployment rates were remarkably low. The Danish krone is pegged to the euro, which has so far resulted in low inflation. Denmark's future challenges include the need for: continued tight budget control; an increase in labour force numbers, especially in the private sector; and better policies to deal with the integration of immigrants.

OECD IDEAS CONCERNING DANISH SOCIAL POLICIES

The labour market is the policy field most frequently addressed in OECD surveys (see Table 3.1) for the past three decades, with a specific focus on high unemployment rates. From the mid-1970s to the late 1990s the same two problems were addressed almost every year: wage increases and high unemployment rates.

It was not until the late 1990s that the surveys addressed two new labour market problems: an insufficient labour supply and early retirement. Overall the OECD fears that the Danish social security system is too generous and creates disincentives to work, thereby causing a culture of dependency on different kinds of public benefits. Accordingly, the OECD has recommended reductions in transfers, lower replacement rates, cuts to the minimum wage and a reduction on marginal taxes for labour. Since the early 1980s the OECD has further recommended stronger support for education, retraining and activation. There is no clear development in the labour market recommendations pointed out by the OECD; in fact, to a large extent the recommendations over the past 30 years have remained the same, though they have become slightly more extensive and radical with time.

In 1985 another policy field, education, is mentioned, though not at any length. The OECD's concern when first addressing this issue was a loss of competitiveness, and it recommended an improved education system in which skills training would be matched to the demands of business and industry, resulting in more education focused on knowledge-intensive lines of business. Later in the 1990s, the focus shifted to the excessively long time spent gaining an education and to the high drop-out rate. The OECD recommended cuts to student grants, reducing the period of time during which students could receive support, and lowering minimum wages to encourage education.

Old age is also mentioned for the first time in 1985, due to concerns regarding the future tax burden of the ageing population. The OECD recommended more flexible retirement schemes and a gradual shift towards supplementary

Table 3.1 Social policy in OECD reports on Denmark

Year	Problems	Criticisms	Recommendations
Employment/Labour market			
1974–90 1998, 1999	Wage increases	Procedures for wage bargaining involve indexation Procedures for wage bargaining are too inflexible High marginal taxes fuel wage increases	Facilitate regular consultations between the government and the labour market Ensure greater wage dispersion and flexibility Make changes to the income tax system
1975–96	High rate of structural unemployment	The Danish social security system is too generous and creates disincentives to work	Reduce transfers Reduce marginal taxes on labour Provide stronger support for education, retraining and activation Lower the minimum wage
1999, 2000	Insufficient labour supply	Benefit levels are too generous for low wage groups The right to reject job offers Average hours worked are low by OECD standards Too much time spent on education	Scale back of paid-leave schemes Reduce replacement rates Put in place a waiting period for unemployment benefits
Education			
1985, 1995–99	Loss of competitiveness		Place a greater focus on education for knowledge-intensive lines of business Improve the education system to focus on skills in demand in business and industry
1989, 1990 1989, 1999			Expand facilities for (re)education Provide youth education and training (*continued overleaf*)

35

Table 3.1 continued

Year	Problems	Criticisms	Recommendations
1995–97	High drop-out rates for formal education	Small wage differentials give no incentives to invest in education	Lower the minimum wage
1997	Denmark falling behind in respect to proficiency in reading, writing, mathematics and science		Provide performance-related payment for teachers as an incentive and increase teaching hours
1997, 1999, 2000	Excessively long time spent gaining education Danish students enter higher education at a relatively old age and spend excessively long time gaining education	No strict upper time limit to finish education	Provide students with loans rather than grants Put in place user fees for training Cut student grants Reduce the length of time during which students can receive state support
	Old age		
1985	Tax pressure due to pensions	Rigid labour market	Make early retirement schemes more flexible Provide private pension schemes
1997, 1999, 2000	Demographic pressures		Make early retirement schemes more flexible Provide private pensions schemes

Source: OECD Economic Surveys on Denmark from 1970 to 2000. The column 'Year' indicates the year of publication of the quoted survey

36

private insurance. Old age is not mentioned again until the late 1990s and although the OECD at that time pointed out the same problem, the recommendations were now different. This time a more consistent and widespread application of user charges and outsourcing were recommended as ways of rationalising and cutting back public expenditure because of demographic pressures.

CONCORDANCE AND DISCORDANCE

Danish Public Policy and OECD Recommendations

In this section we will address the following question: Are the OECD recommendations in concordance or discordance with Danish policy development? The assessment is summarised in Table 3.2 and is followed by a more detailed exposition of the assessment.

Employment

Most reports from 1974 onward have pointed to wage levels and wage increases as the reason for Denmark's lack of competitiveness. As a result, other procedures to regulate the labour market have been recommended. Due to a general consensus in Denmark regarding preference for the 'Danish model', no changes have been made in line with OECD recommendations. None of the various governments have made any clear attempts to create more wage dispersion apart from some changes in the public sector involving more flexibility. When it comes to the income tax system some alterations have taken place, for example a reduction in marginal taxes in 1987 and 1994. On the other hand, Denmark also increased its marginal income taxes in 1982.

According to the OECD, a key problem during the past 30 years has been the high rate of structural unemployment, which has led to a persistent set of recommendations pointing to the importance of reducing both social security transfers and marginal taxes on labour. Again, it is difficult to assess their impact, but from 1982 onwards a number of policies have been adopted to either freeze or slightly reduce certain kinds of benefits (this trend can be discerned in the reform acts passed by the bourgeois government in 1982 and 1987 and by the Social Democrat-led government in 1994). Despite making these adjustments to bring the social security system in line with the OECD's recommendations, it is difficult to assess whether the changes were implemented due to the OECD or it needs to be explained by other factors since the OECD continuously suggests these types of measures.

In the 1996 survey, the OECD seems to have reflected on the apparently conflicting fundamental ideas behind OECD recommendations and the Danish welfare system (OECD 1996, p. 118). The 1996 survey draws attention to the

Table 3.2 Concordance between Danish policy development and OECD recommendations

Recommendations/Criticisms	Concordance
Employment	
Ensure regular consultations between the government and the labour market (74–90, 98, 99)	Unclear/No
Focus on greater wage dispersion and flexibility (74–90, 98, 99)	No
Make changes to the income tax system (74–90, 98, 99)	Unclear/Yes
Reduce transfers (75–96)	Unclear
Reduce marginal taxes on labour (75–96)	Unclear
Provide stronger support for education, retaining and activation (75–96)	Yes
Cut minimum wage (75–96)	No
Scale back paid-leave schemes (99, 00)	Unclear
Reduce replacement rates (99–00)	Unclear
Put in place waiting periods for unemployment benefits (99–00)	Unclear
Make retirement schemes less accessible (97–00)	Yes
Old age	
Make early retirement schemes more flexible. Allow for private pension schemes (85)	No
Gain control over public spending: rationalisation, user charges and outsourcing; shift gradually towards supplementary pension schemes (97, 99, 00)	Unclear
Education	
Focus on more education in knowledge-intensive lines of business (85, 95–99)	Yes
Improve the education system with skills matching the demands of business and industry (85, 95–99)	Yes
Expand facilities for (re)education (89, 90, 99)	Unclear
Provide youth education and training (89, 90, 99)	Yes
Provide more incentives to invest in education by lowering minimum wage (95–97)	No
Give performance-related payment for teachers as an incentive and increase teaching hours (97)	Yes
Provide students with loans rather than grants (97, 99, 00)	No
Collect user fees for training (97, 99, 00)	No
Cut student grants (97, 99, 00)	No
Reduce the period of time during which students can receive state support (97, 99, 00)	No

Note: The policy recommendations stem from the analysis of OECD country surveys (cf. Table 3.1). Details on the assessment are given in the text.

fact that Denmark's design for its tax and transfer system is closely linked to the objectives of the Scandinavian universal welfare model. This welfare state concept differs from other OECD countries insofar as benefit entitlements are linked to social aims as well as demonstrated financial needs, and benefit rights are generally not accumulated through contributions to insurance schemes or to a person's employment record. To combat relative poverty, a whole range of social insurances, offering rather generous replacement rates in the case of either a temporary or permanent loss of income, are provided by the public sector. By drawing these conclusions, the OECD demonstrated its awareness that some of its social policy recommendations conflict with the strong egalitarian profile of the Danish social security system and therefore do not offer possible solutions for Danish social policy.

The OECD brought the problem of an insufficient labour supply on to the agenda for the first time in 1996. Various recommendations were offered, including a scaling back of paid-leave schemes and lower declining replacement rates. It is too early to conclude whether policies in line with these suggestions have actually been put in place, but during the Social Democratic–Social Liberal government in the 1990s some modest attempts at change were made.

Old age
The issue of old age is only mentioned in four surveys. It is first discussed in 1985, with regard to tax pressure due to pensions. The structure of the Danish multitiered pension system remained intact from 1982 to 1993 and total expenditures on old age pensions increased (Kvist 1997). Some adjustments were made in 1999 with a new pre-pension reform but they were only half-hearted. On the one hand, the retirement age was lowered but on the other hand, the reform contained some incentives to remain longer in the labour market and not opt for pre-pension benefits. All in all, from 1985 onward, the Danish pension policy must be judged to be in discordance with OECD recommendations. In the late 1990s the OECD saw the demographic pressure emerging and suggested user charges and outsourcing. These policies have been implemented, but at a moderate level and, moreover, since the administration of old age issues is a local matter, the policies are very diversified. Some municipalities have introduced outsourcing and privatisation whereas others are sticking to purely public models.

Education
Education first emerged as an issue in 1985, and remained prominent throughout the 1990s. A major concern mentioned in several surveys (1989, 1990, 1998 and 1999) is loss of competitiveness. OECD recommendations – including the provision of more education in the field of knowledge-intensive industries and an increase in the responsiveness of the education system to business

demands – were addressed through several policy adjustments throughout the 1990s. Again, it is difficult to assess the policies adopted by the Danish government. At some level, they appear to follow OECD recommendations, but the surveys are not very precise or specific. They only talk about reforms and recommendations in very broad terms.

Improved youth education and training were suggested and during the 1990s several adjustments were made (1993, 1995, 1996, 2000) in an attempt both to motivate more young people to continue their education and also to reform the institution to meet new challenges.

In order to reduce high drop-out rates from formal education, the OECD proposed the lowering of minimum wages. However, this has not happened in Denmark. This is an example of clear discordance between suggestion and implementation.

In 1997 the OECD claimed that Denmark was falling behind in respect to proficiency in general subjects (reading, writing, maths) and the OECD recommended a more competitive education system, including performance-related payments for teachers. Some changes were made both in terms of a new payment scheme (1999) and in regard to improving the quality of teaching and increasing the number of lessons in basic subjects. Therefore we have concordance in this policy area. Also in the late 1990s the OECD criticised the length of time Danish students spent gaining higher education. None of the recommendations have been followed but in 1989 changes were already put in place to reduce the number of years of grant eligibility.

To complete this analysis it is worth stressing that we cannot find any particular pattern showing that governments formed by the right or the centre-right have a stronger tendency to adopt policies in line with OECD recommendations. Governments led by both the Social Democrats and the centre-right have been behind the relatively few policies where we find some concordance between OECD and Danish public policy.

OECD INFLUENCE ON SOCIAL POLICY REFORMS

No studies exist that examine the role or the effects of the OECD on Danish social policy debate in general. During the period under investigation, various governments have undertaken several reforms and adjustments. Two reforms, however, can be considered key reforms because they both altered fundamental patterns which had been followed for several years prior to the reforms. These two reforms were the 1972–74 reform and the labour market reform in 1994. The first was hardly mentioned in OECD surveys. The second reform was not implemented exactly according to OECD recommendations, although some of the ideas are in concordance with OECD policy. It was fuelled primarily by domestic debates and initiatives. It cannot be determined to what extent the OECD influenced the debate in the years before the reforms, and to what extent leading Social Democrats, Social Liberals and civil servants looked to the OECD for ideas.

Analysts examined explicit references to the OECD in political debates between the years 1997 and 2000 by scrutinising parliamentary debates. Most of the 473 references allude generally to the OECD, and are not related to social policy. References to the OECD are made, however, in the course of various debates, and the OECD is often used as an authority to which one can refer in order to give some substance and legitimacy to an argument. There is no pattern to be discerned in terms of one party referring to the OECD with more frequency. Most parties seem to accept the OECD as an objective authority.

An example is provided by Marcussen in his recent study of the OECD (Marcussen 2002). During the Danish election campaign which preceded the referendum vote on Denmark joining the Economic and Monetary Union, the Minister of Economic Affairs Marianne Jelved explicitly referred to a section in the OECD survey in which the OECD mentions that 'Denmark may be better off adopting the euro and thereby gaining the benefits of sharing a single currency with most of its trading partners' (OECD 2000, p. 11). Here the OECD is used as an objective authority in an attempt to persuade opponents about the advantage of accepting the euro.

CONCLUSION

During the period examined, the OECD mainly criticised the structure of the labour market; only in the second half of the 1990s did it focus on other social policy issues such as education and old age. Danish governments have endorsed some of the policies suggested by the OECD but it is impossible to determine how strong the causal link is between recommendation and implementation.

First of all, we cannot tell if the ideas leading to concrete Danish social policies stem from the OECD or from another ideational artist. Other organisations – not least among them the EU – could be a stronger determining force. Or, as is suggested by Goul Andersen, most welfare state policies implemented in Denmark are driven by both domestic problems and political struggles (Goul Andersen 2002) as well as by the manner in which politicians and civil servants perceive and conceive various challenges. Many policies are an outcome of domestic political struggles between different parties but also between the state and municipal levels and the state and interest groups.

From our brief investigation of parliamentary debates and the role of OECD in the Danish media it is quite clear that the OECD is most often used as an objective authority which can be utilised by the government as well as the opposition. This role is probably more evident and apparent than the OECD's role of ideational creator. Danish politicians and civil servants were recently interviewed about the role of the OECD (Marcussen 2002). The research demonstrated that the link between the OECD and Danish policy is difficult to characterise, but most of those interviewed regarded the OECD as an important objective authority to be taken seriously, yet they did not consider it to be nearly as important as the EU.

Another problem in assessing the OECD's role concerns the nature of the recommendations. After analysing the surveys it becomes clear that most of the recommendations are so general in kind that you can almost always argue that certain policies implemented in a Danish context in the years after a survey's publication bear some similarities to the OECD suggestions.

A cautious conclusion could be that the OECD is seen as an objective authority in Denmark. It is, however, far from the only authority politicians look to, and its importance has probably decreased as the number of knowledge producers has grown. Today they include the EU, the IMF, the World Bank, various Danish ministries, universities and other research institutions. The OECD plays a role as a means of legitimising viewpoints and arguments in domestic debates in Denmark. Several politicians and a small but influential sector of the media use it. This role – rather than that of an ideational creator – is probably the OECD's most important contribution in Denmark.

REFERENCES

Esping-Andersen, Gøsta (1990), *The Three Worlds of Welfare Capitalism*, Princeton, NJ: Princeton University Press.

Goul Andersen, Jørgen (2002), 'Velfærd uden skatter: Det danske velfærdsmirakel i 1990'erne', *Politica* **34** (1), 5–23.

Green-Pedersen, Christopher (2001), 'Small states with big success: party politics and governing the economy in Denmark and the Netherlands from 1973 to 2000', paper presented at the annual meeting of APSA, San Francisco.

Jonasen, V. (1998), *Dansk socialpolitik 1708–1998*, Aarhus: Den Social Højskole i Aarhus.

Kaspersen, Lars Bo and Laila Ottesen (2001), 'Associationalism for 150 years and still alive and kicking: some reflections on Danish civil society', *Critical Review of International Social and Political Philosophy* **4** (1), 106–130.

Kvist, Jon (1997), 'Retrenchment or restructuring? The emergence of a multi-tiered welfare state in Denmark', in Jochen Clasen (ed.), *Social Insurance in Europe*, Bristol: The Policy Press, pp. 14–39.

Marcussen, Martin (2002), *OECD og idéspillet. Game over?*, Copenhagen: Hans Reitzels Forlag.

Nørgaard, A. (1999), 'Viden og videnskab om velfærdsstaten', *Grus* **56/57**, 6–39.

Nørgaard, Asbjørn Sonne (2000), 'Party politics and the organization of the Danish welfare state, 1890–1920: the bourgeois roots of the modern welfare state', *Scandinavian Political Studies* **23** (3), 183–215.
OECD [various years], *OECD Economic Survey, Denmark*, Paris: Organisation for Economic Co-operation and Development.
Schmidt, E. I. (1993), *Fra Psykopatklubben*, Copenhagen: Gyldendal.

4. Finland: considering OECD guidelines but within national institutional settings

Pekka Kosonen

INSTITUTIONAL AND POLITICAL CONTEXT

Finland can be said to belong to a Nordic welfare model, or 'Social Democratic regime', more and more so since the beginning of the 1980s. Common goals like universalism, public responsibility for services, equality and full employment have united Denmark, Finland, Norway and Sweden. Based on a system of 'social corporatism', policy-making in these countries deviates in many respects from more market-oriented lines (Kosonen 1998). However, while Esping-Andersen (1990) stresses 'decommodification' in the Nordic welfare states, at least in the case of Finland the basis of the system in a 'working society' should be remembered. It is thus a question of a process in which the normalcy of wage-work has been made compatible with the universalist principle of social citizenship (Kettunen 2001).

In the postwar period, both universalism and earnings-related benefits have characterised the Finnish welfare state. Universalism is in the interest of agrarian population and manual workers, whereas skilled workers and the middle classes have favoured earnings-related arrangements. Many systems like pension schemes, health insurance and public services represent a combination of these two, since both the Centre and Social Democrats (and the labour market partners) have had strong positions on these issues. The most important reforms date back to the 1960s (earnings-related pensions in addition to basic pensions, health insurance) and the 1970s (health care, day care), although the welfare state continued to expand during the 1980s. However, the deep economic recession in the first half of the 1990s (contraction of the GDP by 13 per cent) was associated with both savings and expenditure cuts, although the basic structure of the welfare state remained more or less intact.

While Finnish governments were traditionally formed between the Centre and the Social Democrats, plus some smaller parties, a turn can be detected in 1987 when the Conservatives and Social Democrats formed a coalition. After a break (Centre-right government) from 1991 to 1995, this coalition (together with the Greens and the Left Alliance) governed again until 2003. This could be hypothesised to bring in a policy line more in concordance with OECD recommendations. However, it is likely that the recession of the 1990s, and the slow recovery of employment after that, has been more important in making Finnish policy-makers more open to OECD proposals. An additional factor, not to be forgotten, has been preparation for EU membership (1995) and the third stage of the EMU (1999), which has forced savings in public spending. Thus, multiple factors are at play.[1]

So, what is the role of the OECD, and its annual country surveys in particular, in shaping the policies of its member states? Certainly, the surveys give a lot of information and evaluations on country developments. On the other hand, although the OECD can advise member states to carry out policy changes, it has relatively little ability to push them to do so. For example, in the case of the OECD 'Jobs Strategy', the idea of neoliberal labour market reform was – and is – flexibility in working hours, wage flexibility, reduction in work disincentives, but also strengthening the emphasis on active labour market policies. In a 1997 study on compliance to the OECD 'Jobs Strategies', Finland was among the laggards and got a substantial number of recommendations on how to fulfil the OECD strategy (McBride and Williams 2001). However, it may well be that many of the targets in this strategy contradict Finnish labour market structures and policies.

OECD IDEAS CONCERNING FINNISH SOCIAL POLICY[2]

In the 1970s, the Finnish *labour markets* experienced rapid changes, from almost full employment – even labour shortages were feared – to rapidly increasing unemployment after the mid-1970s. Since, according to the traditional Finnish model of economic policy, monetary and fiscal policies were procyclical, the measures strengthened the ups and downs in both the economy and in employment. In the first half of the 1970s, OECD reports found the main problem to lie in regional and structural imbalances. In the mid-1970s, open unemployment rose. However, this had little room in OECD reports in 1975 and 1977, although later the negative employment outcomes of economic policy are mentioned.

The decade of the 1980s was, from the labour market point of view, relatively stable. The role of incomes policies was increasing in order to guarantee 'moderate' wage increases and to maintain the competitiveness of the export sector. To this purpose, the government could grant some tax concessions, but very cautiously. According to the OECD, labour market mobility should have been greater, and some sectors suffered from the lack of a skilled workforce.

Everything changed at the beginning of the 1990s, and this is reflected in the lengthy criticisms and recommendations of the reports. The main problem during the economic recession was soaring unemployment, with only slowly decreasing figures since the mid-1990s. It was argued that the centralised collective bargaining system was too rigid for market adjustments in wages and working conditions. The criticisms focused specifically on the (collectively-agreed) minimum wages, which hindered the hiring of young, less-skilled persons. Overall, the OECD noted that there was too narrow a wage structure to foster work incentives. Recommendations followed from these criticisms (see Table 4.1).

From 1995 on, during the time when a new 'rainbow coalition' (i.e. almost all major political parties represented) was formed in government, two main lines in OECD reports with regard to employment can be detected. First, flexibility is emphasised even more than earlier. Second, the main point of criticism since the mid-1990s has been associated with the relation between welfare arrangements and employment. The recommendations include: strengthening control over the unemployed, changing the early retirement schemes, applying stricter conditions to earnings-related unemployment insurance, and shortening the unemployment 'pipeline' to pensions and other schemes.

The share of the working-age population to the retired population has long been favourable in Finland, and the OECD began to note *old age* related problems only in the 1990s. In pension policy there are increasing financing problems, in particular with the employment pensions; these are legislated, earnings-related and semi-funded pensions. Criticism is targeted at the low retirement age, which refers mainly to low effective retirement age (under 60 years), but also to the standard retirement age, which is too low. Another criticism relates to the way pensions are funded. The second issue is services for the care of the elderly: the problem is that the system of user charges partly relies on incomes-testing, which may create incentives for individuals to enter into institutional care.

In 1998, the OECD recognised that cost savings had been implemented in *health care*. However, the wide variation in per capita health care costs across regions suggests scope for further progress through the adoption of national best practice standards. This means reducing overlap in service provision and strengthening competition between hospitals.

Considerable achievements on *education* were recognised by the OECD in the 1996 survey, but these, according to the OECD, have been realised at a substantial cost. Tertiary education tends to lack responsiveness to changing demand for specific skills in the labour market. Secondary education tends to result in superficial learning, while vocational education appears to be very narrowly focused on specific skills and occupations.

Table 4.1 Social policy in OECD reports on Finland

Year	Problems	Criticisms	Recommendations
Employment/Labour market			
1970s	In the first half of 1970s low unemployment rate with great regional differences Regional and structural imbalance in the labour market		A more intensive use of incentives for investment and employment in less developed regions Broadening the product and export base of industry An active manpower policy to ensure retraining and mobility
	In the second half of the 1970s increasing unemployment, at its peak 6–7% (1977–79)	Adjustment policy has made progress but at the cost of employment	Investments in competitive sectors Some stimuli to household income and demand Active labour market policies especially in the field of youth unemployment In the medium term, however, great consensus on costs and prices
1980s	Unemployment rate around 5% until late 1980s when unemployment decreases to relatively low level	Some structural rigidities in the labour market, mobility too low	Private investments (in the early 1980s) Stronger efforts to make labour market more mobile, particularly by retraining of manpower
1990s	Unemployment from 3–4% in 1990 to around 18% in 1994 Since then unemployment rate decreasing but remains high around 10% in late 1990s	Government's traditional role as a guarantee of moderate collective wage agreements by fiscal concessions. No scope for expansionary budget policy because of commitment to low inflation and budget consolidation	Reduce non-wage labour costs Reabsorption of unemployment through collectively-agreed real wages without fiscal concessions

continued overleaf

Table 4.1   *continued*

Year	Problems	Criticisms	Recommendations
		Collectively agreed minimum wages an impediment to the hiring of young low-skilled workers	Flexibility in collectively-agreed minimum wages
		Wage bargain mechanism and labour market legislation too rigid for market adjustments and employment. Wage structure too narrow to allow for work incentives and employment of new low-skilled workers	Decentralisation of wage bargaining process/more scope for relative wages
			Deregulation of the labour market by easing job protection, fixed-term contracts, working time rules
		Regional, professional, educational, occupational and skill mismatch in labour markets	Reforms of education and training
			More effective active labour market policies in training
			Increasing the labour mobility by new pension rules
		Welfare state became costly during recession. It distorts labour market, and creates disincentive to work, impediments to better economic performance	Active labour market policies away from subsidised jobs (to training)
			Increasing the employment and labour supply by strengthening the control of the unemployed and by adjustments in social transfers and security with respect to early retirement schemes, unemployment compensation, unemployment 'pipeline', to pensions and other social security schemes/social transfers
		Interaction of taxation ansd social transfers as well as high marginal tax wedge on earned income are weak work incentives	Tax and benefit incentives to work or to work more

Old age

Financing occupational retirement pensions in fast ageing society	Low retirement age Underfunded pension funds	Increase in standard retirement age Increase in effective retirement age Allow pension rights to accrue longer Increasing the funding rate of pension funds
Financing care services of the elderly; the the costs and the popularity of institutional long-term care		Estate charges to finance institutional care services if not distorting effect on savings

Health care

Wide variation in health care costs per capita across regions		Reduce overlapping, improve competition and cost-effectiveness in the provision of services

Education

Costs and relationship to the labour market	Education and skill mismatch in the labour market	'Performance-based' financial incentives to vocational education Measures to improve the efficacy of vocational training and the private apprenticeship system

Source: OECD Economic Surveys on Finland from 1970 to 2000 (cf. note 2). The column 'Year' indicates the year of publication of the quoted surveys

ASSESSING THE POSSIBLE IMPACT

Labour Markets

In the first half of the 1970s, during a period of growth in both exports and employment, the OECD recommendations included a more intensive use of incentives for investment and employment in less developed regions, broadening the product and export base of industry, and an active labour market policy to ensure retraining and mobility. In all respects, Finnish developments followed these lines, albeit in different degrees and for different reasons. The most important – and most problematic – issue has for a long time been the need to broaden the product and export base of industry. However, the state can do little to broaden the industrial base. One exception was the state-owned companies, whose share of production was still quite large in the 1970s.

Incentives for investment in less developed regions such as Northern Finland had already been created earlier, and in 1966 this was extended to 'development areas' that covered all less developed regions. Thus, Finnish policies were in line with OECD wishes. The third proposal, active labour market policy to ensure retraining and mobility, is more difficult to evaluate. Retraining was increased, whereas the amount of people employed in the public labour force dropped in the following years.

The stagflation years from 1975 to 1977 meant a drop in investments and a rapid increase in unemployment. However, this was first reflected in OECD recommendations in 1978, when the recovery had already begun. Some of the main elements behind the recovery were devaluations of the Finnish currency, the markka, and a new effort to strengthen the corporate consensus to have the trade unions accept modest nominal wage increases. Wage demands did remain modest, and as a result, real wages of industrial workers declined from 1977 to 1978 and from 1980 to 1981, facilitating the recovery of investments and manufacturing (Kalela et al. 2001). Falling real wages implied that the proposal on stimuli to household income and demand was not similarly successful. On active labour market policies one can find contradictory developments during the second half of the 1970s. On the one hand, training was not targeted toward the young. On the other hand, enterprises were given support when employing young persons, and municipalities also received more support to employ the young unemployed.

In the 1980s, problems appeared to be minor compared to the previous decade. The theme of structural rigidities and mobility in the labour market was repeated in several OECD surveys. Unemployment rates were not very high. In fact, it was admitted that the situation was not as serious in Finland as it was in a number of other countries; however, flexibilisation, it was recommended, could prevent unemployment rates from growing. In the 1980s, however, the basic focus was not on the retraining of manpower, but in the obligation of the public sector to employ the young unemployed and the long-term unemployed. This line was made legally binding in the 1987 Employment Act, during a time in which unemployment rates as a whole were falling. One part of the act stipulated that the unemployed should preferably get a job in their own home district – which of course contradicts the proposal for increasing geographic mobility.

During soaring unemployment in the first half of the 1990s as part of a deep economic recession, the OECD presented lots of criticisms and recommendations to improve employment. However, the main emphasis of Finnish economic policies was on economic stabilisation, and much less effort was made to reduce unemployment. Several of the OECD recommendations reflect the belief in labour market flexibility as a way to increase employment, and this was also the course that the bourgeois Aho government (1991 to 1995) tried to push through. However, the trade union movement in particular managed to prevent several proposals.

Quite a few recommendations in the 1990s deal with wage-setting and collective agreements, reflecting the assumption that increasing wage differentials create work incentives. In a situation in which some 450 000 jobs (20 per cent of all) disappeared within three years, this emphasis may seem a little strange. The OECD recommended removing minimum wage clauses at least for non-unionised workers. These recommendations have in part been implemented. Also, wage differentials have in practice increased over time.

In the early 1990s, a 'review' of the 1987 Employment Act was required in the name of flexibilisation. This act had guaranteed a job for every young unemployed and long-term unemployed person. The government agreed to cancel the act, mainly for cost reasons. A reduction in non-wage labour costs, referring to employers' social security contributions, was also recommended. In fact, employers' contributions increased first with the rising unemployment, but started to fall after 1994, while the employees' social security contributions (introduced in 1993) have steadily increased (Saari 2001). Finally, no major changes in employment contracts with regard to job protection or working time rules were made in the first half of the 1990s, but the difficult labour market situation in practice contributed to more flexible terms.

In practically all the surveys during the second half of the 1990s, more effective active labour market policies in training and a move away from subsidised jobs are recommended. Thus, 'the emphasis of these [active labour market] programmes should be shifted from subsidised jobs in municipal administrations, which appear to crowd out regular employment, to on-the-job training courses designed to improve the skills of unemployed in line with labour demand in the private sector' (1997). With regard to this issue, concordance can be detected. The number of subsidised jobs in the public (municipal) sector increased first together with the increase of unemployment in the first half of the 1990s, but since the mid-1990s the direction has been away from subsidised jobs.[3] At the beginning of 1998 new labour market policies were launched. The measures included decentralisation of labour market policies, support for small firms that hire new workers, activation of the long-term unemployed, as well as a more exact definition of the rights and duties of the unemployed. In particular, under 25-year-olds lose their right to labour market support (basic flat-rate benefit) if they do not apply for vocational training or for active labour market policy programmes (Kosonen 2000).

Since 1995, the Lipponen government has emphasised the need for structural changes in the labour market. The government set as its main target a reduction of unemployment by half by 1999 (Employment Programme). Economic growth was seen as the central way to achieve this target, but structural changes were also required, referring to flexibilisation and the creation of more work incentives.

OECD recommendations state that control of the unemployed could be strengthened, particularly by strengthening the enforcement of job search rules and work availability; also, the eligibility criteria for unemployment benefits should be strictly enforced. Second, unemployment benefit levels could be scaled down, and benefit duration should be reduced. In reality, many of these changes have taken place. Unemployment insurance has been revised by tightening the entitlement rules for unemployment benefits and by changing the benefit formula for unemployment benefits paid in case of part-time employment. Moreover, the basic amount of social assistance can now be decreased by 20 per cent if the person concerned declines a specified work offer, and by 40 per cent in cases where they repeatedly decline work offers – an example of control and discipline.

The third recommendation deals with early retirement schemes. According to the OECD, there should be a general increase in the early retirement age, and benefit levels should also be scaled down. This is connected to the fourth proposal: to tighten the rules for the unemployed over 55 years old and to increase the minimum age for unemployment pensions. The background for the proposal is the Finnish practice that in the case of ageing benefit recipients, the payment of earnings-related unemployment benefits is extended until the recipient becomes eligible for an unemployment pension (at 60 years of age). This has made it possible for earnings-related income security to continue from age 53 (now 55) until the pensionable age – i.e. the unemployment 'pipeline' to pensions (see Hytti 1998). In practice, radical proposals have not been accepted so far.

Finally, the OECD recommends that the inter-relationship between the tax and benefit system be reviewed in order to create work incentives. Incentive traps had already been identified in the Employment Programme, although politically it was not easy to implement all the proposals. In income taxation, tax rates have been lowered for all income groups, although low-income earners have additionally benefited from increased earnings-related deductions in municipal taxation. In some respects, 'last resort' social policy has been tightened, which should make people more work-oriented than earlier and the number of persons receiving social assistance should decline (Saari 2001). Evaluation reports on these reforms conclude that they were quite successful in removing 'incentive traps', but employment effects were small (Kalela et al. 2001). Table 4.2 provides an overview of concordance between OECD recommendations and Finnish public policy.

Old Age

In pension policy, the main concern of the OECD is that Finns retire too early, which creates financial problems. Therefore, both the standard retirement age and the effective retirement age should be increased. This is made more explicit for the first time in the 2000 survey. One step would be to allow pension rights to accrue until the official retirement age or beyond, which would provide incentives for older workers to continue to work after they have accrued the current maximum benefit level. Another way would be to make early-retirement schemes less attractive, partly by shortening the 'pipeline' to an unemployment pension. Second, in the disability and unemployment pension schemes the old-age accruals during the period of early retirement should be eliminated. Third, entry to the disability scheme should be granted only on purely medical grounds. These two issues have been discussed for some time, but no decisions have been made. On the other hand, in the individual early retirement pensions (a special type of disability pension) the age limit has been increased, whereas the basic pension can be drawn already at the age of 60. However, these pension benefits are reduced taking into account a shortened period of paying contributions and a longer period during which benefits are obtained (see Antolin et al. 2001). This is in part in concordance with the OECD proposals.[4]

During the last few years, the 'effective retirement age' – which is not a clearly defined concept – seems indeed to have increased. The share of 55- to 59-year-old people in employment has increased between 1997 and 2000 from 49 per cent to 61 per cent. Also, the share of 60- to 64-year-old people in retirement has fallen (from 79 per cent to 76.5 per cent), and correspondingly, the share of employed in this group has increased. However, this is mainly due to changes in working life. According to Scherer (2001), the average age of withdrawal from the labour force has been in the decrease since the mid-1970s, but between 1993 and 1998, it increased somewhat again.

An additional concern deals with the funding of the earnings-related

Table 4.2   Concordance between Finnish policy development and OECD recommendations

Recommendations/Criticisms	Concordance
Labour market	
1970s	
A more intensive use of incentives for investment and employment in less developed regions	Yes
Broadening the product and export base of industry	Yes (long run)
An active manpower policy to ensure retraining and mobility	Yes
Investments in competitive sectors	Yes
Some stimuli to household income and demand	No (except taxes)
Active labour market policies especially in the field of youth unemployment	Yes (not in training)
In the medium term, greater consensus on costs and prices	Yes
1980s	
Private investments (in the early 1980s)	Yes
Stronger efforts to make the labour market more mobile, particularly by retraining of manpower	No
1990s	
Reduce non-wage labour costs	Yes
Reabsorption of unemployment through collectively-agreed real wages without fiscal concessions	No (reabsorption), Yes (concessions)
Flexibility in collectively-agreed wages	No
Decentralisation of wage bargaining process, more scope for relative wages	Uncertain (but more wage differentials)
A review of the 1987 Employment Act	Yes
Deregulation of the labour market by easing job protection, fixed-term contracts and working time rules	Yes (in part)
More effective labour market policies in training	Yes (difficult evaluation)
Active labour market policies away from subsidised jobs (to training)	Yes
Increasing the labour mobility by new pension rules	No/Uncertain
Increasing the employment and labour supply:	
• by strengthening the control of the unemployed;	Yes
• by adjustments in social transfers and security with respect to early retirement schemes;	No (except unemployment, pensions)
. . . unemployment compensation,	Yes (mid 1990s)
. . . unemployment 'pipeline' to pensions, and other social security schemes/social transfers	Yes
Tax and benefit incentives to work/to work more	Yes

54

Old age

1990s

Increase in standard retirement age	No (except disability pension)
Increase in effective retirement age	Yes
Allow pension rights to accrue longer	Yes, but earlier
Increasing the funding rate of pension funds	No
Estate charges to finance institutional care services if not distorting effect on savings	No

Health

1990s

Reduce overlapping; improve competition and cost-effectiveness in the provision of services	Uncertain

Education

1990s

'Performance-based' financial incentives to vocational education	No
Measures to improve the efficacy of vocational training	Yes/Uncertain
The private apprenticeship system	No (but somehow with labour market support)

Note: The policy recommendations stem from the analysis of OECD country surveys (cf. Table 4.1). Details on the assessment are given in the text.

pension schemes. An increase in the funded part of these schemes should be considered, and the degree of funding increased. In Finland, there has been a rather stable surplus in the pension funds without major changes in recent years.

In the area of care for the elderly, the OECD recognises that the trend towards institutionalising the elderly (i.e., elderly in public institutional care) has been reversed. Problems are seen in user charges, which partly rely on incomes-testing, and may thus create incentives to enter institutional care. One response might be to make long-term care not only subject to an income test but also to a charge on the estate, if this is not to have distorting effects on savings. However, so far charges have not been essentially changed.

Heath Care

Health care gets attention in 1998; the consolidation of health care expenditures during the 1990s is first praised. However, the OECD argues that there is still scope for efficiency gains. In particular, the wide variation in per capita health care costs across regions suggests scope for further progress through the adoption of national best practice standards. These issues and proposals have been discussed already for some time. Although some efforts have been made, including several background reports in 2002, the objectives have not yet been achieved.

Education

In OECD comments and recommendations on education (1996), cost aspects are emphasised. With regard to tertiary education, it is criticised for lacking responsiveness to changing demand for specific skills in the labour market. However, at that time the government already has begun introducing 'performance-based' funding in the tertiary sector in order to promote training consistent with labour market demands. Hence when the OECD issued such a recommendation it had already been realised. According to the survey, similar financial incentives could be extended to vocational education, which appears to be too narrowly focused on specific skills and occupations. This has not been implemented as of yet. In order to improve the efficacy of vocational training, the OECD recommends placing more emphasis on low-skilled workers and on retraining unemployed persons. Retraining at least has indeed been increased. Finally, in order to improve job opportunities for young people with little practical work experience, the OECD argues that social partners should be encouraged to allow reductions in contractual minimum wages to the level where company-based training effectively becomes profitable to the employer. This should allow for the emergence of private apprenticeship which could usefully supplement the public training programmes targeting unemployed adults. Such proposals have largely been ignored, in particular since the decisions should be made between the 'social partners'.

Reforms and References to OECD Guidelines

In Finnish labour market and social policies, domestic social problems and political forces, including the labour market partners, have been decisive. In planning for policy changes, the most important foreign reference point has for a long time been Sweden, where many reforms were implemented earlier than in Finland. Since EU membership in 1995, EU directives and recommendations have, naturally, been taken into consideration as well. On the other hand, there are many social policy issues which EU policy does not cover. The main exception recently has been the annual employment action plans and Commission feedback on these.[5]

A profound study would be needed to assess direct references to OECD surveys. Instead, I have interviewed some civil servants from the ministries of Finance, Labour and Social Affairs who are familiar with these issues. The main actor is the Ministry of Finance, which also participates in the preparation of the surveys. The picture presented is that the annual surveys get rather wide publicity, and they are read especially by responsible civil servants. They are used also in various working groups and parliamentary committees, but only as one source among several others.

CONCLUSION

In exploring the OECD surveys, it becomes evident that the surveys have little to say about basic labour market and social reforms in Finland. Moreover, most of the recommendations are connected to economic and financial issues, not to social problems as such.

In evaluating the recommendations, concordance is clearly predominant. However, discordance can also be detected, and in many cases this is based on the Finnish decision-making system, which presupposes quite a broad consensus behind any changes. Moreover, the surveys often include criticism and recommendations on issues which in fact are already under scrutiny or changes that have already been made at the time of the report's publication. This implies that the question of impact should not be examined as a one-way effect; rather, the issue should be seen as a mutual process.

ACKNOWLEDGEMENT

Pekka Kosonen is responsible for writing the text. This has not been possible, however, without the invaluable help by Anneli Levo-Kivirikko,who collected and arranged the data, and also prepared Table 4.1.

NOTES

1. Recent studies on labour market and social policies include Kosonen (1998), Julkunen (2001), Kautto (2001), Kalela et al. (2001) and Saari (2001).
2. The subsequent content analysis is based mainly on the following volumes and summarising sections of the *OECD Economic Surveys* on Finland: 1970, pp. 31–34; 1971, pp. 35–37; 1972, pp. 40–42; 1973, pp. 29–31; 1974, pp. 36–38; 1975, pp. 30–32; 1977, pp. 32–36; 1978, pp. 37–39; 1979, pp. 41–43; 52–55; 1981, pp. 40–42; 1982, pp. 43–45; 1983, pp. 39–41; 1985, pp. 37–40; 1986, pp. 44–47; 1988, pp. 74–77; 1989, pp. 98–102; 1991, pp. 98–104; 1992, pp. 76–80; 1993, pp. 73–77; 1995, pp. 91–97; 1996, pp. 116–123; 1997, pp. 1–9; 1998, pp. 1–9; 1999, pp. 7–16; 2000, pp. 9–17.
3. At the same time, local projects have been supported by the EU structural funds.
4. It should be mentioned that in 2001, a working group of the labour market partners concluded an agreement which in principle provided for an overhaul of the early retirement legislation; e.g. new unemployment awards will not be made starting in 2005.
5. The influence of EU guidelines is not to be exaggerated, but they form a reference point for national employment plans (see Impacts of the EES 2002).

REFERENCES

Antolin, Pablo, Howard Oxley and Wim Suyker (2001), *How Will Ageing Affect Finland?*, Economics Department working paper No. 295. Paris: OECD.

Esping-Andersen, Gøsta (1990), *The Three Worlds of Welfare Capitalism*, Cambridge: Polity Press.

Hytti, Helka (1998), *Varhainen eläkkeelle siirtyminen – Suomen malli [Early Retirement – the Finnish Model*, with an English summary], Helsinki: Social Insurance Institution.

Impacts of the EES (2002), 'National evaluation of the effects of the European Employment Strategy', EES evaluation project final report, Helsinki: Ministry of Labour.

Julkunen, Raija (2001), *Suunnanmuutos. 1990-luvun sosiaalipoliittinen reformi Suomessa [Changing the Course. The Social Policy Reform of the 1990s in Finland*; in Finnish], Tampere: Vastapaino.

Kalela, Jorma, Jaakko Kiander, Ullamaija Kivikuru, Heikki A. Loikkanen, and Jussi Simpura (eds) (2001), *Down From the Heavens, Up From the Ashes. The Finnish Economic Crisis of the 1990s in the Light of Economic and Social Research*, Helsinki: Government Institute for Economic Research.

Kautto, Mikko (2001), 'Diversity among welfare states. Comparative studies on welfare state adjustment in Nordic countries', research report 118, Saarijärvi: Stakes.

Kettunen, Pauli (2001), 'The Nordic welfare state in Finland', *Scandinavian Journal of History* **26** (3), 225–247.

Kosonen, Pekka (1998), *Pohjoismaiset mallit murroksessa* [*Nordic Models at Crossroads*, in Finnish], Tampere: Vastapaino.
Kosonen, Pekka (2000), *Activation, Incentives and Workfare in four Nordic Countries. In Comparing Social Welfare Systems in Nordic Europe and France*, Paris: Drees/MiRe.
McBride, Stephan and Russell A. Williams (2001), 'Globalization, the restructuring of labour markets and policy convergence. The OECD jobs strategy', *Global Social Policy* **1** (3), 281–309.
OECD [various years], *OECD Economic Survey, Finland*, Paris: Organisation for Economic Co-operation and Development.
Saari, Juho (2001), *Reforming Social Policy. A Study on institutional change in Finland during the 1990s*, Department of Social Policy, Turku: University of Turku.
Scherer, Peter (2001), *Age of Withdrawal from the Labour Force in OECD Countries*, labour market and social policy occasional papers No. 49, Paris: Organisation for Economic Co-operation and Development.

5. Norway: an amenable member of the OECD

Nanna Kildal and Stein Kuhnle

EMERGENCE OF THE NORWEGIAN WELFARE STATE

Norway's secular social care tradition dates back as far as the twelfth century. Care for the poor without relatives was organised on a local basis. This *legdordning* obliged peasants to offer accommodation and provide for poor people for a limited period of time. This institution lasted until 1900. In 1964, a law on social assistance replaced the poor law of 1900.

Norway introduced compulsory elementary schooling for the whole nation as early as 1827. Although a law for compensation to injured miners was passed as early as 1842, the years 1885–1910 represent the first phase of major social reform initiatives in Norway. A law on compulsory accident insurance for industrial workers, modelled on the German law of 1884, was passed in 1894; subsidised voluntary unemployment insurance followed in 1906; and a compulsory sickness insurance law for workers and employees below a certain income was introduced in 1909 (Kuhnle 1986). Norway was among European latecomers in introducing an old age pension scheme: the first one, means-tested, dates from 1936.

The tradition of public responsibility for welfare was strengthened with the merging of state and church bureaucracies after the Reformation of 1536. But it was only after World War II that Norway developed the so-called institutional – also known as the Scandinavian, or social democratic – type of welfare state (Titmuss 1974; Esping-Andersen 1990). This type of welfare state is characterised by the following features: the strong role of central and local government in the financing and provision of social security and welfare; an emphasis on universal schemes; comprehensive coverage of needs; a significant degree of redistribution; a high level of public employment; and active labour market policies. The Labour Party was at its pinnacle of power during the first two postwar decades, and acted as a major force for the expansion of the welfare state. But postwar developments in Norway were in general characterised by a high degree of political consensus. The most important social reform, the comprehensive National Insurance

Scheme, was introduced by a four-party non-socialist coalition government in 1966.

The welfare state is popular in Norway. No national election takes place without welfare issues of one kind or another reaching the top of the voters' list of concerns. A significant oil and gas sector since the early 1970s has made the country's economy strong. Norway has grown into one of the richest countries in the world as measured by GDP per capita. Labour force participation is high and unemployment is low, at about 3 per cent. Comparatively speaking, welfare state retrenchment has been limited (Kuhnle 2000), but prolonged concern with the rising number of disability pensioners has led to several modifications. On the other hand, the paid maternal (parental) leave scheme has been significantly expanded during the last decade, making it the world's second most generous scheme after Sweden's. In a comparative perspective, it seems justified to characterise the Norwegian welfare state as 'women-friendly' (Hernes 1988) 'family-friendly' and 'work-friendly' (Kuhnle et al. 2000).

OECD IDEAS CONCERNING NORWEGIAN SOCIAL POLICIES

All annual reports[1] on Norway have concentrated on employment issues. Since 1989, most reports have also been concerned with the pension system and demographic pressure on the social security system. Only two recent reports have, respectively, focused on educational issues (1997) and the health sector (1998). No report has ever dealt with poverty.

Problems of inflation, labour market pressure, wage drift and lack of structural adjustments in the economy dominated the reports of the 1970s and 1980s. Yet, during the 1970s, the OECD also praised Norway's 'flexible and effective anti-cyclical policy', the 'stabilisation policy approach' adopted in 1974 which allowed for the lowest unemployment rate in the whole OECD area (1978, p. 5; 1980, p. 58). From 1977 onwards, however, the OECD grew more sceptical of the employment policy, which, together with incomes policies and other attempts to curb the rate of inflation, failed to produce the expected results.

On the threshold of the 1980s, economic growth significantly exceeded that of the OECD average, and full employment was maintained in contrast to most other industrialised countries. Nevertheless, the need for stronger productivity growth and a restoration of international competitiveness was a constant refrain. Towards the end of the 1980s, Norway's inflation rate was below the average of its trading partners (in October 1990 the Norwegian krone was linked to the ECU). However, the unemployment rate had risen to a level above 5 per cent of the labour force, a very high rate by Norwegian consensual political standards, but far below the average of OECD countries. Thus, the rate of unemployment has only intermittently been a topic (1983, 1990–93). In the most recent period, since 1997, labour market concerns have again focused on the issue of a tight labour market, an unusual concern in the West European context.

Old age, health care and education did not appear as issues in the country surveys until the late 1980s. Old age was an issue in the 1989 review, which addressed the problem of pressure on public spending due to changing demographic composition and commitments embedded in the national pension system. The progressive ageing of the population, combined with a foreseeable decline in the oil wealth were, according to the OECD, good reasons for Norway to save a growing portion of the oil and gas revenues in a 'Petroleum Fund', and to control the increase in the numbers of early retirees. In the field of health care, which has received modest attention (1998), the problems focused on are, *inter alia*, the long waiting lists, an under-supply of services in densely populated areas and capacity constraints. With regard to education and training, the general problem in the late 1980s and 1990s is described as a shortage of skilled labour, although Norway's active labour market policies (ALMP) were positively described. A better targeting of higher education on labour market needs is recommended. A summary of social policy evaluations and recommendations reported by OECD is given in Table 5.1.

The OECD sums up the analysis of the Norwegian labour market at the end of the twentieth century, asserting that its performance:

> has been excellent in most respects in recent years. The employment rate is the third highest in the OECD, the unemployment rate is among the lowest and long-term unemployment hardly exists. The effective retirement age is still higher than in most other OECD countries. (OECD 2000, p.12)

CONCORDANCE AND DISCORDANCE

Norwegian Public Policy Development and OECD Recommendations

Are the OECD recommendations in concordance or discordance with Norwegian policy development? Table 5.2 briefly summarises (selective) recommendations and our assessments. The table is followed by some more detailed explications of the assessments.

Employment

All OECD reports from the 1970s were concerned with the rate of inflation. Even if the degree of fiscal stimulus and monetary ease was appropriate from

Table 5.1   Social policy in OECD reports on Norway

Year	Problems	Criticisms	Recommendations
Employment/Labour market			
1970s	Inflation Labour market pressure Wage drift (71–80) Insufficient labour mobility (78)	Too rapid growth in public expenditure	Tighter demand management policy (71) Efficient co-ordination between all major economic parties (72) Less expansion of public expenditure (73) Lower indirect taxation, 'tripartite agreements' (74) Selective restraint through monetary and fiscal policies (75) Encouragement of labour mobility (75, 76, 78 Dec), incomes policy (75, 76) Reduction in selective support measures (78 Jan, 78 Dec)
1980s	Labour market pressure Inflation (80, 81, 85–89) Poor industrial performance Reduced incentives to work and low labour mobility (82, 83, 87) The wage formation system Government subsidies (85, 89) Bottlenecks in labour markets (86, 88) Labour costs Cyclical and structural unemployment (90, 91)	Too low labour mobility Too extensive selective support measures Egalitarian wage policies and taxation and too generous social security system Inability to cope with the structural adjustment pressure The public sector's direct claim on resources accentuates labour market pressures	Reduction in selective support measures (80, 81, 82, 83, 85, 86, 87) Active labour market policies (81, 82, 83) Vocational training programmes (82, 83) Review of the tax and transfer system (82, 83, 87) Review of the wage determination process (81–83), (85–87), 89) Market forces should determine the allocation of resources (85) Reduction in the high level of subsidies (86, 87) Encouragement of innovations and risk-taking (87) Restrictive demand management (88) *continued overleaf*

63

Table 5.1 continued

Year	Problems	Criticisms	Recommendations
1990s	Deterioration of labour market conditions (92–95) Wage pressure (97, 98) Social security system reduces work incentives (97–00)	Fiscal policy too loose Mismatches between supply and demand of labour	Retraining schemes and vocational courses, ALMP (90, 91, 94, 97) Tightening of elegibility provisions (92, 94) Increase in labour market flexibility (93–95), 97, 00) Encouragement of better consistency between wage and productivity levels (94–95) Reduced duration and support level of unemployment insurance (94, 95, 75) Support levels should be kept well below market wages (90) Revision of social security system to strengthen work incentives (97–00) Liberalisation of job placement services, with deregulation of the rules on fixed-term contracts and working hours (00)
Old age			
1990s	Projected increase in social expenditure due to ageing population (89, 93–00) Extension of the early retirement programme (99, 00)	The Petroleum Fund risks being depleted long before the ageing of the population (89, 93–00) High numbers of disability pensioners and early retirees reduces labour supply (99, 00)	Preservation of oil-generated wealth for future generations in the 'Petroleum Fund' (93, 94, 95, 97) Reduction of public pension system costs and a greater reliance on occupational pension schemes in the private sector (95) Tighter state expenditure restraints (95, 00) Increase in the effective retirement age (97) Continued fiscal restraint (98) Revisions to the early-retirement schemes, pensions and early-retirement schemes need to be put on an actuarially-neutral footing (00)

Healthcare

1990s	Absence of price signals as a rationing device of services (98) Under-supply of services in densely populated areas (98) Capacity constraints in sheltered sectors like health care (99) The block-grant funding system has led to long waiting lists and has limited patients' choice of hospitals (98) Weak financial incentives for general practitioners to establish durable relationships with their patients (98) Too strict entry quotas in the retail market for pharmaceuticals (99)	Reforms should be enhanced by the introduction of more ambitious best practice standards for block-grant funding of hospitals, and the government should avoid financial compensation where the reforms entail justified reductions in resources (98) Easing of entry conditions for new suppliers in the retail market for medicine (98)

Education

1990s	Shortage of skilled labour supply (86, 90, 91, 94–97) Education and training must better meet changing skill requirements	Development of the vocational stream of upper-secondary education and a better targeting of higher education on labour market needs (97) Encouragement of human capital investment consistent with emerging employment opportunities (97)

65

Source: OECD Economic Surveys on Norway from 1970 to 2000 (cf. note 1). The numbers in brackets specify the year of publication of the quoted survey.

Table 5.2   Concordance between Norwegian policy development and OECD recommendations

Recommendations/Criticisms	Concordance
Employment	
1970s	
Limit growth of public expenditure	No
Reduce inflation, restore competitiveness	Yes
1980s	
Reduce selective support measures	Yes
Encourage labour mobility	Yes
Review tax and transfer system	Yes
Scale back social security benefits	No
1990s	
Strengthen work incentives	Unclear
Shorten duration and generosity of unemployment benefits	Yes
Create a Petroleum Fund, limit oil dependence	Yes
Tighten eligibility for disability pension	Yes
Develop vocational training, human capital investment	Yes
Old age	
1990s	
Reduce costs of public pension scheme:	
• Rely more on occupational pensions in private sector;	Yes
• Minimum pension;	No
• Earnings-related pensions;	Yes
• Reduce number of disability pensioners, tighten eligibility	Yes
Raise the effective retirement age	Yes
Create Petroleum Fund for future pension commitments	Yes

Health

1990s

Reduce waiting lists	Yes
Introduce price signals to ration services	Yes
Increase labour supply	Yes
Encourage durable relationships between doctors and patients	Yes

Education

1990s

Provide better training to meet changing skill requirements	Yes
Ensure better targeting to higher education to labour market needs	Yes

Note: The policy recommendations stem from the analysis of OECD country surveys (cf. Table 5.1). Details on the assessment are given in the text.

the view of overall demand management, and even if the active role played by the government in reducing the danger of price-wage spiralling effects had been constructive, a marked deceleration of inflation was not achieved. Thus, in 1975, the OECD recommended that Norwegian authorities focus on anti-inflationary strategy as their major policy task. Greater labour mobility, with a likely increase in frictional unemployment, was said to be required if desirable changes in industrial structure were to take place.

In 1978–80 a wage and price freeze was decreed which was consistent with OECD recommendations regarding concerted international reflationary action (1979, p. 45). In 1980, the OECD wrapped up their reviews of the 1970s by observing that the recent re-orientation and improvement in Norwegian economic policies – designed to reduce inflation, restore competitiveness and improve foreign balance – were in harmony with recommendations made by the OECD (1980, pp. 5, 45). However, the re-acceleration of inflation after the termination of the price-income freeze at the end of 1979 was a major policy concern. In order to strengthen the competitiveness of Norwegian industry, the OECD addressed the egalitarian nature of wage settlements, distributional goals in general and the pressures on the labour market. The OECD recommended, *inter alia*, a slower growth of public consumption and public transfers, a faster reduction of subsidies to ailing industries, and more active labour market policies; these measures would all help stimulate structural adjustment and industrial productivity (1981, pp. 43–44).

From this point on, supply-side measures and the encouragement of innovation and risk-taking were key words in the OECD's recommendations to Norway.

In 1986, a sharp drop in oil prices and the subsequent loss of national income (nearly 10 per cent) marked a turning point in the Norwegian 'oil era'. According to the OECD, severe domestic expenditure restraint and a major tightening of demand-management policies were in order. For the first time, the OECD indicated that the necessary economic cure for Norway might involve a scaling back of social benefit transfers (OECD 1987, pp. 7, 40–42).

The OECD suggested that it would be imprudent to use renewed higher oil revenues at the end of the 1980s to alleviate short-term economic problems. It was recommended that the government stick to its long-term strategy of limiting the economy's oil dependence – articulated through the creation of the Petroleum Fund – and expand the traditional sectors exposed to international competition in the mainland economy. With a monetary policy that restricted any increases to the oil-adjusted budget deficit, accompanied by a forceful pursuit of supply-side reforms, the Norwegian economy was expected to follow a non-inflationary path towards higher levels of employment and productivity growth (OECD 1991, p. 65). These recommendations were repeated in the following years, with additional advice to cut subsidies to weaker sectors of the economy, reduce marginal tax rates and curtail the alleged 'abuse of disability benefits' (OECD 1992, p. 95).

By 1993, the OECD estimated that the Norwegian economy was on its way to a slow recovery from the prolonged recession of the 1980s and early 1990s (1994, p. 80). Still, in order to achieve higher output and employment growth in the following years, continuous structural reforms were recommended, *inter alia*, reductions in the very high level of agricultural support and of the public sector, and a restoration of a profitable banking industry. Furthermore, labour market reform was now considered to be of primary importance. Although a 'National Employment Commission' (NEC) was appointed in 1991 in order to develop an overall employment strategy, further improvements were steadily called for, such as better consistency between wage and productivity levels, skill-focused active labour market policy programmes (ALMP) and increased educational opportunities. Furthermore, the OECD recommended a tightening of eligibility criteria for disability pensions, a reduction in the duration of unemployment insurance (to reduce the cost of the system and to enhance work incentives) and better possibilities for hiring labour on a temporary basis. Together with a higher degree of wage flexibility, this last proposal was suggested to facilitate the recruitment of unskilled workers to the labour market (1994, pp. 82–83; 1995, p. 96; 1997, p. 6).

In the latter half of the 1990s, job creation in Norway was substantial, making employment levels among the highest in the OECD. The labour market was especially tight in parts of the manufacturing industry and the health sector, with the result that wage growth was again accelerated. The OECD recommended wage moderation, and in 1997 it praised the current income system – the *Solidarity Alternative* – which involved an agreement from the early 1990s between the government and social partners aimed at maintaining low inflation, restoring full employment and preserving the inter-national cost competitiveness of the mainland industry. Fiscal policy should be geared towards smoothing domestic demand (1997, pp. 1, 2, 5). After the Norwegian economy cooled off in 1999, the OECD questioned the viability of the Solidarity Alternative in regard to both wage-setting and the focusing of fiscal policy to control demand (OECD 1998, p. 3; 1999, pp. 11–13; 2000, p. 11).

Since 1997, the OECD has claimed that the social transfer system and high benefit levels continue to distort work incentives, to create a wage floor and to potentially reduce the labour supply, drawbacks that are exacerbated by high marginal tax rates. In order to improve the functioning of the labour market and create room for a more efficient allocation of resources, the OECD recom-mended, *inter alia*, a streamlining of the welfare system in order to relieve labour supply constraints. Disability benefits, the early retirement scheme and possibly the Family Cash Benefit scheme (implemented in 1998) were perceived to discourage job searches and to run counter to the adjustment needed in view of the ageing of the population and the expected decline in oil revenues (1997, pp. 6–7; 1998, p. 6; 1999, p. 13).

The OECD recommended the development of vocational training and of a higher-education system targeted to labour market needs, that is, to establishing an incentive structure geared towards human capital investment consistent with emerging employment opportunities (1997, pp. 6–7; 1998, p. 6).

The increasing number of disability pensioners and early retirees is considered a weak spot. Consequently the OECD recommended, as before, a tightening of the eligibility criteria for disability benefits and an attempt to make early retirement less attractive. Labour market deregulation and privatisation are seen as essential to the increase of productivity (2000, pp. 16–18).

Old age

Estimates of 'generational accounting' were used in 1991 to indicate that the tax burden would have to increase in the future, and it was recommended that a share of the oil revenues be set aside for the purpose of future pension commitments, and the so-called 'Petroleum Fund' was in fact created that year. The recommendation to strengthen the fund was repeated in most reports during the 1990s. Furthermore, a widening of the indirect tax base was recommended (2000), as well as a tightening of eligibility criteria for disability pensions, fiscal restraint to rein in overall state expenditure, and a revision of the pension system (1995, 2000). In the late 1990s, the OECD suggested reducing the cost of the public pension system by encouraging occupational pension schemes.

The OECD recommendations fit domestic government proposals and decisions actually already undertaken by the parliament in Norway. In 1984, the public committee on social security financing (Trygdefinansieringsutvalget) proposed reducing the ceiling for earning an income-related pension, and in 1992 the parliamentary majority decided on a downward adjustment of future supplementary pension entitlements (Hatland 2001, pp. 108–109). Measures were also introduced to reduce the increase in the number of disability pensioners by establishing stricter medical criteria for allotting disability pensions. On the other hand, the three-party non-socialist minority government in 1997 proposed and gained a parliamentary majority for a substantial increase (18 per cent in real terms) in the minimum pension, a policy not reflecting any OECD recommendation.

Health

A number of problems are listed in the 1998 report on health policy: the tight labour supply in the health sector; the absence of price signals as a means of rationing services; an under-supply of services in the more densely populated areas. The existing rationing mechanisms are said to have led to long waiting lists for treatment, and weak financial incentives have discouraged durable relationships between general practitioners and patients. On all of these accounts, successive governments have promoted reform proposals to correct the malfunctioning of the health system.

Education
Education has been a topic in the annual reports only since 1997, when it was stated that the Norwegian economy would benefit from better education and training to meet changing skill requirements. Quoting a 1994 educational reform, the OECD claims that there is a need for continued efforts to develop the vocational stream of upper-secondary education and a better targeting of higher education toward labour market needs. The main elements of the Labour Party (minority) government's reform proposals for higher education were approved by parliament in June 2001 and may be looked upon as a response to the demand for more labour-market-oriented higher education.

SOCIAL POLICY REFORM AND REFERENCES TO THE OECD

Many policies developed by Norwegian political authorities have been in concordance with recommendations conveyed by the OECD. We can also find examples of discordance, and a further analysis would probably provide ample examples of unsuccessful attempts to follow up OECD recommendations. On the basis of our analysis we cannot establish in what way the OECD country reports have been influential; to what extent OECD recommendations have in effect built upon significant streams of political thinking among domestic policy makers at the time in question; or to what extent reforms and policy decisions would have been developed independently of any messages from the OECD. To make a preliminary assessment of the role of the OECD we have looked at the government's long-term programmes (*Stortingsmelding*), which are presented every four years to parliament (*Stortinget*). These are analytical documents which provide an authoritative overview of the state of political thinking in government circles.

OECD analyses and views are treated with considerable respect in the long-term programmes.[2] All of the programmes refer to the OECD. For example, looking at *Stortingmelding nr. 79 (1980–81)*, which outlines the programme for 1982–85, we find reference is made to: the economic growth in Norway compared to growth rates among OECD countries; the OECD's importance for the liberalisation of world trade; the economic policies followed by 'many OECD countries' (p. 26) concerning strategies for economic development;

policy decisions and recommendations made by OECD ministers concerning an increase of production, reduction of unemployment, and lower inflation; and to the importance of strengthening cooperation with OECD countries in a number of policy fields (economic policy, trade policy, industrial policy, petroleum policy, technological policy, etc.) in order to solve 'common problems' (p. 29) in member countries. In *Stortingmelding nr. 83 (1984–85)* for the period 1986–89, the government states that it will work through the World Bank, the IMF, GATT, and 'in particular the OECD' (p. 19) for better international coordination of economic policies in order to further free trade to the benefit of greater prosperity both in the world and in Norway. A more specific reference says that 'analyses referred to in the *OECD Employment Outlook* from the autumn of 1984 suggest that flexible wage adjustment for youth will make for higher employment'. In *Stortingmelding nr. 4 (1988–89),* for the period 1990–93, reference is made to the high priority given by the OECD to developing means to measure results in the field of education (p.157). Statements such as 'Norway will continue to be an active participant in institutions such as OECD' are made, and the OECD is named first, and not for alphabetical reasons, in the list of seven international institutions in *Stortingmelding nr. 4 (1992–93)* (p. 42) for the period 1994–97. The programmes also state that 'the government has taken the initiative to use the possibilities offered by the EEA-agreement and cooperation in the OECD to establish closer international cooperation for full employment, (p. 121) and 'the government has, in accordance with recommendations from OECD, emphasized a labour market policy based on activation measures rather than passive disbursement of benefits' (p. 128). Reference to an OECD report is made to stress the importance of 'technology and knowledge for economic growth' (p. 200). A comprehensive supplementary analytical report (p. 316) to *Stortingmelding nr. 4 (1996–97)* for the period 1998–2001 includes a great number of references to OECD analyses and recommendations.

CONCLUSION

Norwegian governments, whatever their political colour, have consistently made cooperation within the OECD a high priority. Given the special status of the Norwegian petroleum-based economy during the last 30 years, the justifications for economic and social policies have often deviated from that of other OECD member countries. Thus, some political messages and policy recommendations have not fitted the Norwegian 'political opportunity structure'. Public and social expenditures have not been cut to the extent often recommended by the OECD, and the welfare state has mostly expanded, including in the last two decades. For example, there has been an increase in public employment for local welfare services provisioning; an extension of the parental leave scheme; and a substantial increase in the minimum old age pension. However, as seen from Table 5.2, the OECD and Norwegian governments have gone hand in hand along the road towards tightening eligibility for disability pensions; developing labour market activation policies; developing price signals in the health sector; and changing vocational and higher education requirements according to alleged labour market needs. The OECD is definitely an important point of reference for cooperation, analyses, knowledge and advice for the development of government policies. On the other hand, we can find ample evidence of Norwegian parliamentarians heeding the voice of voters rather than the voice of the OECD when the two sing different tunes.

ACKNOWLEDGEMENT

We would like to acknowledge the preparatory work done by research assistant Hilde Zeiner, who studied most of the annual reports on Norway.

NOTES

1. The subsequent content analysis is based mainly on the following volumes and summarising sections of the *OECD Economic Surveys* on Norway: 1971, pp. 39–43; 1972, pp. 45–48; 1973, pp. 29–31; 1974, pp. 41–45; 1975, pp. 38–39; 1976, pp. 36–37; 1977, pp. 36–38; 1978 (January), pp. 38–40; 1978 (December), pp. 45–47; 1980, pp. 58–60; 1981, pp. 43–45; 1982, pp. 42–44; 1983, pp. 43–45; 1985, pp. 41–43; 1986, pp. 45–48; 1987, pp. 40–42; 1988, pp. 69–72; 1989, pp. 70–73; 1990, pp. 73–77; 1991, pp. 62–65; 1992, pp. 92–99; 1993, pp. 79–83; 1994, pp. 80–84; 1995, pp. 93–98; 1997, pp. 1–8; 1998, pp. 1–10; 1999, pp. 9–18; 2000, pp. 9–18.
2. We have looked at all programmes published since 1968–69 (for the period 1970–73) until 1996–97 (for the period 1998–2001), i.e. eight programmes.

REFERENCES

Esping-Andersen, Gøsta (1990), *The Three Worlds of Capitalism*, Cambridge: Polity Press.

Hatland, A. (2001),'Trygd og arbeid', in A. Hatland, S. Kuhnle, and T. I. Romøren (eds), *Den norske velferdsstaten*, Oslo: Gyldendal Akademisk, pp. 79–117.

Hernes, Helga M. (1988), 'Scandinavian citizenship', *Acta Sociologica* **31** (3) 199–215.

Kuhnle, Stein (1986), 'Norway', in Peter Flora (ed.), *Growth to Limits. The Western European Welfare States Since World War II*, vol. I, Berlin: Walter de Gruyter, pp. 117–196.

Kuhnle, Stein (ed.) (2000), *Survival of the European Welfare State*, London and New York: Routledge.

Kuhnle, Stein, Sven Hort and Aksel Hatland (2000), 'A work-friendly welfare state: lessons from Europe', paper presented at World Bank conference on 'Flexibility and Security: Social Policy and Labor Market in Europe and East Asia', Seoul, 30 November–1 December.

OECD [various years], *OECD Economic Survey, Norway*, Paris: Organisation for Economic Co-operation and Development.

Titmuss, R. (1974), *Social Policy: An Introduction*, London: Allen & Unwin.

6. International organisations and welfare states at odds? The case of Sweden

Eero Carroll

Have the OECD and Swedish decision-makers seen eye-to-eye on the country's social policies? Concordance exists, but is limited – the welfare state has in many ways resisted cutbacks. Sweden has traditionally had high tax rates, a large public sector, and (until the early 1990s) low unemployment. The Swedish welfare state has mainly been seen as a political project of the Social Democratic Party (SPD), particularly since 1932 when the party first gained its sustained control of the Swedish executive (though right-centre coalition governments were in power 1976–82 and 1991–94). The development of Swedish welfare was however in no way predestined, passing through a number of stages.

Compulsory employer liability for work accidents was enacted in 1901. Compulsory health care and sickness insurance followed in 1931 and 1955 respectively. Public occupational superannuation (ATP) was fully enacted by 1962, complementing the citizenship-based basic pensions (People's Pensions) in force since 1947. Finally, increasing state subsidies to the voluntary unemployment insurance system (legislatively sanctioned in 1934) enabled higher coverage and a reduction of individual insurance fees. The expansion of public child care, education, and health care, mainly within local authorities or regional county councils (*landsting*), took longer – not taking off (in tandem with public employment) until the 1970s.

The economic recession of the early 1990s brought about a sea change in Swedish welfare. Unemployment soared, GDP decreased, and social insurance benefits were cut back. The re-ascendant Social Democratic Party enacted the Fiscal Consolidation Programme of 1994–98, which included more expenditure cuts than tax increases. The economy began to recover in 1996 as state finances solidified, but its future prospects are uncertain. Voters punished the SDP for the Consolidation Programme in 1998, and the party only retained power by means of an informal agreement with the ex-Communist Left Party and the Greens. This minority government continued after the election of 2002.

Yet, as noted in one assessment of Swedish welfare which departs from

Esping-Andersen's well-known typology (1990), 'changes within social insurance cannot be labeled 'retrenchment' . . . There is . . . liberalization, but it is no[t] strong' (Lindbom 2001, p. 187). Though social assistance expenditures increased in the 1990s, and thus also the prevalence of liberal regime characteristics, Sweden arguably retains a 'socialist' welfare regime which has resisted systematic dismantling.

The sources of this resilience are both institutional and political. Sweden has a unitary constitution, extensive municipal self-determination with regards to the delivery of social services, and a proportional electoral system with a strong role for political parties. This institutional matrix is characterised by an absence of constitutional 'veto points' against universalist welfare state expansion, which can form its own constituency of subsequent broad support (Rothstein 1994). More ambiguously, trade union wage-setting autonomy and municipal self-determination has led to the creation of corporate and sub-national 'veto points' against government intervention, expansive or contractive. Finally, pressing reasons for retrenchment abated with the macroeconomic problems of the early 1990s. Economic growth in the late 1990s is back to normal, GDP per capita is high,[1] inflation is at or below the (much lowered) OECD average, and unemployment rates are relatively low (if far from the full employment of the late 1980s).

THE OECD'S IDEOLOGICAL EVOLUTION

Trends in OECD diagnosis, criticism and recommendation are depicted in Table 6.1.[2] Recommendations are generally classified by the problem domain to which they are oriented. However, the OECD directed some recommendations (marked by an asterisk) to problems of general economic policy rather than those of employment policy, old-age policy, or social welfare financing as such. I classify these recommendations according to the policy domain within which change was recommended, since it was not possible to classify them according to their proper problem domain. The increasing orientation of social policy recommendations to economic problems (i.e. the privatisation of pensions recommended so as to increase efficiency) constitute part of a larger trend towards economism in OECD thinking. Health care and anti-poverty policies have been non-concerns. Most recommendations address perceived labour market problems – all are presented in Table 6.1.

Trends in problem diagnosis and policy criticism broadly parallel the evolution of OECD policy recommendations. Sweden's labour market problems, diagnosed in terms of external balance problems until the early 1980s, are then (beginning in the mid-1980s) increasingly seen in terms of endogenous and structural factors. Criticism of policy allegedly exacerbating labour

Table 6.1 Social policy in OECD reports on Sweden

Year	Problems	Criticisms	Recommendations
Employment/Labour market			
1970s and 1980s	Increasing labour costs (77, 78) Given unemployment rate associated with stronger labour market pressures and higher inflation High budget deficit burdens employment policy External economic and 'structural' imbalances exacerbate unemployment	Industrial subsidies hinder(ed) restructuring, mobility Devaluation counteracts healthy industry/wage development Regional policy obstructs labour mobility	Increase wage inequality (73) No general demand expansion Income policy Reduction of industrial subsidies* More ALMP
1980s and 1990s	Increasing labour costs Relatively high unemployment among 'exposed groups', e.g. youth Labour market overheating (89, 90) High/rising unemployment (81–82, 94–96, 99) Institutional and structural obstacles to employment (in e.g. wage formation, industrial policy, public sector size, etc.)	High taxes affect work incentives Labour market over-heating worsened by housing subsidies, taxes, deregulation/tax reform sequencing Wage equalisation exacerbates labour misallocation	Increase wage inequality Wage moderation Decentralise wage negotiations Reduce/restrict taxes Reduce transfers/public employment Refrain from devaluations/equivalent (87, 91) Review pension benefit entitlement rules (89) Allow unemployment to increase (91)
1990s only	Too many end up within ALMP programmes during mass recession (92) Inefficient matching of jobs and job seekers (99) Low hours and absenteeism reduce effective labour utilisation (99)	Unemployment benefits too generous, long-term, accessible, state-financed, and/or poorly monitored 'Perverse effects', inefficiency in ALMP; regulatory and social policies generally hinder labour market adjustment, job creation Enterprise training skewed in favour of highly qualified (98)	Increase aggregate wage flexibility Reduce/restructure ALMP Restructure/restrict unemployment insurance Liberalise/decentralise employment protection Harmonise temporary/permanent worker employment protection (95) More favourable, simpler tax treatment of small/medium-size firms (96) More market competition in services (96) Improve educational system output (98) Wage incentive/job access for low-skilled workers (99)

continued overleaf

Table 6.1 Social policy in OECD reports on Sweden

Year	Problems	Criticisms	Recommendations
Old age			
1970s	Pension maturation and an ageing population increase pensioners' consumption level (79)		More solidarity between active and elderly population (79)
1990s		Not enough progress in reform of pension system	Redesign pension system, greater actuarialism; more private pensions*
Education			
1995	Low educational achievement among youth and low private-sector workforce share with high education		Given sharp intake increase, degree quality should be carefully ensured
1996	High tertiary non-completion rates and short length; Not enough orientation to labour market needs for scientific/engineering degrees	Basic research emphasis unhelpful to technological diffusion	Shift support from university-based institutions to cofinanced science parks
1998	Fair-to-middling student results on some international aptitude tests	General student grant emphasis entails increased taxation, non-specific education incentives	Longer teaching hours; Decentralise teacher/wage setting; Extend nationwide testing; Review student loan/grant structure
Financing			
1970s		Uncoordinated local and national taxation (79)	More flexibility on indirect taxation* (74); Capital import financing of public deficit* (76); Expenditure cuts* (79)

1980s–90s	High-rising public deficits/expenditure/debt Taxes too high/complex	Transfers automatically reduced when other revenues rise (89) Tax rates & their differentials result in tax evasion, income capitalisation	Reduce/stabilise 'tax burden'*; expenditure cuts*; broadened tax base/increase consumption taxes to finance marginal tax decreases*
1992	Tax reform entailed revenue losses		No demand stimulation for recovery
1990s	Danger of procyclical budgeting	Uncorodinated and/or excessive local taxation/expenditure Floating exchange rate undermines cutbacks consensus Budget process insufficiently stringent and transparent Extensive tax expenditures	Raise effective retirement age; 'reduce government contingent liabilities in social insurance'

Note: Asterisks indicate that the OECD directed recommendations to problems of general economic policy rather than those of employment policy, old-age policy, or social welfare financing as such.

Source: OECD Economic Surveys on Sweden from 1970 to 1999 (cf. note 2). The numbers in brackets specify the year of publication of the quoted survey.

market problems targets industrial subsidies in the 1970s and 1980s, the tax system starting in the 1980s, and by the mid-1990s labour market programmes and the welfare system itself. The diagnosis and criticism related specifically to pensions are virtually absent, while the contemporary educational system's insufficient completion rates and poor market orientation are seen as exacerbated by reliance on general student grants. Finally, intrinsically high tax rates and transfer levels increasingly motivate recommendations as to the retrenchment of social welfare financing.

Reviewing this ideological trend with regards to demand stimulation, the OECD bias remained Keynesian in the 1970s. OECD reports did express some scepticism about demand stimulation as a labour market policy in the 1970s, preferring selective measures. However, government intervention was not criticised as such. In the early 1980s the OECD recommends increased use of active labour market policy (ALMP), although it questions related policies such as industrial crisis subsidisation and increased public employment. By the recession of the early 1990s, the OECD's stance on demand policy differs totally. In its 1990 economic survey, the OECD thus astoundingly recommends increasing unemployment (see Table 6.1), arguing that 'allowing the over-heating in the labour market to abate and unemployment to increase might go a long way towards damping inflation . . . It would be regrettable if short-term social considerations should prevent this process from taking place and, consequently, put at risk the goal of long-term sustainable low unemployment' (OECD 1990, p. 95). This explicit recommendation to disinflate through unemployment was one which Carl Bildt's right-centre government arguably fulfilled. Earlier attempts at advancing new norms in economic policy-making include the 1987 stand against devaluations, given their negative envisioned labour market consequences, and the stand for pegging the Swedish krona at a fixed exchange rate to the ECU, a policy implemented at around that time.

More marked supply-side concerns also emerge. Thus, OECD reports target pension system design and pensioner labour income taxation for review in light of labour supply constraints in 1989. They recommend more favourable tax treatment of small- and medium-size enterprises in 1996 so as to increase presumably employment-friendly firm startups and expansion. In 1998, OECD reports advocate educational reform and increased wage-contract emphasis on training for similar employment reasons. And, though here in order to address human capital and education sector problems in themselves (i.e. high tertiary education non-completion rates and insufficient incentives to education), the OECD advanced in 1998 numerous ideas for improving the supply of education via reforms of the schooling system (see Table 6.1)[3].

The OECD also expresses recurring, and increasingly anti-egalitarian, concern with wage determination. Thus, beginning in 1973 reports recommend wage and income policy concertation less for its own sake than in order to address cost and price pressures. Later recommendations (1987 and 1996) to decentralise wage-setting lend a certain ambiguity to the OECD's position. From the 1980s on, with wage developments held to be internationally non-convergent, reports recommend wage moderation for employment reasons. Further, trade unions' egalitarianism in wage determination is increasingly seen as causing labour market problems. The first recommendations to increase wage differentiation (in 1973 and the early 1980s) aim to attract workers to export industries by increasing relative wage differentials in these industries' favour. Later support for increased inequality is motivated more by supply-side ideas of increasing returns to human capital. OECD surveys recognise the potential social problems that come with rising inequality, but as time passes dismiss them with increasing brusqueness.

The growing economism of OECD recommendations is evident beyond labour market policy. Beginning in the 1990s it advocates the redesign of pension systems, strengthened actuarialism, and an increased emphasis on private pensions (see Table 6.1). These measures are explicitly oriented to problems of macroeconomic adjustment (indicated by asterisks), rather than those of old-age policy as such. Of all policy recommendations made here, only the implicit stand for wage-indexed pensions in 1979 is oriented to problems of old-age policies themselves. The diagnosis is as follows: the maturation of occupational pensions and an ageing population are together leading to rapid consumption increases among pensioners, which should be brought into line with wage developments for the working population then expected to pay.

Economism characterises many recommendations whose most immediate implications concern social welfare financing. Thus, while the OECD still envisions capital import-financing of deficits in 1976, budget policy recommendations change after the second oil crisis in the late 1970s. Starting in 1979, the OECD consistently recommends reduced spending and taxation (see Table 6.1). Oftentimes, these recommendations are in active search of any clear social policy problems to address. Tax rate and expenditure cuts are seen more and more as intrinsically good, coterminous with reduced economic distortions.

Concerns with liberalisation also increasingly affect OECD recommendations related to labour market problems. Thus, employment problems are held to be exacerbated by unemployment insurance, which beginning in 1992 is repeatedly recommended for contractive overhaul, delimited trade union administration and decreased state subsidisation. OECD surveys, however, begin to criticise active labour market policies in the mid-1990s, recommending programmatic cutbacks (i.e. in subsidised municipal youth employment) in favour of employment exchange services and education reform. The reports also urge change in employment regulations as of the mid-1990s, though not only in liberalizing directions.

WHAT DIFFERENCE DID THE OECD MAKE?

Looking at subsequent policy developments, again assessed separately for labour markets and other policy domains (see Table 6.2), it seems that Swedish taxation and expenditure policies are in increasing accord with the OECD's supply-side policy bias. Tax reforms in 1981–83 and in 1989–91, supported by the Social Democrats, featured marginal tax rate cuts and broadened taxable income bases. This accorded with OECD recommendations to restructure taxation, but not necessarily with a 'reduction of the tax burden', as the reforms were formulated to be revenue-neutral (a formulation not realised in practice, as consumption tax increases did not offset income tax decreases).

Expenditures were also cut as recommended, albeit less consistently. Despite OECD recommendations, the Social Democratic government of 1982 did not undertake broad retrenchment, though industrial subsidies were phased out as recommended. Improved social benefits and greater state financing of municipal child care led to increased spending. It is unclear whether mid-1980s expenditure policies accorded with OECD recommendations for restraint, in that the GDP share of social transfer expenditures stabilised despite nominal expenditure increases.

Both the right-centre Bildt government and the SDP's Fiscal Consolidation Programme (1994–98) pursued expenditure restrictions (if at first unsuccessfully) during the crisis years of the 1990s. Against OECD recommendations to cut or restrict labour taxation, the Consolidation Programme increased state taxation of high incomes from 20 to 25 per cent, yielding a total top rate (with local taxes) of 55 per cent. However, tax increases only accounted for a third of the programme's savings, with expenditure cuts accounting for the remainder. This followed concurrent recommendations to emphasise spending cuts as a means of deficit reduction. Expenditure and benefit increases, not least in social services, defy restraint recommendations contemporaneous with the late 1990s economic recovery.

Finally, pension policies develop concordantly. The reformed pension system adopted in the 1990s (now coexisting with ATP) includes obligatory private and individual pension accounts. The new collective pension is financed by individual contributions comprising 16.5 per cent of one's annual wage, and is augmented by payback and profits from individual accounts (financed with a further 2.5 per cent of one's wage). Total benefits are no longer indexed by prices, but in complex relation to average wages, wage increase norms, and cohort-specific life expectancies. These changes accord with earlier OECD recommendations to revise indexation so as to induce greater pensioner–worker 'solidarity'. Pension policy ignores recommendations for more private pensions to stimulate private savings, made again in 1998 (despite the reformed system's private inroad).

Swedish policy-making is most at odds with OECD recommendations related to perceived labour market problems, notwithstanding individual instances of spectacular concordance. Besides increasing unemployment, the Swedish government maintained fixed exchange rates despite phenomenal costs – if only until November 1992, when exchange rates were floated in discordance with OECD recommendations (see Table 6.1). Yet recommendations regarding wage moderation had unclear consequences, with export sector unions doing anything but moderating their wage claims in the devaluation-expansive 1980s. Recommendations for wage and income policy concertation were mainly rejected, excepting the centralising Rehnberg accords in force between 1991 and 1993. This resistance resulted from the long-standing, insitutionalised autonomy of Swedish unions with regards to wage-setting. Thus, OECD recommendations have met with unfavourable domestic conditions. Concordance with OECD recommendations to allow for rising income disparities varies over time. Income inequality did rise after 1995 (without the recurrence of 1970s-style equalisation), but less specifically in favour of export sectors as in the 1980s – instead rising within all social classes and age cohorts (Fritzell 2001).

Unemployment benefit rates were initially cut as recommended in 1995. Active labour market policy expenditures declined as a percentage of GDP after 1993, and restructuring had by 2000 virtually abolished direct public job creation and youth employment measures.[4] Yet resilience predominates.

Despite attempts by the Bildt government, the voluntary union-administered unemployment insurance system was not abolished as recommended in 1992. Benefits are still channelled through voluntary funds rather than the public employment service as recommended in 1996. And the SDP government's attempts (1996) to liberalise employment law, cut effective unemployment benefit durations, and lower benefit rates were partially abandoned after running into stiff party opposition. Institutionalised policy commitments and pre-existing insurance institutions create their own support constituencies, perhaps resisting change particularly strongly when exogenously recommended for labour markets.

CONCLUSIONS

The OECD began to adopt a supply-side policy bias starting in the early 1970s, and became concurrently more suspicious of the institutionalised

Table 6.2 Concordance between Swedish policy development and OECD recommendations

Recommendations/Criticisms	Concordance
Employment	
All periods	
Increased wage inequality (73, 81, 82, 96, 99)	Unclear
1970s and 1980s	
Refrain from general demand expansion (72, 74)	Yes
Incomes policy (73, 77, 78, 81, 82, 87)	No
Manpower policies to increase labour mobility (80)	Yes
Reduction of industrial subsidies* (82)	Yes
More ALMP (81, 82)	Yes
1980s and 1990s	
Wage moderation (82, 87, 91)	Unclear
Decentralise wage negotiations (87, 96)	No
Increase aggregate wage flexibility (96, 98)	No
Wage incentives and job access for low-skilled workers (99)	No
Reduce/restrict taxes (81, 82, 85, 89, 95, 96, 99)	Yes (80s), No (90s)
Reduce transfers/public employment (85, 95, 96)	No (80s), Yes (90s)
Reduce and/or restructure ALMP (94, 95, 96, 99)	Yes
Allow unemployment to increase (91)	Yes
More market competition in service sectors (96)	Unclear
Refrain from devaluations or equivalent (87, 91)	Yes (87–92), No (92–)
Review pension benefit entitlement rules (89)	Yes
Changes in unemployment insurance:	
• Increase employer/employee financing (92, 96, 99)	No
• Implement compulsory system (92)	No
• Reduce generosity/liberality (94, 95, 99)	Yes (95), No (93, 99)
• Administer benefits through PES (96)	No
• Stricter enforcement of job availability criteria (99)	No yet assessable

84

Liberalise/decentralise employment protection (95, 96, 98)	No
Harmonise temporary and permanent worker protection in employment regulations (95)	No
More favourable and simplified tax treatment of small-/medium-size enterprises (96)	No
Improve formal and/or on-the-job education output (98)	No

Old age

More solidarity between active and elderly population (79)	Yes (90s)
Redesign pension system, greater actuarialism* (91, 94)	Yes
Increased emphasis on private pensions* (90, 96, 98)	Yes (90–96), No (98)

Education

Ensure degree quality given sharp intake increase (95)	Unclear
Shift support from university-based institutions to cofinanced science parks (96)	No
Longer teaching hours (98)	Yes (partially)
Performance pay for teachers, decentralise wage setting (98)	Yes
Further decentralise primary/secondary education (98)	No
More use of vouchers (98)	No
More independent administration, parental influence (98)	No
Nationwide testing extensions (98)	No
Reduce possibilities to proceed with incomplete marks (98)	No
Review structure of student loans and grants (98)	No

Financing

All periods: Reduce/stabilise 'tax burden'* (74, 82, 87, 98, 99)	No (74, 98–99), Yes (82–87)
Before 1979: capital import financing of public deficit* (76)	Yes
Since 1979: expenditure cuts* (79, 80–87, 91–95, 98–99)	No (79–82, 98–99), Unclear (83–87), Yes 91–95)
Broadened tax base/increased consumption taxes to finance marginal tax decreases* (82, 87, 96, 98)	Yes (82–87), No (96–98)
No demand stimulation for recovery (92)	Yes
Raise effective retirement age (96)	No
'Reduce government contingent liabilities in social insurance'* (98)	No

Notes: The policy recommendations stem from the analysis of OECD country surveys (cf. Table 6.1). Details on the assessment are given in the text. Asterisks indicate that the OECD directed recommendations to problems of general economic policy rather than those of employment policy, old-age policy, or social welfare financing as such.

Swedish welfare state. The OECD served primarily as a politically isolated, international 'clearing house of ideas' for Swedish civil servants and politicians with particular domestic policy preferences – that is, as the studio of an 'ideational artist'. Frequent references to the OECD in Swedish policy debates serve as evidence of the organisation's role as an 'ideational authority'. However, OECD statistics are cited much more often than determinate policy ideas. There are only much spottier indications that the OECD acts as a genuine engine of policy change.

Thus, in the 1989/90 parliamentary debate proceedings, when tax reform and economic overheating were major issues, the OECD and tax reforms are co-mentioned during 17 debate sessions (the same is true for 156 debate sessions over the entire 1989–2001 period). In only six of these 1989/90 sessions, however, are the OECD and tax policies mentioned by debators in more or less the same context, and not even in all of these are OECD preferences used as a justification for specific reforms. Tax cuts are usually argued for indirectly via growth comparisons between Sweden and the entire OECD area and/or given competitor country-members. Correspondingly, those sceptical of tax reform criticise such comparisons, and/or the reliability of OECD statistics. At times, OECD sources and contacts are cited to indirectly justify established reforms.[5] OECD statistics and recommendations are also used both in Swedish journalistic and in academic debates, particularly regarding the growth benefits or non-advantages of liberalization (see Schück 2002; Korpi 1996; Henreksson 1996). The 'OECD culture' in Sweden combines knowledge of and an active rhetorical orientation towards the OECD with political selectivity of its influence.

A Member of Parliament worth his or her salt should in Sweden be able to quote OECD statistics at will, but s/he will hardly ever point to the OECD as a source of policy proposals. The same seems to be true of government ministers. Only five government bills co-mention the OECD and pension reform between 1993 and 2001, and never in the same context. In the most definitive pension-reform bills yet adopted by the Swedish parliament (Government of Sweden 1994, 1998), the OECD is not mentioned at all.[6]

Swedish decision-makers often resist OECD recommendations, to a greater or lesser degree depending on the current executive's political colour. The continued (if increasingly gradual) expansion of public social services, as well as the expansionist 1982 budget, defied OECD recommendations for spending cuts. Recommendations regarding labour market problems were resisted particularly strongly. Finally, there appears to have been limited follow-up on education policy recommendations. Certainly, teachers' wage setting was individualised and performance-based in collective agreements in 1995 and 2000, and teacher working hours appear to be growing (even unsustainably) despite re-regulatory attempts.[7] But the Swedish educational system was already highly decentralised by municipalisation in 1991, with further decentralisation through voucher systems and parent–teacher councils remaining limited.[8] Finally, on-going OECD support for shifting public sector resources has gone largely unheeded, and income inequality trends have been inconsistent.

Swedish welfare institutions have not systematically resisted reform in the 1990s – some systemic changes do occur, constituting intermediate-level denaturing (if nothing like total dismantlement). Reformed pensions' equivalence with ATP benefits is still argued on grounds of projected, not real, outputs. Tax reforms constrain financing, and social service privatisation is rapidly increasing (though initial levels were so low that much remains to be accomplished on the path to a neo-liberal 'maximum programme'). Heretofore, the watchmaker company's credo has been realised: the Swedish welfare state 'takes a licking, but keeps on ticking'. Domestic rather than exogenous forces present Swedish welfare its most important future challenges.

NOTES

1. For opposed arguments on Swedish growth's comparative robustness, see sources cited below.
2. The subsequent content analysis is based mainly on the following volumes and summarising sections of the *OECD Economic Surveys* on Sweden: 1970, pp. 34–41; 1971, pp. 44–46; 1972, pp. 40–42; 1973, pp. 32–33; 1974, pp. 36–37; 1975, pp. 41–42; 1976, pp. 38–39; 1977, pp. 41–43; 1978, pp. 40–42; 1979, pp. 44–46; 1980, pp. 52–60; 1981, pp. 46–48; 1982, pp. 48–51; 1984, pp. 45–47; 1985, pp. 52–55; 1987, pp. 58–60; 1989, pp. 85–89; 1990, pp. 94–98; 1992, pp. 96–102; 1994, pp. 99–104; 1995, pp. 92–99; 1996, pp. 1–16; 1998, pp. 1–16; 1999, pp. 9–20.
3. The explosion of educational recommendations relates to the 1998 report's 'special feature' theme, 'Education, training and labour market reform'. Only two other Sweden reports feature special themes ('Employment Creation and Enterprise Growth' in 1996, and 'Structural reform: The tax and transfer system' in 1999).
4. These processes are reflected by expenditure data in the Statistical annexes of the *OECD Employment Outlook* (1997, 2001).
5. Thus, in debate on the SDP government's finance plan in the session of 12 June 1990, the Conservative Party speaker Lars Tobisson argued that government economic policy has led to 'growth this year ... of less than 1 per cent ... the worst among the OECD countries'. He goes on to advocate lower taxes as one solution. The then Minister of Finance, Allan Larsson, counters by referring to his participation in an OECD ministerial meeting some weeks before. Discussions there are held to confirm the government's view of economic conditions, to which it has responded: 'Our finance plan includes important long-range reforms which will lead to increased growth. The most important measure is the tax reform, which will stimulate work and saving' (Protokollnr 1989/90:139, via http://www.riksdagen.se/debatt, logdate 020614)
6. http://www.riksdagen.se/debatt/propositioner, logdate 020617 and 020619.
7. Swedish Teachers' Union, direct information, 19 June 2002.
8. National Agency for Education, direct information, 5 June 2002.

REFERENCES

Esping-Andersen, Gøsta (1990), *The Three Worlds of Welfare Capitalism*, Cambridge: Polity Press.

Fritzell, J. (2001) 'Inkomstfördelningens trender under 1990-talet' in *Public Inquiry Commission Report Series SOU (2001:57), Välfärdens finansiering och fördelning*, Stockholm: Fritzes, pp. 131–187.

Government of Sweden (1994), *Regeringens proposition 1993/94:250, Reformering av det allmänna pensionssystemet*, Stockholm: Allmänna förlaget.

Government of Sweden (1998), *Regeringens proposition 1997/98: 151, Inkomstgrundad ålderspension, m.m.*, Stockholm: Allmänna forlaget.

Henreksson, M. (1996) 'Sweden's relative economic performance: lagging behind or staying on top?', *Economic Journal* **106**, 1747–1759.

Korpi, Walter (1996), 'Eurosclerosis and the sclerosis of objectivity: on the role of values among economic policy experts', *Economic Journal* **106**, 1727–1746.

Lindbom, Anders (2001) 'Dismantling the social democratic welfare model? Has the Swedish welfare state lost its defining characteristics?', *Scandinavian Political Studies* **24**, 171–193.

OECD (1997), *Employment Outlook*, July, Paris: Organisation for Economic Co-operation and Development.

OECD (2001), *Employment Outlook*, June, Paris: Organisation for Economic Co-operation and Development.

OECD (various years), *OECD Economic Survey, Sweden*, Paris: Organisation for Economic Co-operation and Development.

Rothstein, Bo (1994), *Vad bör staten göra?*, Stockholm: SNS.

Schück, Johan (2002), 'Svensk arbetslöshet anses för låg', *Dagens Nyheter*, 4 May, p.C3.

7. Belgium: increasing critique by the OECD

Philippe Pochet

INSTITUTIONAL AND POLITICAL CONTEXT OF THE BELGIAN WELFARE STATE

The foundations of the Belgian social security system are contained in a 1944 agreement of the Employer/Worker Committee, which inspired the Belgian government. Built on the principles of social insurance and solidarity, the Belgian system owed less to the influence of Beveridge and more to the influence of Bismarck. Three separate social security schemes cover the three major categories of workers: wage-earners, the self-employed and public employees. Social benefits are financed mainly by employers and employees (the state also contributes, but its part is decreasing). The funding of social security has been complemented since the mid-1980s by other sources of funding (called alternative funding) and since the mid-1990s by specific levies on incomes (Arcq and Chatelain 1994). Decision-making is shared between the government and representatives of the social partners.

Belgian society is divided into 'pillars' (Socialist, Christian and to a lesser extent Liberal); these pillars have their own institutions in society, covering all facets of life. The education system is shared between public and private schools. The latter are mostly Catholic, and dominant in the Flemish region. Trade union coverage is high at around 60 per cent of the population in the paid labour force. The CSC/ACV (Christian unions) and FGTB/ABVV (Socialist unions) are the main ones. There is also a less important Liberal union. Christians, Socialists, Liberals and the 'neutral' mutualities, as well as the doctors' association are important actors in the health care system. Nevertheless, the social partners and the government have progressively increased their role as the funding question became more central to the debate. While this traditional societal arrangement is progressively subsiding, the linguistic tensions are increasing, leading to the federalisation of the unitarian state. The complex institutional landscape, the multiple veto points and the very complex compromises, often encompassing different social and economic fields, have rendered any dramatic form of change impossible (Arcq and Blaise 1998).

The pensions system is principally based on the first pillar (pay-as-you-go public pension). A reduction in the huge global public debt (100 per cent of GDP in 2002) should allow for future increases in retirement costs as a percentage of GDP. A fund for ageing (2000) was also created in this framework to cover the cost increases in the public pension system. Finally, it is of interest to note that recently the second pillar has been extended, but in line with the principle of solidarity, as the collective convention sets out to extend it at the sectoral level to all workers.

The unemployment benefit system is considered 'passive' in that claimants receive cash transfers with little temporal limitation and control (although control has increased during the 1990s). The consequence is that the social assistance system does not play such an important role in terms of the number of persons who are supported by it. One of the objectives of the social assistance system is to re-integrate the beneficiaries into the mainstream social security system through activation policies.

The links between the labour market and social protection are made through the automatic indexation system between wages and prices, and which is also applied to social benefits. This has created a structural solidarity between the different industrial sectors as well as between active and non-active persons. The indexation system can be considered the cornerstone of the Belgian social system.

Health care is mainly ensured by contributions. This led, at the beginning of the 1990s, to a vivid political debate on the differences in medical consumption between the French-speaking and Flemish-speaking populations. Due to these regional differences, some have called for a regionalisation of this policy area. There have also been proposals to finance it through taxation, because it covers the whole population (Reman 1990). Nevertheless, no agreement has been reached and it remains a federal policy funded by contributions.

During the period from 1975 to 2000, and particularly from the beginning of the 1980s, the major economic problem in Belgium was that of the huge public debt, the budgetary deficit culminating at 14 per cent in 1982. The total public debt attained its highest level – 130 per cent of GDP – in 1995, and then decreased to 100 per cent of GDP in 2001.

After the 1982 devaluation, where the principal goal was the restoration of the account balance and the profitability of the enterprises by freezing wages, the main (if not unique) policy priority of the period 1985–2000 was the adjustment of public expenditure. The 1980s was a period of strong austerity and it was dominated by a political coalition between the Christian and the Liberal parties. It is nevertheless of interest to note that social expenditure was, in relative terms, less affected compared to other areas such as public investment (OECD 1997). At the beginning of the 1990s, public finance expenditure appeared to be under control, but the recession of 1992 led again to a deficit of 7 per cent. At the same time, wage increases were higher than in the neighbouring countries. As in the 1980s, the government took a series of budgetary measures, froze wage increases (except for indexation) and adopted in 1996 a law on competitiveness. During the 1990s, the political coalition was between Christian and Socialist parties. In the 1990s, the second adjustment, due to the need to comply with the Maastricht criteria, was mainly directed toward the reduction of interest rates and the rate of expenditure growth, measures that had fewer negative impacts. It should also be noted that fiscal reforms, lowering the personal income tax levels, have been adopted (1985, 1988 and 2002).

From the early 1990s onwards, debate has centred around alternative funding for social security, a matter with strong 'community' (i.e. Flemish/ Francophone) connotations. The question is whether to distinguish between insurance covered by employee and employer contributions, and universal protection like health care, which should be financed by the general state budget. Since any modification would have regional implications, however, significant changes have been out of the question. For example, because the Flemish are now, on average, richer than the Francophones, a move from contribution-based funding toward a tax on income would have a differential effect on the two linguistic groups.

The period between 1993 and 1996 was particularly rich in events. The aim of the government was to redraw the post-World War II Social Pact (Arcq and Pochet 2000). In July 1993, the Prime Minister announced a broad debate on jobs, competitiveness and the funding of social security in order to conclude a pact similar to the one in 1944. The appeal to the two sides of industry was made in a worsening economic and social context, as well as being in the run-up period to the European Monetary Union (EMU). The positions of the two sides of industry differed greatly. On the trade union side, the CSC/ACV (Christians) looked towards a new social pact that would take into account evolution since the post-World War II pact, as well as the impact of European integration. The FGTB/ABVV trade unions (Socialists) adopted a more defensive attitude by demanding guarantees on social security, commitments regarding jobs, and compliance with collective bargaining agreements and indexation. The employers insisted on the need to diminish the competitive handicap and to reform public finances. The Prime Minister drew up a preliminary draft pact on employment, competitiveness and social security based on the work of a group of experts. The negotiations with the two sides of industry broke down quickly but, despite the ensuing major social conflict, the government adopted the 'overall plan' (*Plan Global*). A new attempt to sign a social pact was made in 1995/96 but it did not materialise. Finally, the government adopted in 1996 a law on competitiveness that limited the maximum wage increases to the average of the three main trade partners: France,

Germany and the Netherlands (Denayer and Tollet 2002). The new deal is based on a systematic comparison with neighbouring countries. After wage comparisons, the next step was the comparison of social security expenditure, with the objective of reaching the average of the three neighbouring countries in a few years (Pochet, forthcoming).

Since 1999, a new government has been in office, comprised of a coalition between Liberals, Socialists and the Greens. With the end of the period of austerity, new room for manoeuvre with the budget has opened up. Moreover, the government adopted the 'active welfare state' concept as its leitmotif. Although its definition remains imprecise, the policy line fits well into the mould of the European Employment Strategy of the European Union.

OECD RECOMMENDATIONS

Three broad periods can be distinguished within the overall analysis of the recommendations the OECD has made regarding Belgium:[1]

1970–82: Belgium is considered a country with no major structural problems. What was to become the principal difficulty of the following decades, the negative consequences of the growing global debt, was minimised through emphasis on the high internal savings rate and the important surplus in the trade balance. During this period, Belgium was often portrayed as exemplary and innovative, although there were problems under the apparently clean surface. These problems would progressively lead to a questioning of the coherence of the diverse policy actions.

1983–93: Doubts about Belgian performance are raised in OECD analyses. Throughout the surveys, the tone of concern appears progressively to be increasing. Let us note that the report of 1984 conducts an in-depth analysis of the Belgian situation, notably raising questions about the overall policy coherence, and attempting to paint a precise picture of the complex institutional situation.[2] This report in particular represents a turning point, after which criticisms progressively increased. One example is that of wage indexation and social security benefits. Previously presented as guarantors of social peace, they were viewed with an increasingly critical eye from 1983 onwards.

The last period begins in *1994*. The Belgian system is no longer criticised in a merely implicit manner, but head on. This culminates with the report in 1997, which proposes a radical overhaul of the Belgian system. The policies and objectives recommended were a reduction of labour costs, an introduction of more work incentives, a re-balancing between activity and non-activity, and an improvement in the qualification and competencies of the active population, notably among the least qualified.

Table 7.1 recalls the principal OECD recommendations.

Table 7.1 *Social policy in OECD reports on Belgium*

Year	Problems	Criticisms	Recommendations
Employment/Labour market			
1977	Growing level of unemployment		More expansionist economic policies
1982	Growing public deficit (13% of GDP) Increase in the costs of social benefits		Reform of how the social protection system is financed Reduction of working time without full compensation
1984	Difference between Belgium and the European average in unemployment rate	Not enough (wage) flexibility Too high labour costs, even when corrected for productivity	Suppression of the automatic indexation of wages More wage differentiation
1986	Labour costs Public employment	Increase in social burden of labour costs and rapid wage increase	Reduce labour costs
1991	Activity rate too low Long-term unemployment	Passive unemployment policies	Reduce the early retirement shcemes
1994	Social security costs	Untargeted	Target social security to those who really need it
1995	High labour costs	Indexation of wage and social benefits	Suppress sectoral bargaining

continued overleaf

Table 7.1 continued

Year	Problems	Criticisms	Recommendations
1997	Inefficient social model	Not enough incentives to work Too much work protection Wage system too rigid Too much early retirement	A general work programme for labour market reform, including a radical change in social security Suppression of the wage indexation system Reduction of unemployment benefits and length, more control and sanctions Suppression of the early retirement schemes
1999	Same problem	Slow pace of structural change	Same recommendations
	Old age		
1990–91	Potential increase in the cost of public pensions of 4% of GDP in 2040	Early retirement programmes too generous	Increase the retirement age for women to align it with that of men
1994	Level of debt		Reduce the public pension
	Health care		
1999	Cost	Reduce regional differences in medical consumption	Introduce more competition in the drug sector Increase the scope of social contributions to incorporate new forms of taxation

Source: OECD Economic Surveys on Belgium from 1976 to 2001 (cf. note 1). The column 'Year' indicates the year of publication of the quoted surveys.

94

ASSESSING THE POSSIBLE OECD IMPACT ON DOMESTIC POLICIES

The Labour Market

The Belgian employment policy of the 1970s was considered innovative by the OECD. The 1979 report even suggests envisaging a generalised reduction in working time. Here, we will concentrate on the three elements of the Belgian system that have been recurrently and stringently criticised since the mid-1980s. They are:

- Automatic wage indexation to price inflation;
- Long-term unemployment benefits (quasi without time limitation) and the passive unemployment policy;
- Generous early retirement schemes (and a very low activity rate among older workers, particularly those over 55 years).

Up to now, there have been no real changes on these issues, although some minor modifications have been made. The only items that were de-indexed from the wage index (which is now labelled the health index) were alcoholic beverages, cigarettes and fuels. The trade unions have strongly resisted any attempts to suppress automatic indexation.

Regarding unemployment, the government adopted some measures in line with OECD recommendations. Currently, unemployment benefits can be halted under certain restrictive conditions if their duration is 50 per cent more than the regional average. More active policies (mainly training) have been adopted during the current legislature (1999–2003) (DULBEA 2002). Nevertheless, this evolution seems to be mainly due to the pressure of the European employment strategy (the employability pillar) (Pochet et al. 2002), rather than that of the OECD.

Regarding early retirement, the OECD report in 1990/91 already indicated that early retirement schemes should be downsized to increase the activity rate and to avoid losses in the workforce. It also underlined the necessity of reducing the incentives for early retirement to avoid limiting the labour supply. In 1997, the report criticised the government for having decreased the retirement age, although it was a targeted and rather limited action. Although the OECD drew attention to this potential problem very early, it was confronted with strong resistance. At the European Council of Stockholm in 2001, a quantified target of increasing the employment rate of older workers to 50 per cent by 2010 was adopted at the European level. It has increased pressure to change the early retirement system. Now the necessity of modifying the rules has become more integrated into the policy discourse of various political and social actors, even if no major modifications in the early retirement scheme have been undertaken (see Table 7.2).

Table 7.2   Concordance between Belgian policy development and OECD recommendations

Recommendations/Criticisms	Concordance
Employment	
1970s	
Make use of demand management	Unclear
1980s	
Deregulate labour market	Unclear
Allow for differential and decentralised wage setting in different sectors/regions of the labour market	No
Suppress the indexation mechanism	No
1990s	
Suppress the indexation mechanism	No
Avoid early retirements	No
Reduce long-term benefit	Yes
Decentralisation, flexibilisation and deregulation of the wage bargaining processes	No
More active labour market policies	Yes
More flexible labour market	No
Old age	
Reduce public pensions	Unclear
Increase the retirement age for women	Yes
Reduce public debt in order to finance public pensions	Yes
Health	
Reduce the cost	Unclear
Reduce the unexplained differences in medical consumption	Yes

Source: *OECD Economic Surveys* on Belgium from 1976–2001 (cf. note 1).

Note: The policy recommendations stem from the analysis of OECD country surveys (cf. Table 7.1). Details on the assessment are given in the text.

Old Age

The 1994 report was the first time that a whole chapter in the OECD report was devoted to the effect of the ageing population on social spending. This chapter was principally of a descriptive nature, and included a presentation of several different scenarios. The effects of ageing on social security were estimated to present a cost of 5 per cent of GDP between 2000 and 2040, in the event of no major structural changes. The message was that it would be necessary to reduce public pensions; however, if the situation of public finances were to improve (cumulative reduction of the public debt), the snowball effect could be reversed and new margins of manoeuvre could be created. The OECD was in line with the dominant political discourse of this period: the difficult budgetary adjustments would be beneficial in the long run since they would allow for public pensions to be guaranteed in the future.

The OECD report in 1990/91 also suggested lengthening the activity periods for women to align them with that of men. This measure was adopted progressively because of European legislation on equality between men and women.

Other Policies

A specific chapter was devoted to the issue of *health care* for the first time in 1999. However, this question was touched upon in the report of 1990/91 in a chapter devoted to the effects of social protection on public finances. The OECD suggests an envelope system (pre-determined maximum expenses) to render (financially) responsible the health care providers. The report also esteems that it is necessary to moderate the differences in medical consumption not reflective of differentiated regional needs. This refers to the polemic mentioned in the introduction, in which some critics in Flanders suspected the Francophones of social security abuse, characterising their behaviour as one of over-consumption which, according to the critics, explained the gap in spending. It proposes a widening of the palette of social security funding (as indicated above, the Belgian debate at one point was focused on a possible fiscalisation of certain branches of social protection, in particular that of health care). However, due to regional tensions, it was not possible to restructure the system and how it was financed. In 1997, the report suggests that a decrease in social security spending should essentially be ensured by savings made in the area of health care.

There is almost nothing on *education* in the OECD reports. It is only in the report of 1997 that the issue is brought up. It is of interest to recall that education has been an area of community competence for the last three decades. Besides the increasing differences in terms of results (see the last classification of the OECD on this topic) it is a sensitive area due to the lack of financial resources in the French-speaking community.

The OECD Recommendations in the National Discourse on Major Social Policy Reforms

During the 1970s, the surveys of the OECD were lenient towards Belgian policies and were not very publicised.[3] One reading of the events is that the debt crisis of the 1980s and the increasingly critical surveys led to their progressively greater political influence. Another reading is as follows: because the government at the time carried out profound reforms for the reduction of social costs, the OECD surveys represented a useful tool with which to justify them. It coincides with the time that the Belgian delegation became more high level (interview with A. Simon, see note 3).

The 1990s have been dominated by a Christian/Socialist coalition. The increasingly critical recommendations of the OECD are at odds with Socialist priorities. The influence of the OECD thus declines. Many consider that what the OECD proposes is what should not be done.

In its 1998 Annual Report on employment in Belgium, the Ministry of Labour explains the reason for the feeble influence of the OECD in Belgium. The report indicates that the analyses of the OECD can be criticised because they are carried out by an international institution, with civil servants who are not well aware of Belgian reality. On the other hand, the European Employment Strategy is more influential due to the involvement of national civil servants and the government in the process.

The limited influence of the OECD reports in national politics was also due to the important role played by the National Bank of Belgium in its contacts with representatives of the OECD and in the process of drafting the report. The recommendations of the OECD are also interpreted in inner political circles as the opinion of the National Bank. Trade unions consider the most recent OECD reports to be so ideological that they should have no real influence in political debate. To illustrate this point, they issued a communiqué after the 1995 report but they judged it a waste of time to respond to the following surveys (interview with T. Dock, see note 3).

CONCLUSION

Overall, it appears that the recommendations of the OECD have not had much effect in Belgium. This is, at least partly, due to the fact that its analysis was not critical enough during the 1970s and the early 1980s, which was not helpful in understanding the depth of the problems in Belgium. During a short period there was a coincidence between the Christian/Liberal coalitions undertaking social reforms and the more critical surveys of the OECD. However, this was short-lived. Since 1995, the OECD recommendations have been radical, calling for an overhaul of the Belgian system. A programme for the overall restructuring of social security was proposed by the OECD, into which labour market reform was integrated. The 1999 report noted that little progress has been made in this direction. The fact that the OECD recommended a radical change in the Belgian model may explain why the recommendations were not taken into account by the governing coalition, which was made up of Christian and Socialist parties. Thus, there has not been any significant impact of the OECD on the central and distinctive elements of the Belgian model, which are indexation, unemployment benefits, low employment rate of workers over 50 years and especially those over 55 years.

In such a complex society where compromises are made between various political families (Christian, Socialist, Liberal) and which is divided along community lines and multiple levels of power, these kinds of (not very contextualised) recommendations have no real possibility of being taken into consideration. Moreover, since World War II, the social partners have played a key and autonomous role in labour relations and, to a lesser extent, on social security. As the OECD recommendations are not targeted toward such actors they can have only a very limited direct effect on the fields covered by negotiation between the social partners (e.g. decentralisation of wage bargaining or flexibilisation of labour conditions).

It is also of interest to note that the quality of the OECD analyses has progressively deteriorated. In effect, the analysis of 1984 had put the finger on the difficulties of the Belgian system through a fine-tuned analysis (the elements highlighted became consensual a decade later; see for example the analyses of the Conseil central de l'économie). However, since then, the OECD changed the nature of its analyses and criticisms. The European Employment Strategy (EES) recommendations, which are globally in line with some OECD recommendations (employment rate, early retirement), were much more influential as they intervened in the national debate in a more subtle way. The main reason for the different influence between the two is that the EES is partly integrated into the domestic political game while the OECD recommendations are considered by most of the players as external.

NOTES

1. The subsequent content analysis is based mainly on the following volumes and summarising sections of the *OECD Economic Surveys* on Belgium: 1976, pp. 28–40, 45–48; 1977, pp. 34–39; 1979, pp. 53–55; 1981, pp. 10–20, 51–52; 1982, pp. 10–21, 46–49; 1984, pp. 33–49, 50–53; 1986, pp. 11–33, 56–59; 1988, pp. 13–29, 79–83; 1989, pp. 91–96; 1990, pp. 76–92,

97–103; 1992, pp. 118–120; 1994, pp. 64–81, 82–89; 1995, pp. 39–45, 92–102; 1997, pp. 1–18, 53–107; 1999, pp. 11–24, 77–102; 2001, pp. 7–20.

2. The analyses of the weaknesses of the Belgian system and its particular industrial structure are later tackled along the same lines of the OECD analysis by some Members of the Conseil central de l'économie, who were playing a key role in the discussions on the evolution of wages (Michel and Denayer, 1997; Denayer and Tollet, 2002).

3. There is no systematic study of OECD influence on Belgian reforms. This brief section is based on material, mainly interviews, used for a study on the influence of the European Employment Strategy (EES) on employment policies (GOVECOR project led by W. Wessels, see www.govecor.org). The interviewed persons are:
   - Denayer, Luc, General Secretary of the Conseil central de l'économie;
   - Simon, André, Head of the research department of the Belgian employment ministry;
   - Dock, Thierry, Member of the research department of the CSC/ACV.

REFERENCES

Arcq, E. and P. Blaise (1998), 'Histoire politique de la sécurité sociale en Belgique', *Revue Belge de Sécurité Sociale* **3**, special issue, 479–711.

Arcq, E. and E. Chatelain (1994), *Pour un nouveau Pacte Social, Emploi, Compétitivité, Sécurité Sociale*, Brussels: Ed. Vie Ouvrière.

Arcq, E. and P. Pochet (2000), 'Toward a new social pact in Belgium?', in G. Fajertag and P. Pochet (eds), *Social Pacts in Europe – New Dynamics*, Brussels: European Trade Union Institute, pp. 113–134.

Denayer, L. and R, Tollet (2002), 'Institutional mechanisms of wage setting in Belgium', in P. Pochet (ed.), *Wage Policy in the Eurozone*, Brussels: P.I.E.-Peter Lang, pp. 177–194.

DULBEA (Département d'Economie Appliquée de l'Université Libre de Bruxelles) (2002), *L'évaluation de la Stratégie Européenne pour L'emploi en Belgique', Final Rapport (31/01/2002)*, Brussels: Convention Ministère de l'Emploi et du Travail-ULB.

Michel, E. and L. Denayer (1997), 'Marché du travail et compromis social: rétrospective et prospective', *Revue Politique du CEPSS* **2**, 45–52.

OECD [various years], *OECD Economic Survey, Belgium and Luxembourg*, Paris: Organisation for Economic Co-operation and Development.

Pochet, Philippe (forthcoming), 'Belgium and monetary integration', in Andrew Martin and George Ross (eds), *Euros and Europeans: EMU and the European Social Model*, Cambridge: Cambridge University Press.

Pochet, P., S. Plasschaert and O. Van der Haert (2002), 'Chapter 7: Belgium', in Ch. Meyer and D. Pyszna (eds), *Self-Coordination at the National-Level: Towards a collective 'gouvernement économique'?*, interim report I, Govecor Project research, May 2002, pp. 82–91.

Reman, P. (alias Leblanc), (1990), 'La fédéralisation de la sécurité sociale', *Courrier hebdomadaire du Crisp No. 1282–1283*, Brussels: Centre de recherche et d'information socio-politiques.

8. France: moving reluctantly in the OECD's direction

Marina Serré and Bruno Palier

INSTITUTIONAL AND POLITICAL CONTEXT

The French welfare state reflects for the most part the Bismarckian tradition: in France, most benefits are earnings-related, entitlement is conditional upon a record of contribution, and the contributions of both employers and employees constitute the system's primary source of financing. The French social welfare system expanded from 1945 to the 1980s, and saw the development of a particular and cohesive set of non-state agencies that fall under the rubric *la Sécurité sociale*. The system is extremely fragmented. It is divided into a number of different sectors covering different policy domains: health care, old age, family and unemployment.[1] The system is also segmented into different schemes covering different occupational groups (for example, there are more than 600 different pension schemes: for those employed in industry and trade, for the self-employed, for civil servants, for public firms' salaried workers, for farmers and so on). Instead of a unified system covering the entire population (as found in universalistic regimes), the system has developed via the addition of specific, particularistic and autonomous schemes for different occupational groups. During the system's expansion from the late 1940s to the late 1960s, many professions defended their specific benefits and resisted integration into the *Régime général*, the most important regime covering salaried workers from trade and industry. The French welfare state therefore deserves the 'corporatist-conservative' label given to it by Esping-Andersen (1990).

Since the mid-1970s, each member of the French population is to be covered by one social insurance fund, and is to receive from it quite generous benefits. Meanwhile, its corporatist fragmentation guarantees that each social group's specific interests will be preserved. As a result of this combination, French social security has developed a large constituency among salaried workers – the well-known attachment of the French to *la Sécurité sociale*. Salaried workers are represented by trade unions. In France (as in other Bismarckian systems), one of the most powerful pro-welfare coalitions is thus headed and represented by trade unions. Trade unions act as both the representatives and defenders of the system. They defend both the interests of the salaried population and their own place within the system.

This political and institutional framework has created a dubious political context for welfare reforms, especially those inspired by the OECD, whose preferences are not shared by employees' representatives. However, many of the OECD's recommendations seem ultimately to have been implemented, though often with a delay, as if France were moving reluctantly in the OECD's direction.

OECD IDEAS CONCERNING FRENCH SOCIAL POLICY

The OECD surveys[2] of France address primarily economic policy and the labour market. Social policy (such as pensions or health care) appears in the 1990s, while poverty and education are rarely approached (see Table 8.1).

OECD recommendations concerning *employment policy* came in three distinct phases. Until 1975, the OECD approach to employment remained Keynesian. From 1975 on, however, the OECD's goals changed to reduced inflation and the support of employment via restrained tax burdens and wages, a set of policies especially difficult to implement in France due to its many labour market rigidities (OECD 1985). In the 1990s the OECD recommended, rather than a policy grounded on unemployment benefits and selective measures, an active policy with increased flexibility and lighter regulations. The OECD is now more concerned by the minimum wage's high level in France than by its existence. It denounces the existence of inactivity and poverty traps and recommends the implementation of conditional benefits. Furthermore, the OECD is convinced of the perverse effects of labour market policies which pursue explicitly social ends, such as the RMI (*Revenu Minimum d'Insertion*) (1991).

In the 1990s *old age policy* became an issue. The OECD anticipated the risk of deficit increases after 2010, when the 'baby boom' generation retires (OECD 1995, 2000). Very generous, both in terms of the income levels and length of social security contributions covered, the French pension system could not be maintained without an economically dangerous rise in contributions. Therefore, the OECD recommended a reform to restore the ratio between active persons and pensioners, wages and pensions (extend contribution period, encourage private pensions funds and so on). The OECD considers France's pension reform of 1993 a first step in the right direction, especially in its introduction of a clear distinction between insurance and solidarity (1994). Still, the OECD criticises the lack of reform to public sector and special pension schemes. These reforms occurred in 2003.

Table 8.1 Social policy in OECD reports on France

Problems	Criticisms	Recommendations
Employment/Labour market High rates of unemployment Labour market rigidities (high wage costs, rigidities in the labour hour regulations, job offers not adapted to demand) Inactivity and poverty traps	Complex, heavy, unstable and expensive regulations Employment policy is too fragmented Unemployment benefits too generous, and the minimum wage high	Increase wage flexibility and total labour hours Redefine the purpose of a minimum wage Reform of employment security: limit restrictions on redundancy and short-term contracts Improve labour qualifications Reform unemployment benefits Improve policies by evaluation
Old age Growing share of the elderly Problem of financing pensions, problem especially after 2010	French pension system is too generous (insufficient requirements concerning the duration of contribution, based on gross wages Public sector pensions have not been reformed (before 2003)	Increase active population (avoid early retirement, extend the age of retirement) Reduce pensions, extend required contribution duration Distinguish solidarity and insurance, develop private pensions funds
Health care Raising health care costs without assuring a better state-of-health in the population 10–20% health expenditures are useless	French health care system induces rising costs (fee for service, liberty . . .) Policies focus on increased financing instead of controlling costs	Change medical suppliers' behaviour; reform payment system, introduce evaluation, medical guidelines and budgetary constraints with sanctions Demand-oriented actions (limited access to specialists) Strengthen competion between medical suppliers and insurance groups
Poverty Inactivity and poverty traps	Perverse effects of employment and fiscal policies	See employment

Source: OECD Economic Surveys on France from 1970 to 2000 (cf. note 2).

Throughout the 1990s OECD surveys label *health care* France's most pressing short-term policy problem, due primarily to what the OECD considers as excessive increases in medical consumption. According to the OECD, the French system itself is partly responsible for this excess. The 'fee for service' mode of payment for doctors provides strong incentives to increase the volume of medical acts, whereas a generalised freedom and the reimbursement of almost all medical expenditures encourage cost increases. The 12 reform programmes of the last 18 years, intended to balance the public health policy accounts, have failed because of their focus on increased financing. Moreover, non-reimbursed spending increased, raising an equity problem. OECD surveys first recommend altering the regulation of medical care's supply side in order to change medical suppliers' behaviour, and to then complete these measures with demand-oriented actions. Prevention is also presented as a way to reduce costs. Although recent reforms (such as of 1995) are seen as 'a welcome break with the past' (OECD 1997, p. 7), the OECD wishes to see greater structural change to the system and insists on the need to restructure the hospital sector (2000).

Only the 1997 survey deals with *poverty*, and then only insofar as it is related to employment policy. The survey argues that the French fiscal and redistribution systems keep some workers in inactivity or poverty even during periods of employment. OECD recommendations generally concern employment and fiscal policies rather than fighting poverty in itself.

OECD ANALYSES AND FRENCH POLICY

In no instance has the French government directly implemented OECD recommendations. French governments have, though with some delay, incrementally implemented reforms that reflect the logic of OECD policy recommendations, at least in the areas of employment, unemployment insurance and pensions. This may be due to the fact that the OECD's policy positions reflect a broader elite consensus shared by French experts and governments. It may also be a result of the fact that OECD surveys on France take into account not only doctrinal preferences but also French specificities. OECD recommendations concerning French social policy in fact vary according to policy area, as does the extent to which national policy and OECD recommendations concur. Concerning employment and pensions, domains in which OECD surveys take into account French specificities, there is limited but clear concordance between OECD recommendations and national policy. On the other hand, with respect to French health care and poverty policies, treated more doctrinally in the OECD surveys, there is little such concordance (see Table 8.2).

Table 8.2   Concordance between French policy development and OECD recommendations

Recommendations/Criticisms	Concordance
Employment	
Increase wages and work length flexibility and refine the purpose of minimum wages:	
• for minimum wage	No
• for work flexibility (through the 35-hour work week)	Yes (relative)
Reform unemployment benefits	Yes (with delayed benefits)
Reform measures concerning employment security: limit restrictions on redundancy and short-term contracts	Yes
Improve active policies by evaluating the programmes introduced	Unclear
Improve labour qualifications	No
Old age	
Increase active population (avoid early retirement, extend the age of retirement	No (in action), Yes (in prescription)
Reduce pensions, extend contribution duration	Yes (relative)
Distinguish solidarity and insurance, develop private pension funds	Yes (forthcoming)
Health	
Change medical suppliers' behaviour: reform payment system; introduce evaluations, medical guidelines, and budgetary constraints with sanctions	No
Demand-oriented action (limited access to specialists)	No
Strengthen competition between medical suppliers and insurers	No
Poverty	
Reform the minimum income schemes so that inactivity and poverty traps disappear; reduce the perverse effects of employment and fiscal policy	No

Note: The policy recommendations stem from the analysis of OECD country surveys (cf. Table 8.1). Details on the assessment are given in the text.

Employment

As OECD attitudes regarding employment policy in general, French employment policy can be divided into three successive stages (Gallie and Paugam, 2000; Barbier and Gautié 2000; Daguerre and Palier 2001). Throughout the 1980s, both the French public debate and the OECD focused on the importance of reducing labour market rigidities: regulatory changes to rules concerning hiring and firing were adopted. Meanwhile, government priorities changed: price stability became the priority, coupled with the implicit acceptance of rising unemployment as an unavoidable consequence of monetarist policy. In this context, French policies focused on supporting the growing number of unemployed, via generous unemployment benefits and what has been called the *traitement social du chômage*. This set of policies, accused of confusing economic and social issues, is far from OECD recommendations.

In the early 1990s, government priorities changed again with the adoption of the Treaty of Maastricht. Structural reforms, in particular the reduction of non-wage costs, were required to reinforce the French economy's competitiveness. The progress towards a single market put French firms in competition with their European counterparts. Faced with the convergence criteria imposed by Maastricht, financing social security deficits with increased employee social contributions rather than cuts in social spending was, after Maastricht, no longer a viable solution. French governments adopted a strategy of retrenchment. After 1992/93, cutting social expenditure formed part of a more general strategy of expenditure and deficit reduction. The OECD looked favourably upon measures reducing both the generosity of unemployment insurance benefits (1992) as well as the level of social contributions (1993). Maastricht thus drove the retrenchment of welfare policy and should be considered an exogenous causal force of greater importance than OECD recommendations.

The third period (1997–2002), concomitant with the development of Europe's 'Luxembourg process', was characterised by a new wave of 'employment-friendly' policies. These innovations took three forms: first, the gradual reduction of the work week from 39 hours to 35 hours. The 35-hour rule took effect in February 2000 for companies employing more than 20 workers but was not effective for small firms until 2002. Second, the introduction of a 'making-work-pay' strategy with the adoption of *Prime pour l'emploi* (January 2001), the French equivalent of the United Kingdom's Working Families Tax. Finally, the adoption of activation strategies for all job-seekers, the *Plan d'aide et de Retour à L'emploi (Pare)*, effective in July 2001. Though the OECD recommends an active employment policy, it judges these measures overly interventionist and expensive for the state and the French firms.

Pension System

The French pension system's development cán also be separated into three distinct phases (Bonoli 1997; Palier 2002). During the 1980s, governments requested reports on future problems, but increased contributions only to deal with immediate problems. The 1990s were characterised by two linked processes: the attempt to cut the overall level of public pensions, successful in 1993 but not 1995; and the probable development of voluntary, privately funded pension schemes.

Pension reform is widely perceived as a politically sensitive issue, and throughout the 1980s governments of both the left and right were inclined to the status quo. Instead of making difficult decisions which would have led to future pension cuts, governments preferred to do nothing, or to simply increase the level of social contributions paid to pension schemes in order to meet current deficits. Employee contributions were increased in 1977, 1978, 1987 and 1989. The delay in reform demonstrates the importance of the social protection system's institutional design. Though pension schemes have faced serious difficulties since the late 1970s, partial reforms were not introduced until 1993. In France, as the OECD acknowledges and criticises, the social partners play an important role in the pension system's administration. Government must negotiate with trade unions representing each individual professional occupation before implementing any reform, and are likely to confront strong popular opposition to any retrenchment proposal.

In 1993, partly in response to the pressure of Maastricht, the newly elected right-wing government undertook an important pension reform aimed at retrenchment. However, it succeeded only in reforming the most important of the basic pension schemes, covering private sector employees. This reform was made possible by its trade of benefit cuts for tax financing of non-contributory benefits, as well as its limitation to the private sector general scheme (Bonoli 1997). Benefit indexation was based on real prices for the initial five-year period, a rule that has since been extended indefinitely. The qualifying period for a full pension was extended from 37.5 to 40 years, and the period over which to calculate the reference salary was changed from the best ten years to the best 25. These reforms are to be introduced gradually over a ten-year period. Finally, a *Fonds de solidarité vieillesse* was created and charged with the task of funding non-contributory benefits. This reform is based on a clearer distinction between assistance and assurance schemes, reflecting the OECD's pension reform recommendations. In 1995, the Juppé government, in control of all the institutional veto points (the presidency and a huge parliamentary majority), failed to extend these measures to the public sector's employee pension schemes. A massive protest movement, which forced the government to abandon its plans, demonstrated both the strong public support for social insurance as well as the extent to which the social partners are involved in its management and defence.

In the spring of 1997, the right-wing government passed a new law to encourage the introduction of company-level pension funds, but upon taking office Lionel Jospin blocked its implementation. Since 1997, his government has sought, with the social partners' agreement, to negotiate another general pension reform, this time including the public sector. However, in the autumn of 2000, the new Finance Minister Laurent Fabius proposed the creation of a *Plan partenariaux d'épargne salariale*. Though not pension funds, these plans are intended to complement contributory benefits cut by the 1993 reforms. The newly elected President Chirac (May 2002) and government are explicitly committed to developing private individual pension funds in the forthcoming years. Therefore, France will eventually develop the type of solution (longer contribution period, introduction of private pension funds) for which the OECD has long advocated.

Health Care

Health care is the domain of French social security which most diverges from OECD recommendations, in part because in this area the OECD is hesitant to recognise French particularities. French governments do not directly control health expenditures. The social partners manage French health insurance, and services are provided by both public and private hospitals as well as independent doctors. The fees for medical care and treatment are negotiated by the social security funds and the medical practitioners' professional organisations. These organisations, especially medical ones, have always fought public regulation, making the control of health expenditure difficult (Hassenteufel 1994). Rather than a limited budget, there exists a system of reimbursed health care expenditures, first paid by the insured person. For medical and pharmaceutical expenses, the insured person initially settles the bill out of his/her own pocket and is then partially reimbursed. Medical care and treatment are reimbursed at up to 75 per cent of the maximum charge. The remainder (co-payment), known as the *ticket modérateur*, varies from 20 to 60 per cent of the total expense, and must be paid by the patient. The system of co-payment is designed to moderate demand. However, complementary insurance (*mutuelles*) very often reimburses the cost of the *ticket modérateur*. Today, 85 per cent of the population purchases some form of complementary health care insurance (Palier 2002)

The growth of health expenditures is often posited as one of social security deficit's primary causes. The proportion of health care expenditure to GDP has increased from 7.6 per cent in 1980 to 9.7 per cent in 1994. Throughout the 1970s and 1980s, governments relied on 'plans' meant to balance social security budget in order to cope with these difficulties. These numerous 'plans' have failed to limit the unstoppable growth in demand for health care. In the same way, the new instruments developed in the early 1990s failed to halt rising health expenditures. In order get this evolution under control, the state has recently stepped up its intervention activities (Serré 2002). The overall tendency appears to defy the model promoted by OECD surveys, which would favour a more market-oriented approach.

Indeed, since the 1995 reform *Plan Juppé*, the state's role in French health care provision has increased. It has been restructured, in particular by the creation of regional bodies charged with the planning of both health care provision and budgets. Half of the members of these *Agences Régionales de l'Hospitalisation* are state representatives. State representatives are also present in the new *Unions Régionales des Caisses d'Assurance Maladie*, in charge of co-ordinating and harmonising the different social insurance funds' various health care policies. These changes do not mean that the system has gone from a corporatist to a statist one, but simply that the state has more instruments at its disposal to control rising expenses.

The most important such reform was the approval of a constitutional amendment (February 1996) obliging parliament to adopt an annual social security budget in a *loi de financement de la Sécurité sociale*. For the first time in France, parliament is taking part in the debate on the social security expenditures, which were previously regarded as separate from the state budget. Parliamentary competence has helped the government control the social policy agenda. Instead of having to justify intervention in domains controlled by the social partners, governments can now regularly plan adaptation measures, especially cost-containment ones. This new instrument has changed the logic of intervention. Rather than searching for ways to finance demand-driven social expenditures, the vote of a *loi de financement* implies budgetary limitations to social spending.

Poverty

The 'new poverty' has been a salient issue in the French political discourse since the early 1980s, and is responsible for a major innovation in French social protection: *Revenu minimum d'insertion* (RMI). It is rather surprising that OECD surveys make almost no mention of poverty (1997 is an exception). This lends credence to the hypothesis that the OECD is concerned primarily with economic rather than social issues, and considers social policy only in its relation to economic policy and outcomes.

In response to growing social exclusion, a number of new programmes have been introduced in France (since the early 1980s) to cover those without access to the labour market, and as such to social insurance. As is the case with health care reform, these programmes generally diverge from OECD recommendations. The first such programmes were employment policies in which the state proposed specific contracts to those excluded from the labour market. Their numbers grew, and by the late 1980s it seemed necessary to create specific social benefits for the excluded, delivered via new social policies aimed at re-insertion (Outin 1997). These policies defy the traditional model of social insurance, in fact emphasising the former system's inadequacy. While traditional social insurance centred on employees, these new policies target the socially excluded. Instead of treating all situations equally and with the same instruments, social re-insertion policies are geared towards specific groups and designed according to local needs, with a high degree of administrative devolution to local authorities. In addition, instead of treating social risks separately (old age, sickness, unemployment), re-insertion policies address a whole range of relevant social problems in an integrated manner (poverty, housing, vocational training . . .).

The RMI, created in December 1988, is the most important of these new social benefits. This new non-contributory scheme, meant for those with little to no income, guarantees a minimum level of resources to anyone aged 25 or over in the form of a means-tested differential benefit. In addition, the RMI has a re-insertive dimension, an explicit contract between the recipient and 'society'. Recipients must commit themselves to participation in a re-insertion programme (job-seeking, vocational training, activities designed to enhance the recipient's social autonomy and so on). In addition to RMI, France now has seven other minimum social incomes. In 2002, more than 10 per cent of the French population received one of these stipends. Through the development of new social policies and minimum income benefits, part of the French social protection system now targets specific populations, using new instruments (means-tested benefits delivered according to need, financed with taxes, and managed by both local and national authorities) with reference to a new logic (combat social exclusion rather than guarantee income and status maintenance).

IS FRANCE SLOWLY CONFORMING TO THE OECD MODEL?

In three successive phases of policy reform, a new architecture, with new principles and instruments, i.e. a new paradigm (Hall, 1993), has emerged for the French welfare state. French governments now accept that the welfare state should be compatible with international competition. It should become 'employment friendly', reducing its costs (especially non-wage costs) and offering benefits that no longer provide harmful disincentives (activation, making work pay). These new norms include the targeting of public expenditure to those whose needs are greatest, as well as the belief that welfare should rely not only on public intervention, but also on the contributions of other actors such as families, NGOs and private firms (Daniel and Palier 2001; Palier 2002).

More than driven by OECD recommendations, these changes should be attributed to European integration. The Maastricht Treaty, especially the preparation of a single currency, imposes more than simply technical criteria on member states. It also implies that all participants have accepted a paradigmatic shift in economic policy. The focus of macro-economic policy has changed from fighting unemployment (through reflation policy) to fighting inflation (through monetarist and strict budgetary policy). Hall (1986) has shown how this shift from Keynesian to monetarist policy transpired in the UK (late 1970s) and in France (early 1980s). The Maastricht criteria reflect this kind of shift at the European level. Limited budget and state deficits and low inflation: these criteria correspond to a coherent, neo-classical economic vision, based on supply-side policy, the promotion of open competition, and budgetary restriction. While with respect to economic policy this paradigmatic shift occurred for most European states in the early 1980s, national social policies generally retained their former (Keynesian) logic throughout the 1990s. The welfare state's crisis also originates in the discrepancy between its internal logic and the new global logic. For most of Continental Europe's welfare state reforms, the issue seems more and more to be the adaptation and realignment of social policy to the new global economic paradigm.

This realignment is driven more by economic than social or political concerns. If this new paradigm can define the economic role of social protection (summarised in the notion of re-commodification), the principles of social justice that underlie them, as well as the political processes and institutions that may provide their legitimacy, are still to be found.

NOTES

1. In France, education is not seen as a domain of social policy since it belongs to the realm of State 'Republican policies'. Therefore, we have chosen not to include education in this study.
2. The subsequent content analysis is based mainly on the following volumes and summarising sections of the *OECD Economic Surveys* on France: 1970, pp. 41–45; 1971, pp. 58–60; 1972, pp. 19–25; 1974, pp. 53–57; 1975, pp. 58–66; 1976, pp. 48–50; 1977, pp. 45–47; 1979, pp. 55–58; 1980, pp. 69–71; 1982, pp. 68–71; 1983, pp. 65–68; 1984, pp. 57–59; 1985, pp. 56–60; 1987, pp. 61–64; 1989, pp. 104–108; 1990, pp. 89–94; 1991, pp. 102–109; 1992, pp. 116–122; 1994, pp. 99–106; 1995, pp. 125–137; 1997, pp. 1–20; 1999, pp. 9–23; 2000, pp. 9–23.

REFERENCES

Barbier, Jean-Claude and Jérôme Gautié (1998), *Les Politiques d'Emploi en Europe et aux USA*, Paris: PUF.

Bonoli, Giuliano (1997), 'Pension politics in France: patterns of co-operation and conflict in two recent reforms', *West European Politics* **20** (4), 160–181.

Daguerre, Anne and Bruno Palier (2001) 'Welfare systems and the management of the economic risk of unemployment, the French case', report for the European University Institute, Florence.

Daniel, Christine and Bruno Palier (2001), *La Protection Sociale en Europe: le Temps des Réformes*, Paris: La Documentation française.

Esping-Andersen, Gøsta (1990), *The Three Worlds of Welfare Capitalism*, Cambridge: Polity Press.

Gallie, Duncan and Serge Paugam (eds) (2000), *Welfare Regimes and the Experience of Unemployment in Europe*, Oxford: Oxford University Press.

Hall, Peter A. (1986), *Governing the Economy: the Politics of State Intervention in Britain and France*, New York and Oxford: Oxford University Press.

Hall, Peter A. (1993), 'Policy paradigms, social learning and the state. The case of economic policymaking in Britain', *Comparative Politics* **25** (3), 275–296.

Hassenteufel, Patrick (1994), 'La profession médicale face à l'Etat, une comparaison France/Allemagne', political science doctoral thesis, Paris I.

OECD [various years], *OECD Economic Surveys France*, Paris: Organisation for Economic Co-operation and Development.

Outin, Jean-Luc (1997), 'Les politiques d'insertion' in M. Vernières (ed.) *L'Insertion Professionnelle, Analyses et Débats*, Paris: Economica, pp. 142–58.

Palier, Bruno (2002), *Gouverner la Sécurité Sociale*, Paris: PUF.

Serre, Marina (2002), 'Le tournant néo-libéral de la santé? Les réformes de la protection maladie en France dans les années 1990 ou l'acclimatation d'un référentiel de marché', Thèse pour le doctorat de science politique sous la dir. de M. Offerlé, Université Paris I Panthéon-Sorbonne.

9. The Netherlands: how OECD ideas are slowly creeping in

Harmen Binnema

INSTITUTIONAL AND POLITICAL CONTEXT

The Dutch welfare state is, in terms of the Esping-Andersen (1990) typology generally characterised as *conservative*, although it has some clear social-democratic traits and – especially in recent years – increasingly more liberal elements too (cf. Kersbergen 1995; Becker 2000; Lamping and Vergunst 2000; Huber and Stephens 2001). In terms of generosity and income equality, the Netherlands are closer to the social-democratic models than to conservative counterparts Austria and Germany, but the architecture is still very much conservative.

First social laws were established in the beginning of the twentieth century and would offer a minimum protection in case of accident, sickness or disability. They were part of a package deal, which has become known as the 'Pacification', also including the equal treatment of private and state schools and universal suffrage. In the inter-war years, the welfare state schemes remained very limited, with a small role for the state and an emphasis on charity. The true build-up of the Dutch welfare state came after World War II, when a Roman–Red coalition (Catholics and social-democrats) headed by Drees (1946–58) introduced a range of new social security laws, starting with the Emergency Act for Old Age Provisions. In the 1950s, this early initiative was extended to a fully-fledged pension system, including a flat-rate universal pension, occupational pensions and private insurances. The pension system is a telling example of the conservative–social-democratic mixture that typifies the Dutch welfare state. Successive governments in the 1960s and 1970s, composed of confessionals and liberals, further expanded the welfare state with laws on health care, children's allowances and unemployment.

The left-wing Den Uyl government (1973–77) increased the (financial) role of the state in providing social protection and linked public wages and social benefits to private sector wages. This development was partially reversed by the governments that followed in the 1980s. Major changes in recent years, initiated by Kok's 'purple' coalition, include the privatisation of the sickness law, reduction of some generous benefits and, more in general, a transformation away from the breadwinner model (e.g. in the pensions scheme). Also, there has been a switch to more active labour market policy instead of passive transfers.

What factors have contributed to the development of the Dutch welfare state? First, we can see the influence of various political parties in government; first and foremost, the role of the *confessional* parties should be mentioned in this respect. Confessional parties have continuously been in government from 1917 till 1994. The Catholic parties in particular, competing with the social-democrats for the votes of the working class, have stimulated the coming about of an extensive welfare scheme. In recent years, it was the purple coalition that pursued changes in a different direction, both in terms of the generosity and the character of the welfare state. Interestingly, this coalition has been more successful than the preceding conservative–liberal coalitions in the 1980s. One explanation might be that a social-democratic party is able to overcome resistance of its traditional clientele, e.g. the unions, since it is believed to reform to ensure viability of the welfare system in the long run (Armingeon et al. 2001). Second, there is the influence of *consociational democracy*. In this type of democracy, many actors are consulted and incorporated in decision-making, which also enhances the social basis for welfare arrangements. Political elites have considerable room to manoeuvre and to close deals on important legislation. At the same time, this type of democracy might also be an impediment to reform: it is very difficult to bring about radical changes (as many governments have experienced). In addition, the role of *corporatism* has contributed to welfare expansion. Tripartite agreements have on several occasions led to welfare reform – most notably the Wassenaar agreement – and the Social Economic Council, in which government, employers and unions are represented, has been important as an advisory board for socio-economic matters (although the government is no longer obliged to ask the Council's advice).

In the late 1970s and 1980s, unemployment rose and the collective burden kept increasing, due to many generous welfare schemes. This trend has been stopped and reversed in the 1990s: currently, the Netherlands is a well-to-do nation, with high economic growth, low inflation and low unemployment. Some have described this as the 'Dutch miracle', for which three policy changes account, according to Visser and Hemerijck (1997): wage restraint, social security reform and active labour market policy. The budget deficit and public debt, both of which increased at high speed in a relatively small time, have steadily been reduced in recent years. There is a balanced budget and the public debt is now around 60 per cent of GDP.

The main problem of the Dutch welfare state, also prominent in the 2002 parliamentary election campaign, is the astonishingly high number of disabled.

Almost one million people receive a disability benefit, despite many efforts to get control over the disability scheme. Inactivity is still high and labour market participation of women and older people (55–64 years) is below EU average. Finally, pressure on the pension system may persist, now that the 'baby-boom' generation will be entitled to public pensions in the next few years.

OECD IDEAS CONCERNING DUTCH SOCIAL POLICIES

The *Economic Surveys*[1] of the Netherlands are rather brief in the 1970s and 1980s, but grow substantially in size during the 1990s. Also, the scope of issues covered is gradually widened. It will show that the first issue – labour market, (un)employment – receives by far the most attention, whereas poverty is not mentioned at all. In the 1970s and beginning of the 1980s, focus is predominantly on the (macro-)economic policy of the Dutch government; little is said about specific aspects of the welfare system. For this reason, three of the five policy fields – health, old age, education – only gain access in the 1990s. Table 9.1 summarises the main criticisms and recommendations.

The OECD considers the extensive and expensive social security scheme an impediment to economic growth and a major cause of rigidities in the labour market. In general, the welfare system is criticised for being overly generous; substantial reductions are proposed, both in terms of the level of benefits and eligibility for benefits.

The points raised by the OECD in the field of employment centre around the issue of *labour market flexibility*. Both unemployment and inactivity are seen as a result of a lack of flexibility. However, the solutions proposed by the OECD differ through the years, nicely showing the development from Keynesianism to neo-liberalism. In the 1970s, the stimulation of investment and demand management are advocated, whereas in the 1980s focus is on cutting social expenditure, increasing pay differentials and lowering or even abolishing minimum wages. In the 1990s, the call for lower public expenditure and an end to wage bargains remains, but to that is added the emphasis on active labour market policy. Moreover, in the last 15 years the problems with the disability scheme have rapidly gained prominence; here the OECD suggests a radical reform, to reduce the number of beneficiaries, as well as level and duration of the benefits.

Old age receives very little attention: the ageing population figures among the demographic and social trends that might put pressure on social spending, the question being whether the basic universal pension is financially affordable. The health system is mentioned as one of the structural factors that cause high social spending; in analogy to other areas, like public transport and utilities, the introduction of market forces is recommended. Two other issues are

Table 9.1 *Social policy in OECD reports on the Netherlands*

Year	Problems	Criticisms	Recommendations
Employment/Labour market			
1970s	Wage/price spiral High unemployment		Shift of demand management toward restriction Stimulate investment
74, 77, 78, 79, 1980s, 1990s		High collective burden	Restrain growth of public expenditure
1980s	Lack of productivity in private sector Inflexible labour market		Reduction in social security benefits for inactive population Decentralised wage bargaining and greater pay differentials
1980s		Generous social security hampers activity and productivity	Relaxation of minimum wage Reduction of labour costs
1980s, 1990s		Many not 'genuinely' disabled receive benefits; disability scheme is far too generous	
1983		Lack of profitability due to rigidities of labour market	
1990s	Disability Low activity Unemployment		Active labour market policy

Old age

Year	Issue	Measures
1989, 1990s	Increasing costs of social security due to ageing	Bring pension system within the tax net Benefit cuts to afford pensions More competition and choice in pension funds

Health

Year	Issue	Measures
1989	Health-supply sector adds to high social expenditure	
1990s	Waiting lists Balance private and social insurances	More exposure to market forces Substantial reform of financing basis and more competition between insurers

Education

Year	Issue	Measures
1987, 1993 1998		Integration of long-term unemployed into the labour market requires more education and fine-tuning with private sector

Source: OECD Economic Surveys on the Netherlands from 1975 to 2001 (cf. note 1). The column 'Year' indicates the year or the period when the issue was raised.

criticised: the appearance of waiting lists (but no advice is offered), and the generosity of the sickness scheme. Finally, the field of education: the discussion focuses on younger people and long-term unemployed (often low-skilled), who should be trained for reintegration into the labour market.

ASSESSING THE IMPACT OF THE OECD

The Criteria of Concordance and Discordance

In this section,[2] I will evaluate to what extent the criticisms and recommendations formulated by the OECD in its surveys, have possibly influenced the social and economic policy of the various Dutch governments. This will be done by using the criteria of concordance and discordance. The first refers to a situation where the policy implemented is in line with measures proposed by the OECD. The second type implies the reverse situation: national policy is not following or even moving away from the recommendations of the OECD. In Table 9.2, an assessment is given of concordance and discordance in Dutch social policy.

To begin with is a more general picture of how the OECD evaluates the policies pursued by the Dutch government. The OECD becomes more and more critical of Dutch policy at the end of the 1970s, stating that 'the limits of successful, but purely conjunctural measures are being reached' (1979, p. 39). On several occasions, the OECD more or less explicitly evaluates whether the Dutch government has acted in line with its recommendations: 'Several of the objectives discussed have been fixed and maintained . . . but results have not matched objectives' (OECD 1983, p. 65). In 1996, the government is praised as it 'moved forcefully in this direction' (i.e. the direction proposed by the OECD). Two years later, the OECD notes that the performance of the Dutch economy 'compares favourably with that of most other European countries, especially in terms of growth and employment . . . with many analysts referring to a "Dutch model" ' (1998, p. 3). Nevertheless, critical remarks concerning public finance and the labour market can still be found.

In various surveys, most notably in the 1990s, the OECD shows its understanding for the Dutch 'consensus approach' and the core values that are at the heart of the architecture of the welfare system. The structural (and sometimes radical) reforms proposed should not be considered as an overturn of these values. But at the same time, the OECD maintains that solidarity has been overemphasised at the cost of economic efficiency and that a better balance between these goals should be found. Both in the reform of employment policy and the social security system, the OECD draws attention to the fact that the gradual and incremental approach that Dutch governments often opt for, leads to slow progress.

Table 9.2   Concordance between Dutch policy development and OECD recommendations

Recommendations/Criticisms	Concordance
Employment	
Shift of demand management toward restriction (70, 71, 73)	No
Stimulate investment (74, 76, 77)	Yes
Restrain growth of public expenditure (74, 78, 79, 80s)	No (70s), Yes (80s)
Reduction in social security benefits for inactive population (80s and 90s)	Yes
Decentralised wage bargaining and greater pay differentials	Unclear
Relaxation of minimum wage (80s, 90s)	No
Reduction of labour costs (81)	Yes
Active labour market policy (90s)	Yes
Old age	
Bring pension systems within tax net (89)	No
Benefit cuts to afford pensions (90)	Unclear
More competition and choice in pension funds (96)	No
Health	
More exposure to market forces (90s)	Unclear
Substantial reform of financing basis and more competition between insurers (90s)	No
Education	
Integration of long-term unemployed into the labour market requires more education and fine-tuning with private sector (87, 93, 98)	Yes

Note: The policy recommendations stem from the analysis of OECD country surveys (cf. Table 9.1). Details on the assessment are given in the text.

Labour market

In the recommendations of the OECD, three elements have been consistently present. First, activity should be increased (requiring more active labour market policy); second, several benefits (notably unemployment and disability) should be lowered to increase incentives to work, and third, wage differentials should be increased (through less centralised wage bargaining). The general heading under which all these proposals can be summarised is labour market flexibility. The Dutch labour market consisted of many rigidities that were deemed disadvantageous for employment and activation.

The Den Uyl government (1973–77) emphasised the stimulation of demand to foster economic growth and employment. This strategy was not against the recommendations of the early 1970s. In later years however, the OECD would state that the limits of this type of measure were reached. The more structural reform that was required – including the reduction of social benefits and increasing competitiveness – was not initiated by the Den Uyl government. The three governments headed by Lubbers (1982–94) to a considerable extent adhered to the OECD recommendations. The 'Wassenaar agreement' between the government and the social partners, was vital in this respect. In this agreement, wage moderation and the shortening of working hours were combined. It would increase profitability and thus lead to higher job creation. It has to be said that the OECD was and still is rather sceptical about the actual success of this 'Dutch model' (cf. OECD 1998): first, it is described as a mere *catching-up* from a previous dismal situation; second, *inactivity* is still high, both compared to other countries and historically and third, job creation consists mainly of *part-time* jobs (limited growth in terms of full-time equivalents). Thus, it may be that the eventual results are more or less in line with the goals formulated by the OECD, but the actual policy that was chosen differs in several respects.

A major reform of the disability scheme was initiated by the third Lubbers government (together with the PvdA): the benefits were decreased and there was a re-examination of all people below the age of 50 that were in the system. Moreover, a first step was made in privatising the sickness benefits, by charging the employer to pay the wages during the first six weeks of sick leave. In particular, the measures concerning disability reflected the proposals of the OECD, which had since the 1980s consistently stressed the need for major reforms.

In 1994, a new coalition was formed, including former rivals VVD and PvdA; the finance minister of the previous cabinet, Kok, became the new Prime Minister. This 'purple' government developed a labour market policy very much in accordance with OECD recommendations. Sickness benefits were privatised and new measures were taken against the abuse of the disability scheme, to significantly reduce the number of beneficiaries and the costs associated with these schemes. More emphasis was put on active labour market policy. In particular, long-term employed and younger people were targeted in the new measures: the latter group through the Youth Work Guarantee Plan, the former by a host of subsidised jobs based on reduction of the employers' share in social contributions. The OECD has also pointed at the need to re-integrate these groups, but the measures proposed were somewhat different. In particular, the creation of subsidised jobs should in the view of the OECD be a temporary measure only. On the other hand, the installation of 'Centres for Work and Income' where social security organisations and employment service work together, approaches the 'one-counter-system' advocated by the OECD (1994, p. 105).

In addition, people receiving social benefits were required to apply for jobs, while the standards for 'appropriate' jobs were lowered (including accepting jobs below qualification). In some respects, the measures of the second Lib–Lab coalition have even gone further than suggested by the OECD, though certainly not against these proposals. Then again, the plea for relaxation of the minimum wage and greater wage differentiation was not reflected in government policy. Finally, the two Kok governments have increased labour market flexibility, which was high on the OECD agenda throughout.

Old age
The OECD has been relatively silent on this theme; therefore, it is hard to assess concordance or discordance. The main problem recorded was the pressure of an ageing population on the size of social expenditure. Indeed, this pressure has been recognised by the Kok government and a special fund has been created (in times of high economic growth) to finance future pensions. The public pension *Algemene Onderdoms Wet* (AOW) that all people from the age of 65 receive is considered almost 'untouchable'. Political parties trying to challenge either the universality or the level of this pension, run tremendous electoral risks (an excellent illustration of the Pierson (1996) argument). As noted previously, the OECD has focused on other benefits when it came to reducing the generosity of social security schemes, and has – like all Dutch governments since 1970 – avoided a discussion on the basic pension.

Health policy
The government has not yet followed the recommendations to bring more market forces into the health care system. As the OECD notes, there is a deep division about the direction that a reform of the health care system should take. Two aspects have been prominent in the recent debates: first, the balance between private insurance and social insurance; second, consumers' choice of health plans. The income-based character of social insurances (which is a reflection of the notion of solidarity) is challenged by some parties. But there

is clear hesitance to give more way to market forces in the health system. The waiting lists for medical treatment have been an important issue for the governments of the 1990s, but despite some efforts to reduce or solve them, policy until now has not been very successful and waiting lists still are on the political (and OECD) agenda.

The government still has tremendous difficulties controlling the problems with the disability scheme. Only small progress has been made in reducing the number of claimants – most of all, those that were not 'genuinely' disabled – and the OECD is dissatisfied with the results of re-examination and a tightening of the eligibility criteria. The privatisation of the sickness scheme has led to a serious reduction of sick leave and the new system, in which employers have a large responsibility, seems to function well. Disability has been prominently on the OECD agenda and measures of the government have partly followed OECD's recommendations, but do not have the desired effect. The privatisation of the sick leave has not been specifically promoted by the OECD, but this policy fits into the more general argument for market forces and limiting social expenditure.

Education
The OECD pays relatively little attention to this issue. When it is mentioned, it is in the context of labour market policy. In that respect, the Dutch government has acted in accordance with OECD recommendations, as the active labour market measures have also focused on re-insertion of long-term unemployed and on offering better opportunities for younger people. On the other hand, the recommendations of the OECD were not detailed enough to evaluate whether the government has followed these. Moreover, when co-operations have emerged between the private sector and the education system, this was not the result of specific government policy.

Explicit Reference

Disability and unemployment, and more in general the costs of social security have been the most prominent and pressing issues between 1970 and 2000. In the previous section, government measures to deal with these problems have been described. What becomes clear is that few major reforms have occurred; instead, many *incremental* changes have taken place, reflecting the consensus approach that characterises Dutch politics. However, the Wassenaar agreement and the successive changes in the disability scheme in the late 1980s and early 1990s can be headed under 'major reforms'. In both cases, there was a clear sense of urgency, which accelerated decision-making. In these cases of reform, we have little reason to assume a direct impact of the OECD.

The strongest case for OECD impact would be explicit references in the political debates on major reforms. To find whether OECD is directly referred to, parliamentary documents from 1995 till 2001 have been analysed.[3] This gave a total of 260 documents; many of these were either reports of small committee meetings or they did refer to OECD, but were not concerned with social security issues. Therefore, documents that were used in the eventual analysis stem from plenary sessions, e.g. the yearly budget debates. All in all, 21 cases remained, in which the OECD was quoted to either strengthen or refute a certain argument.

OECD arguments are more often used by right-wing parties, although the difference is small. Moreover, the majority of references to OECD comes from parliamentarians; government references are from the minister of economic affairs and the finance minister. The VVD has used OECD reports to support its arguments about the 'poverty trap', reform of the disability scheme, competitiveness of the Dutch economy and early retirement. The Socialist Party has mentioned the very high level of broad unemployment and – together with other left-wing parties – has consistently pointed at the low expenditure on education compared to other OECD countries (nb: from other sources than the *Economic Surveys*). Finally, the Dutch government has referred to the problems of inactivity and lack of labour market flexibility. Other references include statistics or comparison with other countries, without a true statement for or against (although these are sometimes used to point at the fact that the Netherlands falls out of line with the rest of OECD). In general, OECD provides the additional, instead of the principal arguments.

CONCLUSION

Evaluating the effect of OECD ideas on Dutch government policy is a little hazardous, considering the modest scope of the analysis presented above. Focus has been, first, on a presentation of the criticisms and recommendations formulated in the Economic Surveys between 1970 and 2000. These proposals have subsequently been compared with the actual policy pursued by the various Dutch governments since 1970.

Some indications for a possible OECD impact can be discerned. An interesting finding here is that many of the measures taken by the Dutch government in line with OECD were implemented several years after the OECD had first formulated them in its surveys. The OECD consistently repeats several recommendations over time. In other words, it seems like some ideas have to be incorporated in the domestic political debate, before they have their effect. It might also be that the delayed effect reflects a situation in which domestic political actors are reluctant to recognise certain problems, since they fear electoral losses when embarking on structural reform. At a certain time however, the urgency of certain problems can no longer be denied and action becomes inevitable.

Which role has the OECD performed, in terms of Marcussen's (this volume) typology? Both the criteria of concordance and discordance and the few cases of direct effect suggest that it is most of all a role as *ideational artist*. The OECD is providing statistics and reports that can be used in political debate, but is not too successful in directly pushing specific policy ideas.

NOTES

1. The subsequent content analysis is based mainly on the following volumes and summarising sections of the *OECD Economic Surveys* on the Netherlands: 1975, pp. 39–40; 1976, pp. 38–40; 1977, pp. 43–45; 1978, pp. 41–43; 1979, pp. 39–41; 1980, pp. 57–61; 1981, pp. 39–41; 1983, pp. 63–65; 1984, pp. 47–49; 1985, pp. 43–46; 1986, pp. 55–59; 1987, pp. 50–52; 1989, pp. 80–84; 1990, pp. 69–73; 1992, pp. 86–92; 1993, pp. 81–87; 1994, pp. 100–107; 1996, pp. 98–107; 1998, pp. 1–17; 2000, pp. 1–18.
2. My overview of Dutch social policy development builds on van Kersbergen (1995), Becker (2000), Hemerijck et al. (2000), Green-Pedersen et al. (2001), Huber and Stephens (2001).
3. For this period, parliamentary documents are available online, which allows for a quick scrutiny, using keywords OESO (the Dutch term) and OECD.

REFERENCES

Armingeon, Klaus, Michelle Beyeler and Harmen Binnema (2001), 'The changing politics of the welfare state – a comparative analysis of social security expenditures in 22 OECD countries, 1960–1998', unpublished manuscript.

Becker, Uwe (2000), 'Welfare state development and employment in the Netherlands in comparative perspective', *Journal of European Social Policy* **10** (3), 219–239.

Esping-Andersen, Gøsta (1990), *The Three Worlds of Welfare Capitalism*, Cambridge: Polity.

Green-Pedersen, Christoffer, Kees van Kersbergen and Anton Hemerijck (2001), 'Neo-liberalism, the "third way" or what? Recent social democratic welfare policies in Denmark and the Netherlands', *Journal of European Public Policy* **8** (2), 307–325.

Hemerijck, Anton, Brigitte Unger and Jelle Visser (2000), 'How small countries negotiate change. Twenty-five years of policy adjustment in Austria, the Netherlands, and Belgium' in Fritz W. Scharpf and Vivien A. Schmidt (eds), *Welfare and Work in the Open Economy, Volume II*, Oxford: Oxford University Press, pp. 175–263.

Huber, Evelyne and John D. Stephens (2001), *Development and Crisis of the Welfare State: Parties and Policies in Global Markets*, Chicago: University of Chicago Press.

van Kersbergen, Kees (1995), *Social Capitalism: a Study of Christian Democracy and the Welfare State*, London and New York: Routledge.

Lamping, Wolfram and Noël P. Vergunst (2000), 'Corporatism, veto points, and welfare state reform in Germany and the Netherlands. Institutions, interests and policies', Paper prepared for the IPSA World Congress, Quebec, 1–5 August.

OECD [various years], *OECD Economic Survey, The Netherlands*, Paris: Organisation for Economic Co-operation and Development.

Pierson, Paul (1996), 'The new politics of the welfare state', *World Politics* **48** (2), 143–179.

Visser, Jelle and Anton Hemerijck (1997), *A Dutch Miracle: Job Growth, Welfare Reform and Corporatism in the Netherlands*, Amsterdam: Amsterdam University Press.

10. Too many rivals? The OECD's influence on German welfare policies

Reimut Zohlnhöfer and Jan Zutavern

THE GERMAN WELFARE STATE: INSTITUTIONAL AND POLITICAL CONTEXT

The German welfare state is a prime example of the conservative model of social protection. Germany was a pioneer in terms of welfare state development, first introducing social security schemes in the 1880s (health care 1883, old age 1889). These schemes shared important characteristics: they were mandatory and financed primarily by contributions of employers and employees, the benefits were earnings-related, and they were segmented by occupational group, thus both preserving status differentials and excluding the non-working population. Until the 1970s the German welfare state continued to expand the breadth of its programmes (unemployment insurance introduced in 1927), the number of its recipients, and the levels of its benefits. Indeed, notwithstanding a number of fundamental political regime changes, the welfare state's basic architecture remained unchanged. Even the introduction of long-term care insurance in 1994 conformed to the contributions-financed model of social insurance. Municipality-financed means-tested social assistance supplements the (federal) system of social insurance. Although post-World War II welfare state expansion took place faster in some countries than in Germany, social expenditure as percentage of GDP has always been clearly above the OECD average. Additionally, the German labour market is highly regulated.

During the period of observation Germany was governed by three different coalitions. A coalition comprised of the social democrats (SPD) and the smaller liberal party (FDP) held office from 1969–82, at which point it was replaced by a government of liberals and Christian democrats (CDU/CSU). This coalition persisted in office until 1998 when the social democrats reassumed power in a coalition with the Greens. However, all these coalition governments operated in an institutional system replete with veto points, among them federalism (which makes Keynesian demand management extremely difficult), an independent central bank that prioritises price stability, an influential constitutional court, and a comparatively strong upper chamber whose majority often diverges from that of the lower chamber, giving opposition parties a real opportunity to influence policy. This institutional setting and the presence of two pro-welfare parties (SPD, CDU/CSU) have necessitated compromises conducive to a large welfare state. In addition, the strong social partners have enjoyed almost unlimited autonomy in the wage setting process. Germany's EU membership and participation in the EMU further constrain government decision-making.

Prior to 1990 Germany was a wealthy country (in terms of GDP per capita) with a successful track record in fighting inflation. However, already in the 1970s unemployment levels rose, and the problem worsened during the following decade. In the 1990s the process of reunification exacerbated these problems. GDP per capita was much lower in the eastern part of the country, and unemployment skyrocketed as a result of the economy's fundamental transformation. The federal government financed unification with immense budget deficits and social security contributions, while its response to unemployment was the standard reduction of the labour supply. This, however, increased the cost of labour, making Germany a prime example of a political economy characterised by welfare without work.

OECD ECONOMIC SURVEYS ON GERMAN SOCIAL POLICIES 1970–2000

Prior to the late 1980s, social policy did not figure prominently in the *OECD Economic Surveys* of Germany.[1] Rather, the German economy's major problems were related to economic policy and industrial bargaining. As Table 10.1 shows, until 1975, the surveys postulated a careful but active use of demand management, a relaxation of monetary policy, and an improvement of unions' and employers' awareness of their mutual responsibility for price and income stability. By 1985, the OECD's orientation had gradually become more supply-side. Tax and subsidy reductions, deregulation, privatisation, decentralisation and the free play of the market became the new magic formulas.

Rising social security expenditures were first mentioned in 1989, when the OECD welcomed two major reforms to the health and pension systems. But any optimism soon dissipated with the onset of unification. Its devastating consequences dominated the surveys until 1994. When social security spending surged again in 1995, the OECD shifted its attention to pension, health care and labour market reforms. The underlying focus of the recommendations became the social insurance scheme's incentive structure: 'What is at stake is not a wholesale dismantling of the welfare state, but rather reforms through better incentives' (OECD 1996, p. 160).

Table 10.1 Social policy in OECD reports on Germany

Year	Problems	Criticisms	Recommendations
Employment/Labour market			
1970–74	Inflationary spiral partly due to lagged wage increases in 1969: restoration of price stability without creating a recession	Policy mix not ideal: monetary policy too restrictive, fiscal measures not developed enough	Make use of demand management instruments; improve coordination of fiscal policies; improve unions' and employers' associations' responsibility for price and income stability
1975	Sharp increase in unemployment		Fiscal stimulus (regardless of budget deficit)
1976–78	Persistence of high unemployment; main reason: low levels of investment in the past	Policy stimulus insufficient to generate self-sustained expansion of private domestic demand	Stabilise wages by close co-operation between government and social partners
1982, 1983	New record level of unemployment, a considerable proportion of which is a result of structural problems	Budget consolidation is beneficial in the medium term, but present speed too high	Lower interest rates, business taxation and personal income tax
1985–1989	Despite upswing, no change in the employment situation	Labour markets not flexible enough, profitability too low, real wages too rigid Budget consolidation not accompanied by sufficient reduction of tax burden, and impediments to free play of the market	Reduce subsidies, lower taxes, deregulate the service sector Introduce competition through privatisation Allow for differential and decentralised wage setting in different sectors/regions
1991–93	Collapse of production and employment in the new *Bundesländer*	Unification process, especially wage catch-up, too fast Public spending hikes too fast Social security outlays too high Responsiveness of labour market institutions to the market too low	For the new *Länder*, improve entrepreneurial culture, temper employment-creation measures, increase incentives to take on a job Decentralise wage-bargaining, accept wage differences, reduce non-age labour cost and subsidies

128

Year	Problem	Recommendation
1994–99	Structural unemployment remains; high risk of long-term unemployment High burden of social security charges Development of private service sector too slow Subsidies still too high Unemployment benefits too generous; wage dispersion too low Working practices inflexible Active labour market policies costly and inefficient	Reduce non-wage labour costs; cut back subsidies; promote part-time work; increase incentives to work Decentralisation and deregulation of labour market and wage bargaining process
Old age		
1995, 1999	Population ageing causing severe pressure on public budgets and non-wage labour costs 1992 pension reform positive, but insufficient measures to counter the trend of early retirements	Provide long-term solution by raising the age of retirement, lowering entitlements; remove legal and tax barriers for private pension funds; avoid early retirements
Health care		
1996, 1997	Surge of health care expenditures, due to ageing population, technological progress, and unification Health insurance conducive to abuse Not enough competition between health funds	Lower incentives for abuse Introduce active purchasing of health care
1999	Inconsistent health reform; supply efficiency exhausted	More competition, more budget flexibility, better capacity utilisation
Education		
1994	Declining quality of Germany as an industrial location	
1996	Growth of higher education Insufficient responsiveness to entrepreneurial needs	Reform high education (shorter and more occupationallay oriented studies), introduce fees

Source: OECD Economic Surveys on Germany from 1970 to 2000 (cf. note 1). The column 'Year' indicates the year of publication of the quoted surveys.

Since 1975, the OECD has focused much attention on the German labour market. Throughout the 1970s there seems to have prevailed a belief that a sound economy and stable wages would ensure job creation. With the onset of the second oil crisis, however, the OECD began to recognise the employment problem's structural component, and throughout the 1980s increasingly pushed for a more consistent supply-side approach to dealing with unemployment. During the unification process OECD surveys harshly criticised the speed of wage equalisation, the low responsiveness of labour market institutions to the market, and misdirected employment-creation measures. After the immediate pressures of unification had eased, attention was redirected to the German welfare without work dilemma. In line with previous recommendations, the OECD prescribed effective and steady supply-side policy measures and, more carefully, a reform of the wage setting process as a whole.

OECD surveys did not cover the health care and pension systems in detail until unification had lost some of its momentum in the mid-1990s. With regards to pensions, the OECD mainly criticised the inadequacy of measures, stemming from the 1989 pension reform, meant to address the problems posed by an ageing population and the trend towards early retirement. In order to relieve the public pension system, the OECD recommended the establishment of supplementary private pension funds. With regards to health care, aside from the problems posed by an ageing population and technological progress, OECD surveys criticised the system's inefficient incentive structure and the inconsistent nature of its reform. Propositions focused on a reduction of the replacement rate, the active purchasing of health care, and the introduction of either real competition among independent funds or of one universal statutory fund.

For the most part OECD surveys dealt with education only indirectly via its relationship to other issues. Thus, recommendations such as the introduction of fees for and the streamlining of higher education come in the context of a labour market strategy in which education reforms assume an instrumental role in reducing unemployment. Finally, the problem of poverty has been totally ignored.

CONCORDANCE AND DISCORDANCE BETWEEN GERMAN PUBLIC POLICY AND OECD RECOMMENDATIONS

Table 10.2 provides an overview of concordance between OECD recommendations and German public policy.

Employment

In the early and mid-1970s, the OECD recommended demand management and improved coordination between the three federal levels, the central bank and the social partners. The policies enacted by the German executive do concur with these suggestions. However, contrary to the OECD's recommendations in 1975 to stimulate the economy by means of fiscal policies, the government introduced a consolidation package. Neither was the recommendation in 1976 for improved coordination between government and the social partners acted upon. In fact, the unions terminated their participation in the Concerted Action this very year. However, the corporatist framework had been declining in importance since 1972. Coordination between the different federal levels, the government and the Bundesbank failed to improve primarily as a result of their respective institutional independence.

OECD surveys in the 1980s increasingly emphasised the necessity of structural reforms to improve the labour market situation. These recommendations were met with a mixed pattern of concordance and discordance. On the one hand, the Kohl government began a moderate deregulation of the labour market by facilitating the use of fixed-term work contracts. The government also passed a three-step tax reform, which brought about a moderate reduction of the tax burden. The privatisation of government-owned companies and liberalisation of the telecommunications sector began in the 1980s, but were of only limited significance. In these areas there is thus concordance between OECD recommendations and government action. These reforms, however, are attributable to the policy preferences of the Christian–liberal coalition and/or the necessary implementation of EC regulations, and thus cannot be regarded as resulting from OECD recommendations.

On the other hand, in many areas, the OECD's supply-side recommendations went unheeded. This is particularly true with regards to deregulation: apart from measures forced on the government by the EC, almost no action was taken to liberalise markets in the 1980s. Only in the second half of the 1990s did the Kohl government begin to enact more ambitious policies in the areas of tax reform, labour market liberalisation, deregulation and privatisation. This shift may have resulted in part from OECD recommendations although other factors (the effects of reunification and European integration as well as an internal shift of power towards the coalition's pro-business wing) are likely to have played a more decisive role.

Measures adopted by the German government in the mid-1990s concerning the regulation of labour markets and labour costs were to a large extent in line with OECD proposals. The federal government lowered unemployment benefits, liberalised dismissal protection and provided a framework for the

Table 10.2 Concordance between German policy development and OECD recommendations

Recommendations/Criticisms	Concordance
Employment	
1970s	
Make use of demand management	Unclear
Wage stabilisation by close co-operation between government and social partners	No
1980s	
Deregulate service sector	Unclear
Deregulate labour market	Yes
Reduce taxes	Yes
Allow for differential and decentralised wage setting in different sectors/regions of the labour market	No
1990s	
Deregulate markets	Yes
Reduce non-wage labour costs	Yes
Avoid early retirements	No (before 96, 99), Yes (else)
Increase incentives to go back to work	Yes
Adopt initiatives in education, training, enterprise creation	Yes
Decentralisation, loosening and deregulation of the wage bargaining processes	No
Deregulate labour market	Yes (before 98), No (else)
Reappraisal of active labour market policies	Yes
Old age	
Raise age of retirement	Yes
Reduce entitlements	Yes (except 98–00)
Remove legal and tax barriers for private pension funds	Yes (since 00)

Health

Lower incentives for abuse   Yes (before 98), No (else)
Introduce active purchasing of health care   No

Education

Reform higher education towards shorter and more occupationally oriented studies   Yes
Introduce fees in higher education system   No

Note: The policy recommendations stem from the analysis of *OECD Country Surveys* (cf. Table 10.1). Details on the assessment are given in the text.

liberalisation of work hours. Additionally, the government took on labour costs by cutting sick pay, limiting early retirement, liberalising labour market policy, and reforming the health care and the pension systems. However, from the OECD's point of view these measures were too modest.

With regards to wage bargaining, the Kohl government largely ignored OECD recommendations to promote greater flexibility. The limited flexibility that did emerge in the form of decentralisation and (barely legal) non-observances of branch wage agreements did not do so as a result of policy pressure from the OECD. The newly elected coalition of SPD and Greens (red–green coalition) planned to re-empower the social partners, not least through the Alliance for Jobs. In this respect we observe a clear discordance between the employment policy of the new German government and the recommendations from Paris. In addition, contrary to the 1998 OECD survey's recommendations, the new government's strategy maintained a strong emphasis on active labour market and job creation measures. Finally, the government did not follow OECD recommendations to further deregulate the labour market. On the contrary, one of the red–green coalition's first policy actions was to reverse the relaxation of dismissal protection.

Old Age

1989 saw the passage of a major reform to Germany's pension system. This reform, whose implementation began in 1992, aimed to reduce future costs by gradually raising the retirement age and eliminating some contribution-free years (for higher education) from the income base for calculating benefits. The concordance between government policy and survey recommendations does not, however, establish in any way a causal relationship, as the latter were not published until the reform process was in its final stage and beyond influence.

Beginning in the mid-1990s, the OECD stepped up criticism of the early retirement regime which had been used extensively to reduce the labour supply in East Germany after the collapse of employment in the new *Länder*. Government actions in line with OECD proposals included the implementation of measures to restrict early retirement, i.e. raising the retirement age, promoting part-time work for the elderly and taxing redundancy payments more heavily.

Retirement pensions were fundamentally reformed once again in 1997. The new legislation strictly rejected OECD suggestions to move to a system of funding. Instead, the reform maintained the pay-as-you-go framework, but reduced the average replacement rate of the former net wage from 70 per cent to around 64 per cent until 2030 by introducing a demographic life-expectancy component to the pension adjustment formula.

The newly elected red–green government overturned some of the above mentioned reforms, in particular the modification of the adjustment formula. The coalition tried to ameliorate the pension system's finances by widening the contribution base and increasing budgetary transfers in its direction. These first steps cannot however be traced to ideas promoted by the OECD. Things look different when it comes to the fundamental pension reform passed in 2001. Amongst other measures this law encourages employees to contribute to a funded pension scheme of their own choosing by subsidising these contributions. In addition, a reduction of the average replacement rate was introduced again. Although this reform failed to implement an obligatory supplementary fund based pension system, it was largely concordant with the OECD's recommendations.

Health Care

As with pension reform in the 1980s, we observe concordance between the German government's health care reform in 1989 and OECD recommendations. However, OECD surveys only commented on the issue after the legislation had been passed in parliament. The Christian–liberal coalition's second health care reform was passed in 1992. Again, no specific proposals concerning the reform's content can be found in the relevant surveys, and indeed the OECD has largely ignored the reform measures. Therefore, OECD recommendations cannot have had any effect on these reforms.

A similar pattern can be observed concerning sick pay. Only when the government took on the issue and cut the replacement rate by 20 per cent was the matter also addressed in OECD surveys. Although we again see concordance, this cannot be explained in terms of OECD's policy influence. Therefore, it comes as no surprise that the OECD's suggestions to implement even more far-reaching reforms in this field went unheeded.

In 1996 the Christian–liberal coalition passed a third health care reform. Its most important elements were an increase in co-payments and the introduction of limited competition between health funds. Although the OECD welcomed most of these measures, this is not a sign of the organisation's impact on the policies as it only commented on the reforms ex-post. On the other hand, the OECD addressed a large number of recommendations to the health sector in its 1997 survey, which came too late to be taken into consideration by the Kohl government.

The newly-elected red–green coalition seemed unwilling to take up these proposals, too. A number of the new government's measures in the field of health policy ran counter to OECD recommendations (the reduction of co-payments, the introduction of spending budgets for hospitals and doctors, and the introduction of a positive list of pharmaceuticals to contain expenditures). Other measures were more in line with the OECD's 1997 proposals, notably the extension of contract possibilities between health funds and suppliers, the introduction of a more performance-oriented price structure for hospital services and the strengthening of general practitioners' position in relation to specialists.

Education

Education policy in Germany is for the most part a matter of the individual *Länder*. Regarding higher education, the federal legislator can regulate only the basic university framework. This basic framework (*Hochschulrahmen-gesetz*, HRG) was reformed in 1998, the Christian–liberal coalition's last year in government. The reform aimed to enhance the competitiveness of German higher education and to reduce the time students must invest to earn their first degree. To this end the government, among other things, made possible the introduction of new university degrees – a measure clearly in line with OECD proposals. The 1998 reform included no regulations concerning fees for higher education. This decision could be interpreted as concordant with OECD proposals, as opposition parties in the Bundestag pushed for a general prohibition of such fees in the HRG. The failure to include such a regulation allowed for the introduction of such fees at the *Länder* level.

Although the current government once more reformed the university system's regulatory framework, it did not address the issues promoted by OECD surveys in this field. The red–green coalition abstained from introducing fees for higher education and instead tried to promote the status of younger academics by abolishing the *Habilitation* (post-doctoral lecturing qualification) and introducing junior professorships.

OECD RECOMMENDATIONS IN THE NATIONAL DISCOURSE

Since no general studies of the effects of OECD recommendations on German social policy discourse exist, we analyse only references to the OECD made in parliamentary deliberation. We further restrict our analysis to those cases in which concordance exists between the proposals from Paris and German public policy, as it is highly unlikely that the OECD influenced reforms which did not implement its recommendations.

Even in instances where such concordance exists, there is little evidence that OECD proposals directly impacted German social policy. Parliamentary deliberation surrounding legislation deregulating the labour market (1985 and 1996) does not once mention the OECD. The same can be said about reforms of the pension and health care systems which the current government as well as its predecessor implemented in the 1990s. Simply put, there was absolutely no reference to the OECD in any of these deliberations.[2]

Though at times OECD surveys (1998, pp. 11 ff) suggest that a particular reform can be traced to its previous critiques (as in the case of the reform of the Work Promotion Act in 1997), parliamentary discourse provides these suggestions no supporting evidence. In this case, the OECD was referred to only during the speech of a single Christian democrat. More recently, regarding the red–green coalition's employment policy reform in 2001, two MPs, one Christian democrat and one liberal, criticised the government's failure to deregulate the labour market by pointing to OECD recommendations.

Assuming that parliament is at least one of the core arenas in which democratic political discourse unfolds, it can be concluded from these findings that OECD's impact on national discussions of social policy is rather limited. However, one particular OECD study was recently widely discussed by the German public, namely the Programme for International Student Assessment (PISA), which judged the performance of German pupils below average. The effects of this study on future legislation cannot yet be assessed. However, it seems extremely likely that the PISA results will find expression in new programmes meant to rectify the under-achievement of German students.

CONCLUSION

Social policy did not play a prominent role in OECD surveys of Germany prior to the late 1980s. Although unemployment was a dominant issue throughout the period in question, OECD surveys do not establish a link between employment problems and the institutions of the German welfare state before the late 1980s. Instead, in the mid-1970s fiscal stimuli were recommended, and not until the mid-1980s did the OECD's economic and social policy advice assume a marked supply-side orientation. We obtained mixed results concerning the concordance of OECD recommendations and German public policy, and found that the OECD is only rarely referred to in parliamentary deliberation defending reforms. These findings lead us to believe that the OECD's impact on German welfare reform has indeed been rather limited. The OECD is certainly not seen as an infallible point of reference for the defence or attack of German social policy reforms. One plausible explanation for this finding is that there are numerous other institutions providing economic and social policy advice in Germany, above all the Bundesbank and the Council of Economic Advisers. These two institutions are frequently invited to hearings of Bundestag committees, and the federal government is obliged to comment on the Council's annual report. Therefore, only where there is no other ideational authority, as is the case in education policy, can the OECD exert some impact. In other social policy domains, it seems highly likely that OECD's limited influence is due to the multitude of alternative sources of advice – there are just too many rivals.

NOTES

1. The subsequent content analysis is based mainly on the following volumes and summarising sections of the *OECD Economic Surveys* on Germany: 1970, pp 46–49; 1971, pp 40–42; 1972, pp 53–55; 1973, pp 53–56; 1974, pp. 52–55; 1975, pp. 33–35; 1976, pp. 33–34; 1977, pp. 48–49; 1978, pp. 56–57; 1979, pp. 58–60; 1980, pp. 54–55; 1981, pp. 52–53; 1982, pp. 55–57; 1983, pp. 54–56; 1984, pp. 49–51; 1985, pp. 54–56; 1986, pp. 61–64; 1987, pp. 60–63; 1988, pp. 75–79; 1989, pp. 101–106; 1990, pp. 84–89; 1991, pp. 125–136; 1992, pp. 86–93; 1993, pp. 101–106; 1994, pp. 117–123; 1995, pp. 127–134; 1996, pp. 149–160; 1997, pp. 1–16; 1998, pp. 1–14; 1999, pp. 9–24.
2. The analysis is based on the German parliament's database, published on the Internet (http://dip.bundestag.de/). The parliamentary documents (government draft, committee report, 1st and 2nd reading) of the relevant reforms were analysed using the site search function. Search terms used successively were 'OECD', 'Organisation', 'wirtschaftliche Zusammenarbeit' and 'Entwicklung' (bearing in mind that OECD translates 'Organisation für wirtschaftliche Zusammenarbeit und Entwicklung'). Reforms included were the Employment Promotion Acts of 1985 and 1996, the reforms of the Work Promotion Act of 1997 and 2001, old-age pension reforms of 1997 and 2001, health care reforms of 1996 and 2000, the tax reform of 1997 and the reform of university organisation in 1998.

REFERENCE

OECD [various years], *OECD Economic Survey, Germany*, Paris: Organisation for Economic Co-operation and Development.

11. Little contention: Switzerland and the OECD

Klaus Armingeon and Michelle Beyeler

THE SWISS WELFARE STATE – INSTITUTIONAL, POLITICAL AND ECONOMIC CONTEXT

In international perspective, the development of the Swiss welfare state began early but became delayed thereafter. Only recently has it caught up with the typical continental welfare state. Swiss welfare state development began early with the government introduction of a factory law in 1877 regulating labour conditions, among them child labour and maximum working time. However, between 1890 and World War II, the expansion of the national welfare state was, to a large extent, stalled. This was mainly due to the failure of the governments to get major new laws accepted in popular votes. Using the three-fold classification of welfare states (Esping-Andersen 1990), until World War II, Switzerland could be classified as a liberal welfare state: there were many means-tested benefits, subsidies to private insurance instead of public schemes financed via compulsory contributions or taxes, and few universal schemes. By and by, Switzerland added other schemes to this liberal core. These can be classified as social democratic or conservative. The first pillar of the pension scheme, introduced in 1948, is social democratic: it is a general insurance for all citizens that covers the basic needs of pensioners. This scheme is highly redistributive since contributions are a direct function of income (except in the very high income brackets), while the variation of maximum to minimum benefits is only two to one. The second pillar of the pension scheme (effective 1985) is conservative: it covers employed people and contributions and benefits are strictly a function of income. The third pillar is liberal: it is a voluntary savings scheme. These savings are tax deductible.

Health insurance has been liberal for a long time, since it has been (in most cantons) voluntary and state-subsidised until 1996, when universal health insurance came into effect. After 1996 the liberal traits are still discernible since – with few modifications – contributions are paid on a per capita basis. Compulsory unemployment insurance has been in effect since 1984. Its benefits are based on contributions. Hence the Swiss welfare state has a liberal core with significant social democratic and conservative elements. It has been a lean welfare state throughout most of the postwar era, and it is only in the 1980s and 1990s that, due to demographic and other reasons, welfare state expenditures underwent a sudden increase.

Direct democracy, federalism, corporatism, consociational government and a weak pro-welfare coalition in society and in the political system are of utmost importance for Swiss welfare state policy. Popular votes, which are frequently taken, are an important condition for any reforms, particularly if these imply raising taxes and contributions. Some delays of the Swiss welfare state are related to failures of welfare state reformers to gain majority support in society. On the other hand, once schemes are established, it is hard to gain majority support for welfare state retrenchment. Federalism is well developed in Switzerland, giving states (cantons) and local communities much autonomy. Most social assistance as well as the educational system is organised by cantonal and local authorities. Taxes are levied at the sub-national level, and federal tax is marginal in contrast to revenues going to states and local communities. Implementation of national policy is done by state administrations. This makes the federal government heavily dependent on sub-national governments. Policy options like massive national deficit spending or a national policy for income equality through redistributive federal taxes are hardly feasible in this context.

Swiss corporatism, on the other hand, creates a strong social partnership and industrial peace, conducive to economic competition in world markets. However, this type of arrangement between employers, unions and the state never included a deal between wages, prices and social and fiscal policies, as it has for example in Scandinavian states. Consociational democracy includes all major political actors in the government of the country. Hence compromise, a lack of sudden policy changes, and muddling-through instead of alternating government policies, characterises Swiss policy development. Finally, compared to other European countries, social democracy is weak in Switzerland, and so is Christian democracy in comparison with neighbouring countries. Accordingly, the liberal–conservative bloc is very strong in society and politics. Hence, the coalition that propelled the welfare state in most European countries – social and Christian democracy – is relatively weak in comparison to the forces that impeded strong welfare state expansion in Switzerland. In addition, conservative attitudes – for instance, with regard to the role of women in the economy and family – are more widespread than in the average European country.

Switzerland is a rich country in terms of GDP per capita. The economy recovered rapidly from the second oil price shock (1979) and grew steadily during the 1980s. It was only in the first half of the 1990s that a prolonged recession brought with it the problems of unemployment and public deficits.

In general, however, due to many obstacles to public sector growth, Switzerland is a country with sound public finances. In addition, it is a country with below-average inflation. There is neither an expansionist federal government, nor are there costly corporatist deals or high welfare state expenditures driving up inflation. In addition, an independent national bank pursues a non-accommodating policy of price stability. Switzerland – although not a member state of the European Union or the European Economic Area – is increasingly Europeanised through bilateral treaties with the EU and procedures to make Swiss law compatible with European legislation. The latter is called *autonomer Nachvollzug*; i.e. adopting EU rules for Switzerland without giving up its formal sovereignty.

OECD IDEAS CONCERNING SWISS SOCIAL POLICIES

In general, OECD's accounts of Swiss social and economic policies arrive at a positive evaluation, notwithstanding a number of specific criticisms[1]. When the OECD referred to Swiss public expenditure during the 1970s, it mainly pointed to the inadequacy of the instruments available to the central government to use fiscal policies. Until the 1990s, the OECD never criticised the level of social security expenditures in Switzerland for being too high. On the contrary, during the 1980s the OECD even suggested that with its high per capita income and the sound financial situation of the public sector, Switzerland could expand public activities in some specific areas (higher and professional education, policies targeting the elderly). However, in the 1990s the tone changed and the OECD got increasingly worried about 'the primarily structural nature of the deficit and the high speed of expenditure growth' (OECD 1992, p. 106).

When comparing specific policy fields (cf. Table 11.1), the most prominent issue for the OECD has been employment. Over the 30 years under study here the representation of the problems of the Swiss labour market has changed considerably: during the 1970s the OECD proposed supporting activity by using active fiscal and monetary policies. In the 1980s the OECD's main concern has been to address the problem of labour shortages by changing the incentive structure of the social security system and by increasing foreign labour. The recession of the 1990s brought the problem of structural and long-term unemployment to the forefront. The OECD recommended increasing activation measures and removing incentives for inactivity/unemployment in the taxation and the social security system.

Old age, health care and education did not become issues in the country surveys until the late 1980s. Because of the lack of coverage in earlier surveys it is not possible to trace the development of OECD ideas concerning these

Table 11.1 Social policy in OECD reports on Switzerland

Year	Problems	Criticisms	Recommendations
Employment/Labour market			
1970–74	Inflexible labour supply		Relax constraints to foreign labour inflow
1975–77	Decreasing activity rate	Monetary policy is too restrictive	More active use of fiscal policies to support activity Relaxation of monetary policy
1980, 1985	Insufficient labour supply		Review social security regulations; vocational training, encourage labour mobility, more use of foreign labour
1993, 1996	Social security system impedes labour mobility		Stronger emphasis on structural measures such as increasing labour market skills of foreign workers and removing obstacles to equal treatment of men and women with respect to work time
1993	Structural and long-term unemployment		Increase resources of employment offices, activation, more flexibility and efficiency on running the unemployment insurance scheme
1996	Problematic incentives of ALMPs	Maximum duration of benefits is too long	Careful evaluation of ALMPs: prevent a shift from full-time, high-paid jobs to part-time, low paid jobs
1997, 1999	Moral hazard effects of unemployment insurance		Shorter duration – spend the money on policies aiming at employability and training

Old age

1988, 1989, 2000	Growing share of the elderly	Increase active population: raise immigration/naturalisation, increase participation of women, higher retirement age, family policies
1988, 2000	Inefficiencies in governing pensions funds	Stronger and more coherent rules governing fund valuation and more proactive and consistent oversight by the regulators
2000	Problems with future financing of first pillar	Careful planning of further extension of the age of retirement; use labour cost neutral taxes
2000	Moral hazard problem of complementary incomes-tested benefits	Limit access to or reduce the amount of complementary benefits during early retirement; improve or extend income-related pension provision for low-income earners
2000	Rising costs of long-term care of frail elderly	Measures to increase individuals' ability to stay in their homes

Health care

1989, 1991	Rapidly rising health care costs	More competition among medical suppliers; incentives for suppliers of health care to use less expensive treatments (e.g. professional home care services instead of hospitalisation), better co-ordination at the federal level and between cantons, exploit economies of scale by optimising the capacity of hospitals

continued overleaf

Table 11.1   continued

Year	Problems	Criticisms	Recommendations
Education			
1988	Low levels of tertiary education		Spend more on higher education
1997		Switzerland's education and training system is too expensive	Reconsider teacher's salaries, raise ratio of students-to-teachers. Research effective allocation of educational resources, more private competition
1997		The financing of university education is inefficient and unfair	Lend students money to contribute towards tuition and living costs and require repayment through tax system

Source: OECD Economic Surveys on Switzerland from 1970 to 2000 (cf. note 1). The column 'Year' indicates the year of publication of the quoted surveys.

policy fields. With regard to old age policies, the OECD in general praised the Swiss three pillar system: 'Switzerland stands out for being relatively well prepared to deal with the fiscal problems of ageing' (OECD 2000, p. 14). Still, the OECD pointed out some aspects of the pension system that could be improved and recommended the implementation of measures to increase the active population. In the field of health care, the OECD's main concerns were the rapidly rising health costs and the deficiencies in the organisation of the sickness insurance. The educational and training system in general was judged by the OECD to perform rather well. According to the OECD the system is, however, quite expensive. Additionally, higher education opportunities as well as how universities are financed could be improved. Social assistance or housing policies have never been addressed.

OECD RECOMMENDATIONS AND SWISS PUBLIC POLICY DEVELOPMENT

Are the recommendations the OECD gives in concordance or discordance with Swiss policy development? Table 11.2 briefly summarises the recommendations and our assessments.

In the 1970s the OECD proposed the use of more active fiscal policies in order to cure the *labour activity* problem. In the construction sector in particular 'fiscal packages' have indeed been used to support activity. However, strong federalism, an independent central bank and public rejection of budget deficits inhibited more effective use of fiscal policies despite it being repeatedly addressed by the OECD. It is difficult to assess whether Switzerland's policies have been in concordance or discordance with the OECD in this field. During the 1980s in particular, the OECD praised Switzerland for the consistency of its economic policies.

The OECD proposed that the problem of *labour shortages* be addressed by increasing foreign labour. However, the rigid system of controlling the inflow of foreign labour was not modified. As the OECD acknowledges, this can be explained by domestic economic and especially political factors (OECD 1980, p. 50; 1985, p. 60; 1990, p. 95). By changing the system of occupational pensions in order to increase the mobility of employees, Switzerland's policies developed in concordance with the OECD. Switzerland also reacted in line with the OECD recommendations when it introduced the principle of activation in labour market policies in the 1990s. However, when it comes to the duration of unemployment benefits, the disincentives to take up part-time employment were not in line with OECD suggestions.

Two policy measures to address the problem of an *ageing population* have been in concordance with the OECD: First, an increase in the legal age of

Table 11.2 Concordance between Swiss policy development and OECD recommendations

Recommendations/Criticisms	Concordance
Employment	
1970s: Measures to support labour activity:	
• Use of active fiscal policy, monetary discretion	Yes
1980s: Measures to address labour shortage:	
• More use of foreign labour	No
• Encourage labour mobility by reviewing regulations of pension fund	Yes
1990s: Measures to fight unemployment:	
• Activation and evaluation of the new system	Yes
• Shorter duration of unemployment benefits	No
• Remove obstacles for part-time employment	No
• Increase skills of foreign labour and women	Unclear
Old age	
Measures to increase active population:	
• Raising immigration and naturalisation	No
• Increasing retirement age for women	Yes
• Increase female labour force participation and provide family policies to reconcile work and family	No
Measures to address the possible financing gap of the first pillar:	
• Labour cost neutral financing	Yes
• Further increase of the retirement age in the future	Not yet assessable
Measures to increase efficiency in the governing of the second pillar	No
Measures to address the moral hazard problem rising from supplementary benefits and early retirement regulation:	
• Limit access to complementary benefits during early retirement	Unclear
• Extend income-related pension provision to low-income earners	Unclear
Measures to increase individuals' ability to stay in their homes	Unclear

146

Health

Measures to reduce costs:
- More competition among medical suppliers — Yes
- Incentives for health care suppliers to use less expensive treatments — Yes
- Better co-ordination at the federal level and between cantons — Yes

Education

Spend more on higher education — Yes
Reconsider teachers' salaries, raise ratio of students-to-teachers — No
Research effective allocation of educational resources, more private competition — No
Lend students money to pay for tuition and living costs, repayment through tax system — No

Note: The policy recommendations stem from the analysis of OECD country surveys (cf. Table 11.1). Details on the assessment are given in the text.

147

retirement for female employees was introduced in 1995 together with more gender equality in the system of basic pensions. This was an uneasy compromise between the left parties (particularly in favour of gender equality) and those actors who were primarily interested in the consolidation of the pension system. Second, in consolidating the system of basic pensions (first pillar), Swiss politicians increasingly rely on indirect taxes (value added tax) to supplement work-related contributions. With these measures, increases in wage costs are partly de-coupled from the steep increase of resources needed for the system of basic pensions. OECD proposals of using indirect taxes for the financing of the social security system are in line with these policy changes.

With regard to family policies supporting fertility and the compatibility of family and employment roles, Switzerland still lacks co-ordinated action by the federal government. In 1999 a federal law on maternity insurance was rejected in a public vote. This discordance with OECD recommendations can be explained by the strength of liberal ideologies, the distribution of competencies and resources between the cantons and the federal government, the weakness of those actors that are in favour of family policy (social democrats, Christian democratic party, trade unions), and the conservative stance of the Swiss population with regard to gender equality.

Still in the early 1990s, Switzerland had the highest rate of cartels of any OECD country. In the 1990s in particular, Swiss authorities supported enforced competition in the economy and society. The move to more competition also applied to *health policy*. Here, certain elements of competition and 'cost-consciousness' have been introduced – for example, in the financing of hospitals.

The OECD has repeatedly criticised Switzerland for lacking competition in various fields. Recent changes are in concordance with the recommendations from Paris. However, there are few doubts that the strongest incentives for more competition are based on the increasing international mobility of capital, the requirements of the World Trade Organization, the process of Europeanisation of Switzerland (*autonomer Nachvollzug* – see above) and – in the health system – the unsustainability of the former system due to the deficits of the states (cantons), which are in charge of financing a large part of the system of public health.

Switzerland extended tertiary *education* by creating and strengthening Universities of Applied Sciences (*Fachhochschulen*). Although this development is concordant with OECD recommendations, there are other, and probably much more important explanations for the establishment of these schools than the OECD proposals: (a) Swiss business complained about the difficulties of finding highly-qualified employees; (b) polytechnics have existed in Germany for a long time and with good success. With regard to the latter factor, it may be a case of some diffusion of the German model to Switzerland. No major moves in the direction of reducing the costs of education and of changing the system of university financing as proposed by the OECD in 1997 have been made up to now.

MAJOR REFORMS AND EXPLICIT REFERENCES TO THE OECD

Swiss *labour market policies* are marked by two major reforms. First, after a massive decline in total employment in the 1970s,[2] compulsory unemployment insurance was introduced. Plans for a compulsory insurance among administrative elites had existed long before, and were waiting for an obvious problem in response to which politicians and the population would be willing to accept another compulsory insurance (cf. Freiburghaus 1987). The OECD has never explicitly criticised the lack of a compulsory unemployment scheme in any of the country surveys. Only after Swiss authorities had already envisaged the reform was this judged to be an appropriate step by the country surveys (OECD 1975, p. 47; 1976, p. 48). Except for this support for an already pursued path, there is no indication that the OECD influenced the reform process. Second, active labour market measures have been established on a broad base in Switzerland in the mid-1990s. The OECD had criticised Switzerland's backwardness on active labour market policies. Hence, there may have been some indirect effect as politicians who favoured more active measures could use OECD recommendations to strengthen their arguments.

Concerning *old age policies*, a major reform of the first pillar took place in 1995, following proposals launched by national politicians to eliminate the discrimination against women in old age schemes. In the 1990s the problems in financing the pension system became obvious. These problems are related to the demographic changes, scrutinised by a research team composed of experts from various federal ministries. The reform of the basic pension in 1995 tried to combine certain measures to enhance fairness with regard to women with a reduction in future cost pressures. The expert report on the future costs of pensions did not explicitly take into account OECD critiques. The other major reform has concerned the second pillar. It became compulsory in 1985. Here again, no impact of the OECD can be discerned in the sense of explicit references to the OECD by national actors.

In 1996, *health policy* was substantially reformed – at least with regard to the type of health insurance. Until then, health insurance had been voluntary, although some cantons did already have compulsory schemes for their populations. However, due to the enormous financial risks of sickness, more than

90 per cent of the population were members of private schemes prior to 1996. Given this, legislating compulsory health insurance did not change much, either for the insurance companies or for the general population. In 1994 attempts were also made to control the rising health costs through structural changes. The most pronounced move in that direction was increasing competition on the supply side (hospitals, doctors, pharmacies), which was concordant with OECD recommendations. Apart from that, there is no obvious evidence of the influence of OECD recommendations in these reforms. It has mostly been the concern of national political actors and organisations (political parties, health insurance companies, public health administration, cantons) that has triggered the policy changes.

In the case of *education* no major changes can be detected. Until this point, the OECD's critiques with regard to inefficiencies, unfairness and cost have not even caused a major debate, let alone any reform.

Explicit reference to OECD ideas in Swiss reform processes is fairly rare. This statement is supported by a content analysis of parliamentary debates. As of 1995, the minutes of both houses of parliament are available on CD-ROM and as files on the World Wide Web. This opens possibilities for simple computer-aided content analyses. A first search included a search for the acronym 'OECD' or the French equivalent 'OCDE' in all statements in these minutes. References to the OECD were made 271 times during these six years under study. In a second step we considered whether the statements concerned the labour market, pension system, health policy, education or poverty, and found 36 entries. In most of them the OECD was mentioned as a geographical area – e.g. 'in most OECD-countries demographic change is a challenge for the pension system' or as a producer of statistics and scientific studies – e.g. 'according to OECD statistics, 13 to 19 per cent of adults have difficulties in reading and writing'. Only in the case of 12 references were OECD reports or analyses used for criticising or defending certain policies and policy changes.[3] In no case did OECD recommendations have a prominent function in the sense that politicians used it as a key argument. Rather, the OECD is quoted as providing further support for the goals pursued by the respective politician. The statements of the international organisation are used to defend both left-wing and right-wing arguments.

CONCLUSION

Swiss welfare state policy has not been fiercely criticised in the OECD economic surveys. In general, Switzerland was ahead in already having implemented policies that the OECD began to propose. Given this, we can hardly expect a direct and decisive effect by the OECD on Swiss policy making. On the other hand, the OECD has been more volatile with regard to ideas than Switzerland has been with regard to policies. In the 1970s, the OECD recommended an interventionist and active central state, which was not feasible in federal Switzerland where popular votes are used as a major decision-making technique. In the 1980s and 1990s, in turn, the OECD recommended more liberal policies. These suggestions, however, could not be realised, since the institutional and political make-up of the Swiss political system is not amenable to coherent sets of policies precluding broad compromise.

When Swiss decision-makers refer to the OECD, they mostly cite scientific studies and statistics. The OECD is perceived as a politically neutral, scientific and objective entity that produces legitimate knowledge. However, the Swiss do not accept the OECD as an ideational authority, in the sense that its recommendations are conceived to be the reference point of domestic reform efforts. Rather, the OECD in Switzerland plays the role of an ideational artist.

The absence of a direct, visible link between welfare reforms and the suggestions made by the OECD in its annual economic surveys should not however be interpreted as evidence of lack of any impact of OECD reports on Swiss policy making. A chief economic advisor in the Swiss Ministry of Economics pointed during an interview in July 2002 to more subtle and indirect effects of the OECD. At OECD meetings, national economic advisors tend to build consensus on adequate, 'reasonable' strategies based on shared ideas and axioms of mainstream economics among themselves. Back at home they try to convince politicians and the public of the appropriateness of these analyses and recipes. In this sense, our interviewee stresses that 'one should not underestimate the OECD's impact'.

NOTES

1. The subsequent content analysis is based mainly on the following volumes and summarising sections of the *OECD Economic Surveys* on Switzerland: 1970, pp. 33–37; 1971, pp. 36–38; 1972, pp. 57–60; 1974, 53–56; 1975, pp. 46–49; 1976, pp. 46–49; 1977, pp. 52–54; 1978, pp. 52–54; 1979, pp. 50–53; 1980, pp. 49–51; 1982, pp. 55–58; 1983, pp. 46–47; 1984, pp. 49–51; 1985, pp. 58–61; 1987, pp. 65–67; 1988, pp. 79–83; 1989, pp. 92–96; 1990, pp. 93–98; 1991, pp. 107–114; 1992, pp. 103–110; 1993, pp. 101–106; 1994, pp. 100–106; 1995, pp. 107–113; 1996, pp. 125–134; 1997, pp. 1–13; 1999, pp. 9–22; 2000, pp. 9–23.
2. This did not lead to a serious rise in registered unemployment, since outflow of foreign labour has not been compensated and many unemployed did not register at the employment offices.
3. *1995*: The federal government argues that an OECD report supports the thesis that liberalisation of telecommunications is beneficial to the citizens.
   1996: The federal government defends the present structure of the Swiss welfare state by pointing to recent OECD findings demonstrating that the Swiss welfare state is much larger than often thought.
   1996: A liberal politician points to the critique made by the OECD that there is not enough theoretical training in apprenticeships.
   1996: A social democrat complains that the OECD has anti-union statements in its report on the labour market situation in Switzerland.

1997: A conservative politician (Swiss People's Party) argues that from the OECD it is well known that shorter working times lead to increased wage costs, thereby increasing unemployment.

1997: A liberal politician criticises unemployment compensations having been extended, although the OECD has proposed to make them dependent on participation in measures of active labour market policy.

1997: A social democrat argues that even the OECD proposes to expand domestic demand.

1998: A Christian democrat pleads for shortened periods of unemployment compensation, as proposed by the OECD.

1998: The federal government counters the social democratic wish for less working time by pointing to OECD studies that show no strong correlation between that measure and employment growth.

1998: A social democrat substantiates her opposition to a rise in the age of retirement by arguing that under certain conditions the OECD does not recommend increasing the age of retirement as a means for improving the financing of the pension system.

1999: A Christian democrat takes issue with the social democratic proposal of improved protection against dismissals by arguing that OECD studies demonstrate that such protections decrease the employment chances of women.

1999: The federal government takes issue with the social democratic proposal of a four-day working week by pointing to OECD studies demonstrating that reduction in working time does not automatically lead to more employment.

REFERENCES

Esping-Andersen, Gøsta (1990), *The Three Worlds of Welfare Capitalism*, Princeton, NJ: Princeton University Press.

Freiburghaus, Dieter (1987), *Präventivmassnahmen gegen die Arbeitslosigkeit in der Schweiz*, Bern: Paul Haupt.

OECD [various years], *OECD Economic Survey, Switzerland*, Paris: Organisation for Economic Co-operation and Development.

12. OECD views on Greek welfare: not European enough

Blanca Ananiadis

INTRODUCTION: THE GREEK WELFARE STATE

In Greece, the twenty-first century opened with a broad wave of welfare reform proposals. This process, begun in the mid-1990s, first aimed at rectifying existing economic and financial 'structural imbalances' (a concept used in all OECD surveys). In fact, most social reforms were either constituent elements of (labour market, social security), or resource-dependent upon (education, health), the financial restructuring that paved the way to successful entry into the Eurozone. Since the mid-1990s, the social agenda has become more decisively reformist. Negotiated and still negotiable, politically costly and plagued by the uncertainty of its outcomes, reform plans have helped to further unveil a deep layer of 'structural imbalances' in the Greek socio-economic configuration.

Until recently, Greece represented a near ideal-type 'Southern-syndrome' welfare state, referring to the categorisation proposed by Ferrera (1996) (an addition to Esping-Andersen's well-known 'three-worlds' typology). Frequently cited in the welfare literature, that syndrome refers to a particular mixture of nominal universalism in health care and dualism (i.e. sharp disparities in benefits resulting in 'hyper-protected' and unprotected sectors) and fragmentation in occupationally-based income maintenance and pension systems. In the Greek case, this dualism was exacerbated by a culture of politically endowed privileges associated to clientelistic practices, centralised welfare provision and consistently low – when compared to both European and OECD standards – levels of social expenditure. Pension-heavy social protection (around 50 per cent of the social budget since the early 1980s), restricted and meagre unemployment benefits, and the narrow scope of social services provided an environment ripe for the persistence of familialism as an alternative to officially established social safety nets.

In the 1990s this model was challenged by the imperatives of a multifaceted Europeanisation of institutions and policies, resulting in an approximation to other EU members with regards to the diagnosis and solution of social problems. It is important to note that one of this transformation's primary agents has been a political party with no social-democratic tradition. More accurately, the reformist drive of the Panhellenic Socialist Movement (PASOK) is related to a *contemporary* version of European social-democracy. However, the complex institutional ('path dependent') setting that constitutes either the basis for or the obstacle to transformation in mature welfare states is not present in the Greek case. A populist, rather than pluralist, consociational or neo-corporatist, legacy makes the Greek model of social protection especially adaptable to the exigencies of Europeanisation. That is, the ambiguous nature of organisations and policy inherent in populist regimes[1] allows for greater flexibility and receptivity in the implementation of European policy packages. It is not the burden of entrenched legal–rational practices, but rather Greek society's party-centred clientelism with which reformists have to contend. In practice, the consistent internalisation of 'Europe' has changed a number of traditional decision-making patterns. This ongoing process has helped to highlight those political antagonisms particular to Greece but whose negotiated solution might also depend on developments related to a more broadly European social project. In this sense, the EU has become part and parcel of the domestic scene. No such role can be attributed to the OECD. Perceived as a more distant and hybrid instance of supranational surveillance, the organisation preserves the prerogatives of 'external' authority, a beyond-frontiers world of expertise and reliability untainted by the current nuances of domestic and European politics.

Greek welfare policy in the period under consideration should be placed against the background of a politically turbulent twentieth century. The Civil War (1946–49) and the military dictatorship (1967–73) are usually cited as the darkest moments in the battered republic's post-World War II history. The seven-year period following the fall of the Greek Junta witnessed the end of a political role for hitherto powerful institutions (the monarchy, the military) and foreign intervention. It did not mark, however, the reconstitution of social forces within the new constitutional parameters. Rather, initially strong political parties grew to massive entities, and subsequently 'colonised' a public sector presided over by a '. . . ubiquitous, overinterventionist, overregulating, paternalistic and protectionist state' (Diamandouros 1997, p. 27).

Amidst an economic downturn following 13 years of high-growth (1960–73), in 1974 the fledgling democracy was challenged by both the Turkish invasion of Cyprus and spiralling inflation (a recurrent feature of the economy for years to come). 1981 was yet another year of lasting political significance, marking Greece's accession to the European Community and the rise to power of the Panhellenic Socialist Movement (PASOK). Since then, Greek welfare's contemporary history is directly associated with PASOK's self-transformation, partial reversals during two short-lived opposition-led governments (1989; 1991–93) notwithstanding.

Before referring to the OECD's portrait of Greek socio-economic development, a number of puzzling dualisms detected by the welfare literature (e.g. Petmesidou 1996; Matsaganis 2003; Venieris 1997; Symeonidou 1997) should be pointed out. Truncated industrialisation only partially explains the state's role as a major employer in a country with Europe's largest self-employed sector (46 per cent). Despite social reforms aimed at incorporating hitherto excluded sectors of the population, the 1980s witnessed the reinforcement of a redistributive system grounded in partisan and political criteria. A veritable pyramid of privileges in social benefits was the result of discriminating access to both employment and funds. On the other hand, in correlation to extensive 'self-employment' and the high proportion of small enterprises in industrial and tertiary sectors, Greek society was characterised by both weak private sector unionisation, concomitant low benefits (Kravaritou 1999, pp. 93–95) and rampant tax evasion.

'Watered down' legislation in the fragmented social insurance sector, subsidies *in lieu* of services, and a thriving private health care network in a system nominally universal since 1983 (Matsaganis 2000; Petmesidou 2000) are but few of the 'structural imbalances' reforms have attempted to overcome since the mid-1990s.

OECD VIEWS ON GREEK SOCIAL POLICIES

OECD surveys[2] analyse Greek social policy through a prism of macroeconomic concerns and projections. Expectedly, analyses of the labour market have been (and remain) pivotal components of these reports. Moreover, the manner in which the OECD discourse takes stock of rapid changes to prevailing economic philosophies is noteworthy. Hence, the concern with full employment, 'development', and 'long-term planning' characteristic of the early 1970s (1971, 1972) had virtually disappeared by the mid-1970s. Thereafter, the surveys departed from Keynesian economic assessments, though still referring to the exigencies of 'demand management'. This concept is now used in the context of recommendations aimed at tackling some of the quantifiable symptoms of structural imbalances: accelerated inflation, increased balance of payments and budget deficits, poor investment, and a loss of competitiveness. From the mid-1970s through the 1980s the surveys focused on stabilisation, calling on the public sector to redress problems of excessive intervention, poor taxation, inefficiency, extensive public employment, subsidisation and expansionary policies. Repeatedly, OECD assessments refer to the steady increases in nominal income as a major source of inflation and to the growth of non-agricultural employment as taking place at the expense of productivity. Although in one instance quite uncharacteristically admitting that '[g]iven relatively low

pay levels in many sectors, especially in the private sector, some income distribution was probably justified on social grounds' (OECD 1986, p. 38), OECD
reports for the most part ignored the initial low base of wages and salaries and
their role as instruments of income distribution. Further, in the early 1990s
analyses of the income/consumption question skip any references to historico-
institutional constraints (other than those brought about by the troubled state
sector), geopolitical considerations, and/or social priorities. Besides, in the
same period the section of the surveys devoted to income and consumption
often resorted to textbook 'rational expectation' explanations of the following
type: 'Greek households do not take into account future increases in taxation
or reduction in transfers when making decisions about savings and consumption' (OECD 1991, p.15).

Changing economic philosophies have, over time, also manifested themselves in self-contradictory advice: while contraction of labour-intensive
activities in the early 1970s was seen as compromising full employment
(OECD 1972, p. 49), as of the mid-1970s their expansion is perceived as the
culprit of dwindling productivity (e.g. OECD 1979, p. 49).

As noted above, central to the reports are labour market analyses (see Table
12.1), which in the early 1980s portray a market plagued by 'rapid wage
increases, longer holidays, shorter working hours and weak productivity
trends' (OECD 1983, p. 18). References to 'flexibility' and 'structural rigidities' – which become commonplace in the 1990s, particularly after the launch-
ing of the Job Strategy – appear as early as 1986 (OECD 1986, pp. 64–67). In
contrast to the academic focus on 'flexible specialisation' (the potential for
development of flexible small and medium industrial and service ventures),
OECD surveys concentrate on wages, labour costs, and flexible work hours to
boost 'the supply responsiveness of the economy' (ibid, p. 66). As of the mid-
1990s, reassured that 'the macroeconomic fundamentals of the Greek economy have strengthened remarkably' (OECD 2001, p. 19), the OECD made
employment one of the reports' central concerns (1996, 1998, 2001). A Job
Strategy tailormade for Greece proposed a revision of the entire institutional
framework.

Regarding pensions, while in the 1970s OECD surveys mentioned social
security contributions only in the limited contexts of taxation and nominal
income (1979, p. 7), references to the subject steadily picked up in the 1980s,
pointing at their foreseeable effect on deficits and imbalances (1983, 1997,
1989). Despite the fact that, by 1990, Greece had the OECD's highest pension
expenditure/GNP ratio (OECD 1991, p. 60), gloomy OECD forecasts fell
short of providing a set of specific policy recommendations. The surveys did
not include a full review of the system until 1997, at which point drastic
corrective measures were finally urged.

Aside from passing references to its impact on labour, OECD surveys did

Table 12.1 Social policy in OECD reports on Greece

Year	Problems	Criticisms	Recommendations
Employment/Labour market			
1970s	Inflation Fast increase in nominal income Low productivity	High wage settlements High public employment	Combat tax evasion to stop growth of non-wage income; expand tax base Consensus wage settlements; stop public sector hiring Combat inflation through stabilisation policies led by government sector's deficit reduction
1980s	Stagflation High income, low productivity Low participation in employment	Raising labour costs; sharp loss of competitiveness Costly transfers to protected sectors Growing public sector employment Poor macroeconomic management	Abolition of the wage indexation system; more restrictions on new government hirings; strengthening of labour market flexibility Labour market would benefit from: less state involvement in the economy; tax reform & control; elimination of direct government intervention in banking activities and sharp reduction of external and internal deficits; enhancing supply-side responsiveness Opt-out clauses in labour agreements
1990s	Unemployment Dual labour market	Rigidities Labour costs still high	Eliminate legislation on dismissals More working time flexibility, more ALMPs less subsidies

continued overleaf

Table 12.1 *continued*

Year	Problems	Criticisms	Recommendations
Old age			
1970s and 1980s	Imbalances Sudden fall of dependent employment Adverse demographic trends	Government should not finance transfers to problem funds Farmers and professionals virtually exempted from contributions	Better linkage between contributions and benefits Control social security tax evasion
1990s	Highest pension expenditure/GNP ration in OECD Widened gap between expenditure and contributions	Long transition period in reforms Lax eligibility criteria High ceilings and replacement rates in public sector	Need to lower expectations; realistic contributions Overhaul the entire system; rethink 'acquired rights'
Health care			
1990s	Low quality services Uneven coverage, poor primary care	Centralisation and low competition No incentives in public sector	Managerial autonomy Introduce mobile rural/island centres and urban primary care centres Differentiated incentives for doctors
Education			
1980s and 1990s	Duplication of tasks in public/private secondary education High unemployment among university graduates Insufficient training Shortage of managerial skills, training programmes and R&D	State monopoly of higher education Centralisation of programmes and resources Lack of rigorous evaluation of teaching at all levels	Better training and job-related education Monitoring and evaluation of teaching and programmes Develop links industry/university Set time limits for obtaining university degrees Decentralisation

Source: OECD Economic Surveys on Greece from 1970 to 2001 (cf. note 2). The column 'Year' indicates the year of publication of the quoted surveys.

not extensively describe the pitfalls of Greece's education system until 1992. An oblique initial reference to problems with Greek health care appeared this same year. While the surveys subsequently relate educational matters to the vicissitudes of training and the Jobs Strategy, as of 1997 health care has become the object of special attention. The surveys do not, however, address poverty and issues related to the insufficiency of social services.

OECD RECOMMENDATIONS AND GREEK SOCIAL POLICIES

Assessing whether public policy in Greece has conformed to OECD proposals in the areas under consideration requires the introduction of a number of provisos. First, for most cases in which public policy adheres to OECD suggestions, the time lag between recommendation and implementation is significant enough as to preclude the assumption that the two are causally linked. In fact, the timing of policy implementation is clearly related to the 'maturing' of certain patterns of economic reasoning in the political arena, to the likelihood of domestic consensus, and to the strength of government resolve and partisan support. Second, in the analysis of Greek social policy reforms, the OECD's impact cannot be isolated from that of other inter-governmental organisations (IGOs). 'Cross-fertilisation' amongst IGOs in the realm of ideas as well as concrete interactions between the OECD and the EU Commission are fairly evident. These mutual influences are especially apparent with regards to employment policy in the 1990s. Third, as seen in the instances described below, the fact that the 'spirit' of reform is in line with broad OECD recommendations does not imply an equivalent measure of concordance when it comes to these reforms' more concrete proposals. Finally, the passing of a reform bill did not necessarily entail its full implementation or monitoring. This latter proviso applies with special relevance to health care (Petmesidou 1996, p. 115), social security (starting with the 1934 law creating the Social Insurance Organisation [IKA]) (Venieris 1997; Matsaganis 2000) and labour relations (Kravaritou 1999). In addition to these specific obstacles, a politico-administrative system traditionally characterised by 'a low degree of institutionalisation, a gap between formal rules and informal practices, and fragmentation' (Spanou 1998, p. 475), has constituted a more general impediment to social reform.

Table 12.2 offers a description of the relevant recommendations included in OECD surveys, by period. It also includes an assessment of the extent to which social policy measures approximate OECD proposals. The table provides a broad summary of OECD recommendations, and the Greek state's corresponding responses (or lack thereof), in the policy areas under investigation. Hence,

Table 12.2 Concordance between Greek policy development and OECD recommendations

Recommendations/Criticisms	Concordance
Employment	
1970s (all surveys)	
Measures to address the effect of high nominal income on structural imbalances and inflation:	
• Reduction of non-wage income and control of tax evasion	No
• Reduction of PSBR and public sector employment	No
Measures to enhance competitiveness and productivity in line with other OECD countries	No
• Curtailment of state involvement in manufacturing and finances	No
• Restriction of credit, subsidies and aid to protected sectors	No
1980s	
Measures to reverse expansionary policies and severe structural imbalances (83, 85, 86):	No
• Sharp reduction of government spending, transfers to protected sectors and public sector hiring	No
• Taxation of self-employed sectors (farmers, liberal professions)	No
• Elimination of the automatic indexation adjustment (ATA) of wages	No
• Enhancement of labour flexibility and removal of legal and practical barriers to dismissals	No
1986–87/1990–93	
Structural measures aiming at reversing the trend from expansion to restraint (87, 89, 90, 92, 93):	
• Application of the Adjustment (1985–87) and Stabilisation (1991–93) programmes as well as the 'Convergence' budgets (1992, 1993)	Yes
1990–95	
Measures to combat unemployment by enhancing labour flexibility and competitiveness (90, 92, 93):	
• Reforms aiming at decentralising collective bargaining in wage settlements	Yes
• Removal of the system of automatic wage indexation	Yes
• Increased unemployment benefits as a trade-off for relaxation of employment protection legislation and practices and removal of ceilings to dismissals	No
• Lower minimum wages and higher wage differentials	No

160

1996–01
Policy guidelines to comply with the Greek OECD Jobs Strategy (96, 98, 2001):

I Increase of labour, wage and working-time flexibility:
- Introduction of opt-out clause from collective bargaining in areas of high unemployment — Yes
- Further reduction of the role of middle tier of collective agreements — No
- Limits and premiums for overtime to be determined by individual collective agreements — No
- Reduction of non-wage labour costs — Unclear
- Promotion of part-time employment — Yes

II Enhancing active labour market policies and labour force skills:
- Development of training programmes, employment promotion centres and private placement agencies — Yes

III Fostering liberalisation of publicly controlled enterprises. — Yes

IV Promotion of new technology and innovation — Unclear

Old age

1980s
Measures to reverse deficitary trends in social security funds (83, 86, 87):
- Better linkage between benefits and contributions — No
- Control of social security tax evasion; separation of funds from contributions and general taxation — No

1990–95 (90, 92, 93)
Measures to reverse social security deficits:
- Raising pensionable age and rates of contributions — Yes
- Linking pensions to contributions and setting much lower rates than last salary — No

1996–2002 (96, 97, 98, 2001)
Measures aiming at structural reform of the pension system:
- Reversal of early retirement trends — No
- Unification of social security funds; better organisation and autonomy of the system — Yes
- Tightening of eligibility criteria, lowering replacement rates, extension of contribution period, involvement of the private sector — (under review)
- Speeding-up reforms — No

continued overleaf

161

Table 12.2   continued

Recommendations/Criticisms	Concordance
Health	
1990s–2001 (97, 98, 01)	
Measures to improve supply of health services:	
• Development of a decentralized network of urban and rural primary care centres	No
• Restructuring of health funds	In progress
• Improvement of health management organization; decentralization	Unclear
• Restructuring of the price system and reduction of expenditure on pharmaceuticals	Yes
Measures to create pecuniary incentives for public sector doctors:	
• Introduction of fee-paying services in public hospitals	Yes
Education	
1990s–2001 (96, 98, 01)	
Measures to strengthen links between education and the labour market:	
• Improvement of training centres, vocational programmes and job-related education	Yes
• Introduction of monitoring and evaluation of teachers and programmes at all levels	Yes
• Development of links industry/university	Unclear
• Setting of time limits for obtaining university degrees	No

162

Note: The policy recommendations stem from the analysis of *OECD Country Surveys* (cf. Table 12.1). Details on the assessment are given in the text.

it does not contain the important background descriptions of recent policy history included in the surveys. It is however in such detailed analyses that criticisms of previous administrations become bolder, almost daring, whenever the incumbent government's policy falls in line with OECD recommendations. In these instances, the assessment's political nature is frankly explicit. This is most evident during the PASOK administration's turn-around between 1985–87 (OECD 1986, 1987). It resurfaces during the New Democracy (ND) Party interregnum (OECD 1991–93), adding explicit references to PASOK's legacy of 'clienteles' (1991, pp. 62–63), 'friendships', and 'vested interests' (1992, pp. 57, 59). As of 1996, and coinciding with the current administration's advent, this discourse has acquired a more dialogical tone.

Employment

Government policies from the mid-1970s through the mid-1980s (and again between 1987–89) went against both the spirit and the letter of virtually all OECD recommendations. Pursuing expansionary and protective policies at a time when austerity reigned in most of Europe, successive Greek governments could not forestall dwindling investment and industrial production. Record external deficits and PSBR levels (at 8 per cent and 17 per cent respectively by 1985) spurred short-lived policy reversals, most often rapidly followed by new bouts of expansionism. In this context, the automatic inflation-indexation wage system (ATA) established in 1982, along with rising nominal wages and further public-sector job creation, became the surveys' primary targets. OECD reports from the early 1980s tacitly recognise this clash of economic philosophies, acknowledging that the Five Year Plan for Economic and Social Development (1983–87) provides for an even 'greater role of the public sector and for the "socialisation" of certain activities' (OECD 1983, p. 50). A partial fit between longstanding OECD recommendations and policy reform appears in the Adjustment Plan (1985–87) as well as the Stabilisation (1991–93) and Convergence (i.e. Maastricht targets, 1992–93) programmes pursued by the New Democracy administration. Developments since the mid-1990s bear the imprint of both the OECD Jobs Strategy (1995) and the European Union's Employment Strategy and Guidelines (1997). Annual National Action Plans (NAPS) and various pieces of labour legislation (dealing among other things with employment and training (law 2434/1996), industrial relations (2639/1998) and job creation (2874/2000)) have attempted to tackle pressing social issues: one of the lowest employment rates in the OECD (55.4 per cent in the year 2000), high unemployment (11.1 per cent), particularly amongst women and the young, inadequate legalisation of migrant workers, and a downturn (2002) in the share of part-time work.

Most adopted measures have been in line with OECD recommendations and EU guidelines. Furthermore, these supranational organisations' criticisms regarding the sub-par implementation of existing measures, such as the 'opt out' clause in sectoral labour agreements, coincide impressively (e.g. OECD 2001 and European Commission 2001, pp. 61–62). However, the ongoing three-way dialogue (OECD assessments/EU evaluations/NAPS) on labour issues places the OECD surveys at the radical end of policy proposals regarding labour flexibility. While a portion of the European Commission's recommendations and directives in the sphere of the social (e.g. equal opportunity policies and related care services, disability and anti-ageism policies) are echoed by the latest Greek NAPs, OECD surveys exhibit no concern with social issues *for their own sake*, and in matters of labour policy tend to adhere to criticisms voiced by the employers' Federation of Greek Industries (SEV). One such instance involves the recent (2001) reduction of overtime hours, their annualisation on a voluntary basis, and the increase in overtime premiums. Arguing that 'these measures would tend to increase labour costs and reduce labour supply' (2001: 58), the survey reinforces SEV's arguments as to the rising costs of labour. According to the Economist's Intelligence Unit, these arguments 'are as yet unsupported by data and appear[s] to have been made for political effect to discredit the law, which the federation dislikes' (July 2001).

Old Age

During the 1980s OECD surveys briefly recommended the monitoring of social security tax evasion (1983, p. 49), discrimination between contributions and taxation, and the search for a solution to the problems caused by funds relying on financial injections (e.g. The Farmers' Social Insurance Organisation (OGA)) (1987, p. 47). Given that, until the mid-1990s, OECD reports are chiefly *reactive* to government legislation, the assessments of compliance referred to in Table 12.2 are based on analyses of OECD criticisms rather than on concrete recommendations. Despite acknowledging that, reforms notwithstanding, the social security deficit would 'still remain much higher than in OECD countries generally' (OECD 1993, p. 80), a comprehensive review of the system was not forthcoming until 1997. Subsequently, the subject figures prominently in the surveys, which point either at the 'insufficiency' of reforms (e.g. the 1998 'small reform', tightening entitlements and merging some funds) or their delay (2001). Although government plans seem to be moving in the same direction as OECD recommendations, public opposition has hitherto defied the rationality of domestic studies, EU proposals and OECD surveys. In 2001, a wave of strikes and mobilisation, unprecedented during the current administration, led to the withdrawal of a radical reform bill. A substantially watered down bill was passed by parliament in June 2002.

Other Policy Fields

The *health reforms* still underway (1997, 2002) constitute a typical case of delayed and/or shirked implementation of (rather than discordance with) the surveys' recommendations. A reform that addresses structural deficiencies, in line with a number of OECD proposals (1997) and related to the restructuring of social security funds, proceeded amidst opposition from social insurance doctors and the private health sector.

In the field of *education*, OECD proposals are chiefly job-related, geared towards the effectiveness of training and linked to activation policies. Both the NAPs and the Greek Ministry of Education are pursuing (EU-funded) targets that conform to those proposed by the surveys. Comprehensive educational reforms (2000 and 2001) undertaken by the current administration, involving important changes to secondary and tertiary education, have not elicited OECD assessments.

EXPLICIT REFERENCE TO OECD

OECD studies, and especially the economic surveys, are systematically referred to in the Greek press. Perceived as an external authority, indisputably beyond the boundaries of daily domestic concerns, the surveys are also a source of ideas that have gained acceptance in the socio-political world of advanced-industrial economies. This technical expertise, however, does not always translate into smooth policy-making. In fact, the organisation's 'technical' character might be at best ignored, at worst questioned, whenever it ventures social recommendations that derive strictly from prevailing macro-economic analyses. A glimpse at Greek parliamentary debates which refer to the OECD will help exemplify this phenomenon.

Tables 12.3 and 12.4 provide a fairly self-explanatory quantitative summary of interventions in which the organisation is mentioned.[3] The surveys are at

Table 12.3 The OECD in Greek parliamentary debates (Jan. 1997–Feb. 2002): main political parties' references

	Surveys/studies as source of data	Surveys backing arguments	Mentioned with other IGOs	Negative reference
PASOK	43	44	14	–
New Democracy	41	39	6	–
Communist Party	7	–	7	24
Left Coalition	–	13	4	–
Total	91	96	31	24

The OECD and European welfare states

Table 12.4   The OECD in Greek parliamentary debates (Jan. 1997–Feb. 2002): references to OECD by subject and political party

	PASOK/Cabinet MPs/Total			New Democracy	Communist Party	Left Coalition
Economy	27	15	42	20	5	13
Industry/technology	11	4	15	5	3	–
Public sector/service	6	3	9	9	4	3
Environment	3	1	4	1	–	–
Employment/labour	2	3	5	3	1	–
Education	10	4	14	24	9	7
Social security	–	–	–	3	3	–
Health	2	2	4	8	1	3
Social services	–	–	–	–	–	3
Budget & other	–	–	16	13	4	2
Total			109	86	30	31

points 'appropriated', by government and opposition alike, to back a variety of arguments. Although it is not possible to ascertain in all cases whether references made pertain to the economic surveys or to other OECD studies, it is clear that the great majority refer to the surveys. Expectedly, data and recommendations regarding the state of the economy figure prominently. However, the most surprising result of this brief analysis is that mention of employment and labour market relations is almost insignificant. While 'productivity' figures are referred to in discussions of the economy's overall state, when it comes to un/employment issues or labour questions the OECD seems to lose its aura as a technical authority. Given the subject's prominence in all the surveys analysed, it would be reasonable to assume that Greek parliamentarians and their constituents perceive employment issues as more than just another economic variable. A similar conclusion obtains with regards to references in the context of pension reform. The social policy area with the highest number of entries is education, a prominence probably linked to the magnitude of reforms rather than to their (scant) treatment in the surveys. In sum, it is clear that the OECD is not a source of political momentum for reforms. In fact, there seems to exist a certain reluctance to refer to the Organisation's opinions on subjects that are charged with both political meaning and, potentially, political costs. Whether the translation of OECD ideas from purportedly technical assessments to national policy is somehow mediated by European Union politics is an open question.

CONCLUSION

An economic transaction is a solved political problem. Economics has gained the title of queen of the social sciences by choosing solved political problems as its domain. (Abba Lerner, 'The economics & politics of consumer sovereignty', *American Economic Review*, 1972)

In the preceding pages I presented OECD views of Greek social policy and the Organisation's likely effect on the domestic scene. As a source of established ideas and prevailing economic philosophies the OECD seems to have the vantage point of a safe political distance. As was the case in the early years of Europeanisation, in Greece the external parameter is also a point of reference. It can either operate as a mirror-like incentive, a measure of national accomplishment, or as a justification for the implementation of reforms. The country is today however coming to terms with its role as the part of a broader unit, with the building of a common (though as yet undefined) social project. Although the perceived political obstacles to recurrent OECD recommendations might be at times filtered through European Union politics, that unassailable 'social Europe' dimension is not present in the OECD surveys. In this sense, given their exclusively macroeconomic lenses, their proposals in the sphere of the social might be construed as over-ambitious.

NOTES

1. There is a copious literature on the populist character of PASOK under the leadership of Andreas Papandreou. The contributors to the collection edited by Richard Clogg (1993) succeed in presenting the regime's most salient characteristics.
2. The subsequent content analysis is based mainly on the following volumes and summarising sections of the *OECD Economic Surveys* on Greece: 1971, pp. 46–50; 1972, pp. 52–57; 1975, pp. 36–40; 1976, pp. 35–43; 1978, pp. 39–45; 1979, pp. 46–49; 1980, pp. 47–50; 1983, pp. 51–52; 1986, pp. 64–66; 1987, pp. 51–52; 1990, pp. 70–75; 1991, pp. 79–84; 1992, pp. 76–83; 1993, pp. 79–84; 1996, pp. 97–106; 1997, pp. 1–17; 1998, pp. 1–16; 2001, pp. 9–18. For the sake of completeness, subjects that elicited succinct treatment in the concluding/introductory chapters were supplemented by detailed material from the relevant sections of the surveys.
3. All entries with over 3 per cent relevance from parliamentary sessions in which the OECD is mentioned.

REFERENCES

Clogg, Richard (ed.) (1993), *Greece 1981–89: The Populist Decade*, London: Macmillan.
Diamandouros, Nikiforos (1997), 'Greek politics and society in the 1990s', in Graham Allison and Kalipso Nicolaidis (eds), *The Greek Paradox: Promise vs. Performance*, Cambridge, MA: MIT Press, pp. 23–37.
Economist Intelligence Unit (2001) *Country Report: Greece*, July.
European Commission (2001), 'Report on the implementation of the 2000 broad

economic policy guidelines' in *European Economy No 2*, Brussels: European Communities.

Ferrera, Maurizio (1996) 'The "Southern model" of welfare in social Europe', *Journal of European Social Policy* **6** (1), 17–37.

Kravaritou, Yota (1999), 'Greece' in M. Gold and M. Weiss (eds), *Employment and Industrial Relations in Europe, Volume 1, European Foundation for the Improvement of Living and Working Conditions*, The Hague: Kluwer Law International, pp. 87–110.

Matsaganis, Manos (2000), 'Social asistance in southern Europe: the case of Greece revisited', *Journal of European Social Policy* **10** (1), 68–80.

Matsaganis, Manos (2003), 'The suspended reform: the welfare state and modernisation of society' in Dimitrios Venieris and C. Papatheodorou (eds), *Challenges and Prospects for Social Policy in Greece* (in Greek), Athens: Hellenica Grammata.

Ministry of Labour and Social Security (2001), *National Action Plan on Employment: Greece*, Athens: Ministerial Report.

OECD [various years], *OECD Economic Survey, Greece*, Paris: Organisation for Economic Co-operation and Development.

Petmesidou, Maria (1996), 'Social protection in Southern Europe: trends and prospects', *Journal of Area Studies* **9**, 95–125.

Petmesidou, Maria (2000), 'Social protection in Greece in the nineties: reforming the "weak" welfare state', in Achilleas Mitsos and Elias Mossialos (eds), *Contemporary Greece and Europe*, Aldershot: Ashgate, pp. 303–330.

Spanou, Calliopi (1998), 'European integration in administrative terms: a framework for analysis', *Journal of European Public Policy* **5** (3), 467–484.

Symeonidou, Haris (1997), 'Social protection in contemporary Greece', in Martin Rhodes (ed.), *Southern European Welfare States: Identity, Problems and Prospects for Reform*, London and Portland: Frank Cass, pp. 67–86.

Venieris, Dimitrios (1997), 'Dimensions of social policy in Greece', in Martin Rhodes (ed.), *Southern European Welfare States: Identity, Problems and Prospects for Reform*, London and Portland: Frank Cass, pp. 260–269.

13. Italy's adaptation under external pressures: whose influence?

Fabio Bertozzi and Paolo Graziano

INSTITUTIONAL AND POLITICAL CONTEXT

The Italian welfare state has often been depicted as a member of the so-called Southern European welfare model, since its model of social protection shares several characteristics with other Southern European states (Greece, Portugal and Spain) such as a particularistic pattern of benefit distribution and the low institutional capacity of public administration (Ferrera, 1996). Nevertheless, during the 1990s numerous reforms have been implemented and new trends in Italian social policy have begun to emerge: relevant pension reforms have been adopted (1992 and 1995), important health insurance reforms have been implemented (1992–93), and labour market (1997) and social assistance reforms (2000) have been introduced. But what have been the reasons for such reforms? Or, better said, what reasons predominated over others? In fact, both endogenous and exogenous explanatory factors have been identified (Ferrera and Gualmini 2000; Sbragia 2001). In this chapter we shall focus on the external challenges such as OECD guidelines and budget constraints required by the Maastricht Treaty. In fact, due to reforms of the welfare state and cutbacks in public expenditure (which had relevant repercussions on social protections in the Italian welfare state), Italy was able to meet the criteria set in Maastricht and to enter the European Monetary Union in 1998. These reforms had initially seemed very difficult to pass in the Italian political and institutional context. They occurred during a decade in which the economic performance of the Italian economy was not as positive as in the 1960s, when important reforms of the Italian welfare state had been implemented. Nevertheless, the Italian governments of the 1990s, and in particular the Prodi government (1996–98), were able to implement reforms that have limited pension benefits to a certain extent, further decentralised the management of health insurance schemes, and introduced new elements of flexibility to labour market regulation.

OECD RECOMMENDATIONS ON ITALIAN SOCIAL POLICIES

Since the early 1970s, the OECD has highlighted the domestic sources of imbalance in the Italian economy (strengthened by the world recession).[1] The price–wage inflationary spiral, the management of public finance (in particular social security expenditures) and the resulting large budget deficit receive particular criticism (see Table 13.1).

Despite a trend toward recovery in the 1980s, the major disequilibria of the Italian economy continue to worsen: growing unemployment and social expenditure and a widening gap between the south and the north of the country. On the contrary, the 1990s represent a turning point in Italian political economy. Whereas the main economic indicators show worsening performances, Italy performs 'the biggest financial retrenchment in this period among major OECD countries . . . pruning spending in four major areas: public employment, pensions, health care and local authorities' finances' (OECD 1994, p. 101). The OECD welcomes the performance of the Italian government, but at the same time recommends pursuing the reduction of public spending, especially in the field of social transfers, in order to consolidate the progress toward convergence necessary for participation in the EMU. Finally, 'as a result, in May 1998 Italy became one of the eleven founding members of EMU, achieving a primary political objective' (OECD 1998, p. 22).

In the OECD surveys on Italy, not all social policy issues have been considered in the same way. Since the 1980s, constant attention has been paid to employment and pension policy, whereas policy on health and education has been considered only intermittently. Anti-poverty policy has been completely neglected in the surveys.

In the field of *employment*, the decline of the Italian labour market was already pointed out by the surveys in the 1970s. While up to 1976 the OECD still recommended developing public investment and measures aimed at reducing the social costs of recession, since 1977 the main focus has been on labour market rigidities and the risk of a price–wage inflationary spiral. During the 1980s, a similar situation is described: a high and growing unemployment rate among women and young people in particular, persisting north–south labour market disparities, high labour costs and a price–wage inflationary spiral. At this time, the OECD stressed the rigidity of the wage indexation system (sliding scale system). The recommendations during this period were to introduce greater flexibility into the labour market and to adapt labour supply to demand. The further increase in the unemployment rate in the early 1990s led the OECD to formulate new recommendations such as government policies to increase temporary and part-time work and the need for more

Table 13.1 Social policy in OECD reports on Italy

Year	Problems	Criticisms	Recommendations
Employment/Labour market			
1970–76	Growing unemployment and fall in the participation rate		Limit the number of hours worked, public investment and public works projects, provide a guaranteed minimum income
1976–2001	Price wage inflationary spiral and high labour costs	Rigid wage indexation system (sliding scale)	Modify the wage indexation system, reduce labour costs
1979, 1981, 1987–91, 1996, 1999	North/south employment and unemployment cleavage	Inadequate regional wage differentials, insufficient education and training	More market-responsiveness regional wage differentials, decentralise the wage-bargaining system, improve education and training systems
1986–2001	Persistently high structural and long-term unemployment (high proportion of women and young people)	Excessive regulations and rigidities	Greater labour market flexibility, ease barriers to employment, improve labour market-oriented policies (ALMPs, education and training, work organisation)
1999, 2001	Low female participation rate	Insufficient part-time jobs	More flexibility in employment arrangements, increase in part-time work, loosen regulations on job protection
Old age			
1980–89	Rapid increase in the number of persons entitled to pension benefits and growing expenditures	Reform attempts are rarely enacted intact	Need for radical reforms to rationalise expenditure

continued overleaf

Table 13.1 continued

Year	Problems	Criticisms	Recommendations
1991–2000	Generous pension provisions and high expenditures	Early retirement incentives too strong	Tighten eligibility criteria for early retirement, anticipate the elimination of the 'seniority' pensions, increase retirement age and remove disincentives to work after 65, increase the role of private pensions, introduce a fully-funded second pillar to roll back the public system
1995–2000	Very long phasing-in period of the pension reforms	Transition period too long	Shorten phasing-in period, move all workers into a 'pro-rated' system
Health care			
1980–1985	Sharp rise in expenditures	Decentralisation makes expenditure control more difficult	Improve expenditure control and analysis of the financial implications of the planned reforms
1992, 1997	Inefficient health service and long waiting lists	Unexploited opportunities to increase efficiency	Stimulate competition in the medical sector, establish competition between public and private health providers, increase the use of preventive medicine
1992, 1997	Inefficient health administration and distorted means management	Uneven implementation of the reforms across regions	More efforts to guarantee an effective implementation of the reforms all over the country
Education			
1996, 1999, 2001	Deficiencies of the educational system	High dropout rates, compulsory schooling ends at 14, insufficient capacity to provide high-quality technical training	Fast implementation of reforms
1960, 2001	Need to develop well-skilled human capital	Mismatch between high school courses and business requirements	Education and training reforms need to be accelerated

Source: OECD Economic Surveys on Italy from 1970 to 2001 (cf. note 1). The column 'Year' indicates the year of publication of the quoted surveys.

labour market-oriented policies (improving education, training, the public employment service, targeted measures for problem groups and also enhancing the ALMPs).

In the field of *pension* policy, the OECD emphasised in the 1980s the rapid increase in the number of persons entitled to benefits and the existence of inequitable and costly policies. It recommended radical reforms to face these problems. At the beginning of the 1990s, the OECD highlighted the generosity of the Italian pension system in international perspective and its negative consequences on public expenditure. From 1995 to 2000, the surveys welcomed each reform of the pension system that was implemented (the Amato reform in 1992, the Dini reform in 19952 and the Prodi reform in 1997), but stressed the need for further reforms in order to accelerate the stabilisation of pension expenditures. The OECD recommended shortening the transition period to the new scheme, tightening eligibility criteria for early retirement, anticipating the elimination of 'seniority' pensions, moving all workers into a 'pro-rated'[3] system and introducing a fully-funded second pension pillar in order to increase the role of private pensions.

The sharp rise in public expenditures in the area of *health care*, induced by the decentralisation of expenditure management to the regional level, attracted the attention of the OECD in the 1980s. In the 1990s the surveys underlined the inefficiencies within health services and administration while also recognising considerable regional variation. The OECD recommended reinforcing regional financial responsibilities and stimulating efficiency through a stronger competition between public and private health providers.

The OECD highlighted the main deficiencies of the Italian *educational* system only after the mid-1990s. The problems that are emphasised are linked to the need to improve human capital in order to reduce labour market insertion difficulties, i.e. the short period of compulsory schooling (ending at 14), high drop-out rates, insufficient capacity to provide high-quality technical studies, and a mismatch between high school courses and business sector requirements. The reforms and their implementation, according to the OECD, need to be accelerated in this field.

CONCORDANCE AND DISCORDANCE

Italian Public Policy Development and OECD Recommendations

Employment
In the 1970s the OECD suggested that public investment and public works projects be increased, and that the number of hours worked be limited. In fact, much was done by the Italian government during the 1970s in the direction

envisaged by the OECD, but there is no evidence in the literature that the change was induced by external factors (such as the suggestions of the OECD). In fact, the Workers Statute (*Statuto dei Lavoratori*), which was passed in 1970, was not a product of international factors but rather the first achievement of the new convergence between trade unions and pro-labour social movements. Therefore, the policy change was endogenous, not exogenous. The 1970s were years of clear trade union empowerment: Italian union density grew from 33.4 per cent to 44.1 per cent between 1970 and 1980, and the influence of unions was very relevant during the whole decade.

Furthermore, the OECD, in order to prevent the price–wage inflationary spiral, proposed that the government modify the system of wage indexation in order to use more active fiscal policies to cure the low activity problem (see Table 13.2). On the contrary, during the 1970s the wage indexation system, quite favourable to workers, was not reformed. Requests for modification were made only by employers' associations (*Confindustria*) and were not on the agenda of either the government or the trade unions.

The scenario began to change during the 1980s and the early 1990s, when the influence of the trade unions declined following the Fiat defeat in 1980 – when Fiat resisted a strike promoted by the trade unions with the help of over 40 000 employees – and wage indexation reform was implemented in 1984 under the first government led by a socialist (Craxi). Furthermore, during the 1990s deregulation of the labour market – introduced by the 1992–93 and 1997 reforms – took place. Therefore, some of the suggestions stemming from the OECD proposals were translated into law. There is not much evidence that during the 1980s the OECD or other international organisations played a role in the formulation of the reforms, whereas during the 1990s some causal links between OECD and European Union suggestions have been proposed by the literature (Ferrera and Gualmini 1999, 2000). In sum, the main reforms of the 1970s (the above-mentioned *Statuto dei Lavoratori*, the vocational training system reform of 1978) were a result of national policy-making where the main actors during the entire decade were the trade unions, whereas those of the 1980s and the 1990s seem to have been influenced by external factors as well. Among the external factors, however, we find EU pressures rather than OECD influence. Currently, growing international constraints and declining power have led trade unions in the 1990s to abandon anti-reform positions and to accept flexibility as necessary to fight high unemployment (Samek Lodovici 2000, p. 274).

Old age

With respect to old age, the OECD began to provide sound advice only during the 1980s. The most pressing suggestion during the 1980s focused on the need for radical reforms to rationalise expenditure in order to prevent inequitable

Table 13.2   Concordance between Italian policy development and OECD recommendations

Recommendations/Criticisms	Concordance
Employment	
1970s	
Measures to support employment rate:	
• Wage indexation system reform	No
1980s	
Measures to reduce territorial disparities and labour cost:	
• Greater labour market flexibility	No
• Territorial wage differentiation	No
• Wage indexation system reform	Yes
1990s	
Measures to fight unemployment:	
• Greater labour market flexibility	Yes
• Territorial wage differentiation	No
• More active policies	Yes
Old age	
1980s	
Measures to reduce expenditures and inequalities:	
• Radical rationalisation of expenditures	No
• Prevent inequitable outcomes (public/private workers)	No
1990s	
Measures to reduce generosity of public and private pension schemes:	
• Implement pension reform more rapidly	No
• Tighten eligibility criteria for early retirement	Yes
• Increase the minimum retirement age	Yes
• Introduce a fully-funded second pillar scheme	Unclear

continued overleaf

Table 13.2 continued

Recommendations/Criticisms	Concordance
Health	
1980s	
Measures to reduce costs:	
• Analysis of financial implications of reform (1978)	No
1990s	
Measures to improve efficiency and reduce territorial disparities:	
• More competition among medical suppliers	Yes
• More co-ordination between levels of government	Yes
Education	
1990s	
Measures to reduce deficiencies in the education system overall:	
• High school and university education reform	Yes
• More vigorous policy action	Unclear
• Development of human capital	Unclear

Note: The policy recommendations stem from the analysis of OECD country surveys (cf. Table 13.1). Details on the assessment are given in the text.

outcomes. In fact, during the decade no substantial reforms were made and, in fact, the pension schemes became even more generous than in the past following the 1969 introduction of the 'seniority' pensions (*pensioni di anzianità*).

In the 1990s, things began to change. In fact, the 1992–93 and 1995 pension reforms followed some of the recommendations suggested by the OECD. A new (and gradually less generous) pension scheme was introduced. It significantly tightened pension eligibility criteria and provided for a gradual realignment of public pension schemes to private ones. Nevertheless, suggestions such as shortening the transition period to the new scheme, moving all workers into a 'pro-rated' system, anticipating the elimination of 'seniority' pensions, increasing the minimum retirement age, removing disincentives to work after 65, introducing a fully-funded second pillar allowing for a rollback of the public system, and increasing the role of private pensions, remained somewhat absent from the reform agenda of the Italian governments.

But what is the specific role of the OECD in the development of pension reform? No specific study has been carried out on this topic, but the secondary literature underlines the relevance of international (i.e. European) influence on the reforms (Cazzola 1995; Antichi and Pizzuti 2000; Ferrera and Gualmini 2000). Nevertheless, trade unions (whose 'old age' affiliates now represent over 45 per cent of total membership) showed strong resistance to radical changes. They were more inclined towards 'fine tuning' adjustments, and therefore pension reform has only been partial and has included only some of the suggestions contained both in OECD recommendation documents and in European Union policy recommendations. Here more empirical research is needed in order to distinguish between two different (if not competing) causal factors.

Health care
As with old-age policies, the OECD did not deliver specific recommendations during the 1970s but began to do so in the 1980s. This was after the 1978 reform – which introduced a universal health care scheme provided by the National Health System (*Servizio Sanitario Nazionale*) – had already been implemented. The reform delegated many powers of implementation to the regions, but both the programming and the financing of health care policies remained national. The reform did not follow OECD guidelines; in fact, the OECD expressed several concerns regarding the reform, particularly the financial implications since the reform was seen as very expensive and unsustainable in the medium and long term.

During the 1990s, important reforms were carried out in the health care policy field; the so-called 'reform of the reform' of 1992–93 introduced competition in the medical sector (between public and private health providers), promoted preventive medicine and addressed some of the difficulties in guaranteeing effective implementation of health care policies across all

Italian regions. These innovations are very much in line with the suggestions advocated by the OECD, but – once again – is there a causal link between OECD recommendations and health care reforms? Not much evidence to this effect is provided, and in fact one of the most accurate studies of health policy in Italy (Maino 2001) demonstrates that there has been external influence but that it came from Europe (although indirectly) rather than from the OECD. Hence, once again it is Europe that has some influence over Italian social policies.

Education

During the 1970s and the 1980s the OECD recommendations did not cover education policy because it was perceived as of secondary importance with respect to other social policies. Nevertheless, in Italy in 1978 a vocational training reform was passed in which control over implementation was transferred to the regions. The reform proved to be inadequate, and in the early 1990s the OECD recognised that the national education system in Italy had to address its deficiencies. The OECD noted that problems such as a high university drop-out rate, insufficient capacity to provide high-quality technical training, and a mismatch between high school courses and business requirements in particular had to be addressed for the Italian welfare state system to function overall. In fact, two very important reforms were made in Italy during the 1990s: the pre-university educational system reform (1999) and the university education reform (1999–2000). Both reforms were (and still are) very contested, and as of yet it is unclear whether they will be fully implemented. In any case, the reforms were driven by the 'Olive Tree' government that sought to reduce the educational disparities between Italy and the other European countries (Ventura 1998; Capano 1998). The OECD policy recommendations were not very influential. Instead, European programmes such as Erasmus and Socrates (and the need for European uniformity in the field of educational policy) have played a major role in bringing about reform.

OECD RECOMMENDATIONS ON SOCIAL POLICY REFORM

At this stage of our research, it is not easy to assess whether and how OECD recommendations may have been included in key national political debates on major social policy reforms. Therefore, what follow are informed impressions. Nevertheless, a systematic analysis of parliamentary debates has been carried out and our first impression has been confirmed by a more analytical study.[4]

Labour market policies have been on the top of the reform agenda of both the Prodi and D'Alema governments. In particular, the 1997 reform on labour market flexibility that went under the name of *pacchetto Treu* – following the name of the Minister of Labour of the time – has introduced several new types of flexible jobs (such as temporary work) and increased short-term work contracts. But the OECD has not been much present in the political debate on labour market reform; instead, Europe and the need to bring Italy in line with European labour standards have first led the debate and then accompanied implementation. In fact, if we take a closer look at the parliamentary debates that led to the adoption of the reform we can easily see that a lot of attention was devoted to European Union constraints (the rationale for the reform being: 'we have to reform our labour market in order to compete with other European states and to not be left behind'). OECD guidelines, on the other hand, were not taken into consideration. In fact, neither one of the political coalitions (centre-right or centre-left) have introduced OECD recommendations into the political debate, whereas both have referred to European Union policies or policies of other European countries. Only the *Rifondazione Comunista* (created by a minority of former Communist Party members) was very critical towards the core issue of the reform: flexibility. In sum, at first glimpse it seems that a European influence has played a stronger role than any other international influence.

With regard to *pension policies*, major pressures came not only from the OECD but also (and perhaps even more vigorously) from the European Commission. Three major reforms were passed during the 1990s (1992, 1993 and 1995) which have changed (although not completely) Italian old-age policies. Nevertheless, the OECD appears to have played a stronger role here than in other policy areas, since it clearly pointed out the policy deficiencies of the Italian system, and Italian experts used OECD databases in order to show how 'bad' the Italian system was and how 'good' others were. Also, the policy measures adopted have been very similar to those suggested by the OECD. Nevertheless, it is quite difficult to distinguish between pressures from EU political discourses and from OECD guidelines. Whatever the predominant source of pressure was, the formulation phase of the reforms has been delayed by the strong opposition put forward by the trade unions. Therefore, although the reforms seem to be in line with OECD (and European) recommendations, their implementation still follows old Italian policy-making patterns, i.e. trade unions – having decided to co-operate with centre-left governments in the 1990s – are still able to block those policy measures that imply too many sacrifices for their constituents. In sum, the role of the OECD in the national political debate on pension reforms is difficult to assess. Whereas OECD recommendations may have influenced the choice in reform orientation, direct pressure for reforms came much more clearly from the EU, especially through the need to comply with the Maastricht criteria in order to participate in the EMU.

Health policy has also recently been reformed by the Italian governments.

More federalism, competitiveness and vigorous cost containment have been the keywords for both government decisions and OECD recommendations. Furthermore, health care policy reform has been very much influenced by the so-called new public management approach, often advocated by international organisations such as the OECD and European institutions such as various Directorate Generals of the Commission. Therefore, there is an indirect impact of international guidelines on Italian health care policy, but once again it seems that the European Union and its quest towards more policy convergence is more relevant in national political debate than is the OECD.

Education policies have undergone relevant reforms as well. Although implementation of educational reforms is not yet completed, it seems that this is the area where international influences have been the strongest. In this respect, a significant component of national political debate has been centred on the internationalisation of careers and the need to upgrade the Italian educational system in order to enhance Italian human capital and its capacity for business innovation. Present in the political discourse has also been the relevance of Europe and the new European labour market where Italy now belongs. Given this, not much space was left for those who did not conform to the OECD and European Union vision in the policy discussions. In this vision, the mismatch between high school courses and business requirements had to be overcome in order to foster a better connection between education (high school and university) and the labour market. However, it is very difficult to assess whether the OECD has played a specific role in the debate given the clear predominance of the European Union.

CONCLUSION

The preliminary results of this study reveal a minimal (if not irrelevant) influence of the OECD on the evolution of the Italian welfare state. In fact, both the politics and the policies of the European Union seem to have been more influential (Ferrera and Gualmini 2000; Sbragia 2001). European pressures (and examples) have been pivotal in the government justifications for labour market reforms in particular. With regard to pension reforms, the need to meet Maastricht criteria has clearly played a central role in the 1990s, at least in terms of adapting the existing system better to the European context. In general, in the Italian case the EU seems to have played a much more determinant role than the OECD in stimulating and orienting reform in all social policy areas under consideration here.

Nevertheless, a more in-depth analysis must be carried out in order to understand and differentiate the role of the EU vis-à-vis other international organisations better, in particular the link between the EU and the OECD.

Indeed, the question that is still unanswered is how influential OECD guidelines have been on the evolution of European policies and ideas. In other words: first, have the OECD and the European Union lined up their 'policy recommendations' due to the existence of one 'international political discourse' based on cost containment and welfare recalibration or retrenchment – as the political discourse on pension reform might suggest? Second, do EU policies have some autonomy from other international policy proposals or are they dependent on the broader neo-liberal ideological frame of 'less public, more private'? Further research and analytical effort is needed, but here we have outlined some of the possible directions for future reflection.

NOTES

1. The subsequent content analysis is based mainly on the following volumes and summarising sections of the *OECD Economic Surveys* on Italy: 1970, pp. 47–53; 1971, p. 41–44; 1972, pp. 54–56; 1975, pp. 43–49; 1976, pp. 36–38; 1977, pp. 39–45; 1979, pp. 61–64; 1980, pp. 52–55; 1981, pp. 45–47; 1982, pp. 51–54; 1984, pp. 49–51; 1985, pp. 50–52; 1986, pp. 59–62; 1987, pp. 58–61; 1989, pp. 88–94; 1990, pp. 82–88; 1991, pp. 94–98; 1992, pp. 98–104; 1994, pp. 100–105; 1995, pp. 102–109; 1996, pp. 118–128; 1997, pp. 1–18; 1998, pp. 9–23; 2000, pp. 9–22.
2. This reform is described as being 'a milestone in Italy's attempts to break the rising trend of pension payments' (OECD 1996, p. 121).
3. Where benefits would be determined according to the length of time workers have spent under each programme.
4. We have chosen to focus on the so-called *pacchetto Treu* (law 196/97), which is one of the central reforms in the field of labour market policies in Italy in the 1990s. We have compared the references to the OECD and to the EU in the parliamentary debate which led to the adoption of this law. Whereas there is no single explicit reference to the OECD in the whole debate, references to EU regulations and recommendations are frequent. This does not exclude any influence of the OECD recommendations, especially in the elaboration of the law by administrative actors. However, it provides some clear indications regarding the role (or lack thereof) played by the OECD recommendations in the actual political debate.

REFERENCES

Antichi, Massimo and Felice Roberto Pizzuti (2000), 'The public pension system in Italy: observations on the recent reforms, methods of control and their application', in Emmanuel Reynaud (ed.), *Social Dialogue and Pension Reform*, Geneva: International Labour Office, pp. 81–96.

Capano, Giliberto (1998), *La politica universitaria*, Bologna: Il Mulino.

Cazzola, Giuliano (1995), *Le nuove pensioni degli italiani*, Bologna: Il Mulino.

Ferrera, Maurizio (1996), 'The "Southern Model" of welfare in social Europe', *Journal of European Social Policy* **6** (1), 17–37.

Ferrera, Maurizio and Elisabetta Gualmini (1999), *Salvati dall'Europa?*, Bologna: Il Mulino.

Ferrera, Maurizio and Elisabetta Gualmini (2000), 'Italy: rescue from without?', in Fritz W. Scharpf and Vivien A. Schwarz (eds), *Welfare and Work in the Open Economy, vol. 2*, Oxford: Oxford University Press, pp. 351–398.

Maino, Franca (2001), *La politica sanitaria*, Bologna: Il Mulino.
OECD [various years], *OECD Economic Survey, Italy*, Paris: Organisation for Economic Co-operation and Development.
Samek Lodovici, Manuela (2000), 'Italy: the long times of consensual re-regulation', in Gøsta Esping-Andersen and Mario Regini (eds), *Why Deregulate Labour Markets?*, Oxford: Oxford University Press, pp. 271–306.
Sbragia, Alberta (2001), 'Italy pays for Europe: political leadership, political choice, and institutional adaptation', in Maria Green Cowles, James Caporaso and Thomas Risse (eds), *Transforming Europe. Europeanization and Domestic Change*, Ithaca, NY and London: Cornell University Press, pp. 79–96.
Ventura, Sofia (1998), *La politica scolastica*, Bologna: Il Mulino.

14. The OECD and the reformulation of Spanish social policy: a combined search for expansion and rationalisation

Santiago Álvarez and Ana M. Guillén

INSTITUTIONAL AND POLITICAL CONTEXT

The Spanish welfare state was created in 1900 with the passing of a law that established employers' liability for labour accidents. In 1906, a National Institute for Social Provision was created with the aim of fostering voluntary insurance among low-income workers. However, little advancement was made until the Second Republic (1931–36), when the introduction of compulsory insurance for health care, retirement pensions and invalidity was proposed. The Civil War broke out before the legal reform could be passed, so that it wasn't until the mid-1940s that compulsory insurance for low-income industrial workers became a reality.

The system expanded throughout the 1960s and early 1970s by incorporating more and more categories of workers. Especially after 1967, when the Basic Law of Social Security (passed in 1963) began to be implemented, the social protection system was broadened significantly, following a conservative model. By 1975, over 80 per cent of the Spanish population had access to public health care. Nonetheless, some aspects of social policy, such as unemployment subsidies, non-contributory benefits and care services remained clearly underdeveloped. Division of gender roles under the authoritarian regime was very strict, so that the breadwinner model was applied to its full extent. The care of children, the elderly and disabled people was placed in the hands of women in the domestic sphere. Thus, female participation in the labour market and the development of public care services was delayed.

Such was the situation when the transition to democracy began in 1975. Furthermore, although a free-market economy had been well established and economic growth rates were spectacular during the 1960s and early 1970s, some aspects of the economy were still problematic. Among them, one could point to the absence of a fully-fledged taxation system and very deeply ingrained labour market rigidities. Spain was an authoritarian regime until 1975 and this circumstance may well have influenced OECD-recommended policies (both economic and social) in the 1970s.

Since 1975, five distinct periods may be ascertained in the evolution of the economic situation. It is important to note that, in the Spanish case, social policy measures have been highly influenced by economic policy recommendations, both from the OECD and from the EU.

The first period took place between 1975 and 1980, during which the protracted growth period of the Spanish economy (initiated in 1959) came to an end and the effects of the oil crises could be discerned. OECD recommendations were in line with the application of Keynesian policies. Expenditure on social policy and the participation of the state in the financing of social protection grew dramatically during this period.

The second period, from 1980 to 1985, was marked by further contributions to the economic crisis (drop in activity, high inflation rates, dramatic growth of unemployment rates). Contrary to the previous period, no crisis-mitigating measures were proposed but rather structural reforms focused on correcting the fundamental disequilibria of the economy. Given this situation, the necessity of rationalising social protection in order to contain the deterioration of public accounts was stressed.

Strong economic expansion took place between 1985 and 1990, leading to high figures for job creation. However, expansion was not used to correct inflation and budgetary imbalances. In this period, the OECD underlined the successes of the Spanish economy but also stated the necessity of deepening the liberalisation of the structural macroeconomic rigidities, and making them more flexible. In the social protection field, the OECD voiced concerns about the continued deterioration of social security accounts after a decade of expanding transfers and services.

Between 1991 and 1995, a significant deterioration of the economic situation took place. Public expenditure control was needed at this time in order to comply with the Treaty of Maastricht conditions for access into the EMU. Such factors explain the failure of the Convergence Programme designed by the Spanish government for the period 1992–96. OECD recommendations followed the line of international compromises to which Spain was signatory, and were thus centred on budgetary adjustment through the reduction of public spending.

Lastly, the period from 1996 to 2001 registered an amelioration of the internal economic situation again, favoured by an international growth trend that allowed Spain access into the EMU and encouraged significant employment creation. However, a zero deficit in public spending and austerity in public social spending continued to be pursued.

OECD RECOMMENDATIONS CONCERNING SPANISH SOCIAL POLICIES

During the quarter of a century analysed here, the OECD economic surveys[1] for Spain have emphasised two basic issues, namely labour market problems and pensions. Other social policy domains such as health care, education, social transfers and the fight against poverty have received less attention (see Table 14.1).

Social Transfers

In the 1970s, emphasis was placed on the lack of equity in public policies and on the need to adopt active policies that would help solve economic problems and reinforce social justice (OECD 1977, p. 38). To this aim, a thorough fiscal reform was seen as inescapable in order to increase public revenues and to distribute fiscal burdens more evenly (OECD 1977, p. 37). In conjunction with these efforts, social transfers were to be increased, with the aim of placing them at the same level as the average for OECD countries and helping diminish the social consequences of the economic adjustment (OECD 1977, p. 37; 1978, p. 45).

By the end of the 1980s, the intense growth of public spending may be ascertained – from 23.4 per cent of GDP in 1973 to 41.1 per cent in 1986. Public social spending followed a similar trend, increasing from 11.6 per cent to 20.4 per cent of GDP in the same period. There was a need to introduce reforms in public management (OECD 1989, p. 59). It was proposed that an analysis of the costs and benefits of different social programmes be carried out (OECD 1989, p. 71).

Labour Market and Employment Policies

The economic crises of the 1970s revealed the problems the Spanish labour market faced in incorporating an active population, problems that had been mitigated thus far by high emigration rates (OECD 1975, p. 37). Measures to reduce the long working days (among the highest in Europe) were proposed (OECD 1976, p. 40), as well as increases to passive unemployment protection, thus far very low, and an extension of unemployment subsidies to young people searching for their first job (OECD 1977, p. 37; 1978, p. 12).

In the 1980s preoccupations were centred on labour market rigidities. The new Labour Charter (*Estatuto de los Trabajadores*), which made industrial relations and wage agreements more flexible, was greeted positively (OECD 1980, p. 48), despite the fact that the measures adopted were considered insufficient, and demands were voiced for new liberalising measures (OECD 1982,

Table 14.1 Social policy in OECD reports on Spain

Year	Problems	Criticisms	Recommendations
Social transfers			
1976–79	Lack of equity in the application of public social policies		Extension of social protection to correct impact of the crises and situate Spain closer to the European average Reform of the fiscal system
1989	Need to introduce advancements in equity and efficiency of public supply		Analysis of costs and benefits of different programmes Control of services and application of stricter criteria in public supply Amelioration of public management
Employment/Labour market			
1975–79	Slow down of economic activity Price/salaries spiral and inflation grows Severe effects of recession on unemployment	Unemployment protection too low	Sectorial employment policies: provision of help to sectors in crisis Active budgetary policy Reduction of working hours Increase of unemployment benefits Extension of unemployment benefits to young people in search of first job
1980–90		Labour market rigidities High wage increases hindering competitiveness and increasing prices	Wage growth contention: salary increases dependent on productivity Liberalisation of labour market Lowering of rigidities in collective bargaining
1991–2001	'Gulf Crisis' increase of costs of economic adjustment Increase in unemployment	Dual labour market: excessive protection of permanent workers and low protection of temporary ones Unemployment protection too high	Measures fostering mobility Reform of unemployment benefits; decreased passive protection; activation measures

Old age

			Private employment agencies
			Search for social pacts with social interlocutors
			Modulation of unemployment benefits according to redundancy payments
1976	Need to introduce public policies to increase social justice		Extension of transfers
1980–86	Deterioration of social security accounts	Employers' contributions too high; negative influence on labour market insertion Inquities among social security regimes High level of fraud	Contention in transfers
1989			Need to correct structural deficiencies in financing Internal reorganisation of the system
1994–2001	Worries about future balance of the system		Need to correct structural deficiencies in financing Internal reorganisation of the system Increase of minimum contributory pension Revision of rights granted to special social security regimes Fostering of private pension funds Toledo Pact provisions on the rationalisation of the pension system valued positively

Health care

1976			Increase of public spending on health care and social services
1986, 1989			Attainment of universal coverage and internal reorganisation of health care system valued positively

continued overleaf

Table 14.1 continued

Year	Problems	Criticisms	Recommendations
1993, 1996, 1998	Increase of health care costs		Introduction of measures aimed at greater efficiency of health care expenditure Cost-control measures in public pharmaceutical spending
	Education		
1976, 1979			Increase of education supply with the aim of curbing unemployment Extension of professional training
1989		Maladjustment between education (especially professional training) and labour supply	Recognition of spectacular advancement in all levels of the education system
1996		Maladjustment beween education and labour supply continued	Limiting the 'academic' orientation of the education system

Source: OECD *Economic Surveys* on Spain from 1975–2001 (cf. note 1). The column 'Year' indicates the year of publication of the quoted surveys.

188

p. 46) as well as for the elimination of the rigidities encountered in collective bargaining. Besides, the OECD insisted on the necessity of adopting wage contention strategies in order to foster employment creation, control inflation and enhance economic competitiveness (OECD 1980, p. 52; 1981, p. 46; 1984, p. 55).

In the 1990s, the dual character of the labour market (i.e. the division between core workers and marginal/informal ones) was highlighted. The existence of strong protection for indefinite contracts yet much lower levels of protection for temporary workers was considered a negative trend (OECD 1991, p. 81). It was also determined that redundancy payments were too high and that they were not justified by the existing high levels of unemployment protection, which, in turn, hindered participation in the labour market by raising the reserve salary under which workers are not willing to join the labour market (OECD 1994, p. 92). It was argued that employment creation during the 1980s was possible thanks to the liberalisation of certain labour market segments and the application of activation policies (OECD 1994, p. 91). The need to insist on activation policies was also put forward.

Pensions

In the 1970s, references to the pension system were scarce and could be summed up by the need to increase the amounts received by beneficiaries (OECD 1976, p. 40). In the 1980s, references to pensions went hand in hand with increased worries about unemployment. Thus, it was stated that an increase in employers' contributions would play a part in raising labour costs (OECD 1980, p. 50).

In 1986, the OECD analysed the deterioration of the financial situation for social security. The problems were provoked by the reorganisation of the system in 1977–79, which led to a significant increase in coverage and in the average amount received in pensions (OECD 1986, pp. 28–30). Structural deficiencies were ascertained, given that despite the fact that social contributions were among the highest in the OECD, the total resources of the system did not surpass the average (OECD 1986, p. 29). This situation was explained by the existence of significant levels of fraud and due to the presence of inequities within the social security schemes. In particular, imbalances existed among the 'general scheme for dependent workers' and other special schemes (the 'agrarian regime' revealed persistent and high deficits). The restrictive reforms introduced to the pension system in the period 1984–86 were valued positively (OECD 1986, pp. 31–32). Such reforms consisted of an increase to the minimum contributory period (from eight to 15 years) and to the number of salaried years used to calculate the amount of the pension (from two to eight years).

In the 1990s, worries about the financial balance of the system were again voiced, and the rationalising measures proposed in the Toledo Pact were welcomed. The Toledo Pact of March 1995 was forged with the cooperation of all political parties with parliamentary representation. Employers' associations and unions also adhered to it. The Pact was derived from the works of a parliamentary commission whose goal was to ensure the future viability of the pension system. Despite all the restrictive proposals included in the Toledo Pact, the OECD insisted on the need to further increase the minimum contribution periods, to revise the rights of special regimes, and to foster private complementary schemes, all in order to avoid a recurrence of budgetary imbalances (OECD 1996, p. 132; 2001, pp. 111–157).

Health Care

As noted above, the general OECD assessment of Spanish social policies in the 1970s underlined the insufficient nature of public efforts at social protection. Health care was no exception, and the OECD recommended a much stronger effort to augment public expenditure on health care services (OECD 1976, p. 40). In the 1980s, the advancements achieved through the universalisation of health care and the reorganisation of health services was acknowledged (OECD 1989, pp. 62–63). Lastly, in the 1990s, emphasis was placed on the increase in health services costs and on the need to attain higher levels of efficiency and to control the growth of public pharmaceutical spending (OECD 1996, pp. 130–131). Efficiency measures and pilot programmes already adopted by autonomous regions (enjoying full responsibility for health care) were in this respect greeted positively (OECD 1998, p. 85), but the OECD surveys insisted on the necessity of carrying out a more systematic reform in order to counterbalance the effects of the impending trend toward population ageing (OECD 1977, pp. 84–87).

Education

The OECD clearly welcomed developments in this policy field, especially regarding the increases in public availability at all levels of the education system and the universalisation of compulsory education (OECD 1989, pp. 65–66). However, the lack of adjustment between workers' skills and the needs of the labour market was also noted. This lack of adjustment led to a situation in which – despite the high rate of unemployment – some jobs remained unfilled because of a scarcity of qualified personnel (OECD 1989, p. 67). In order to alleviate this situation, an extension and amelioration of professional training was recommended (OECD 1979, p. 39). Moreover, the exaggerated 'academic' orientation of the Spanish educational system was criticised (OECD 1996, pp. 96–97).

CONCORDANCE AND DISCORDANCE

Social Transfers

Broadly speaking, it can be argued that Spanish social policy has followed the path of OECD recommendations in this respect. An in-depth reform of the fiscal system was carried out in 1979 in order to make it more progressive and allow the state to tap the necessary resources to broaden social policies. Social transfers were indeed broadened (leading to an increase in the number of beneficiaries) and made more generous from the beginning of the 1980s. Most relevant has been the introduction of non-contributory transfers for the elderly and the disabled; the increasing use of complements to minimum pensions; amelioration of widows' and orphans' pensions; the improvement of paid maternity leave; and the introduction of minimum income programmes (in this case done by the autonomous regions). In parallel, cost–benefit measures, an amelioration of the public management of social programmes, a fight against fraud and abuses, and support for rationalising measures have all been pursued, especially in the 1990s. Therefore, we can conclude that concordance between OECD recommendations and social policy developments has taken place in this policy domain (see Table 14.2).

Employment, Labour Market

Broadly speaking, both unemployment and labour market policies also show a great degree of concordance. Where employment polices are concerned, unemployment benefits were raised both in terms of the amount paid out and the people protected by them, reaching a peak at the end of the 1980s (with 82 per cent of the unemployed receiving benefits). Nonetheless, passive protection for young people in search of their first job has never been included in the Spanish unemployment protection system. The second half of the 1980s also witnessed the most intense investment in and development of activation policies. In the 1990s (1992 reform), however, and in line with OECD recommendations, passive protection was drastically reduced, whereas active labour market policies were continued but did not grow significantly despite OECD insistence on the need to develop them further.

As regards labour market policies, some industrial sectors in crisis did receive backup from the state and statutory working hours were reduced. The process of wage growth contention was achieved by the attainment of several social pacts starting in the late 1970s until the mid-1980s. Also, the first wave of labour market liberalisation took place in 1984–85, allowing for a rise in temporary contracts but leaving the already existing indefinite full-time contracts untouched. From this point on, women and young people became

Table 14.2   Concordance between Spanish policy development and OECD recommendations

Recommendations/Criticisms	Concordance
Social transfers	
1970s	
Measures to correct the lack of equity in the application of public social policies:	
• Extension of social protection	Yes
• Reform of fiscal system	Yes
1989	
Measures to introduce advancements in equity and efficiency of public supply:	
• Analysis of costs and benefits of different programmes	Unclear
• Control of services and application of stricter criteria in public supply	Yes
• Amelioration of public management	Yes
Employment	
1970s	
Measures to support activity and fight unemployment:	
• Help to sectors in crisis	Yes
• Active budgetary policy	Unclear
• Reduction of working hours	Yes
• Increase of unemployment subsidies to young people	No
1980s	
Measures to fight labour market rigidities:	
• Wage growth contention	Yes
• Liberalisation of labour market	Yes
• Lowering of rigidities in collective bargaining	Yes
1990s:	
Measures to fight unemployment	No
• Measures of fostering mobility	Unclear
• Reform of unemployment benefits	

• Private employment agencies	Yes
• Search for social pacts with social interlocutors	Yes
• Modulation of unemployment to redundancy payments	Yes
1970s	
Extensions of transfers	Yes
1980s	
• Contention in transfers	Yes
• Measures to correct structural deficiencies in financing	No (Yes in the 1990s)
• Internal reorganisation of the system	No (Yes in the 1990s)
Old age	
1990	
Measures to guarantee the future balance of the system:	
• Increase of minimum contributory pension	Yes
• Revision of rights granted to special social security regimes	Yes
• Fostering of private pension funds	Yes
Health	
1970s	
Measures to increase public spending on health care and social spending	Yes
1980s, 1990s	
Measures to reduce costs	
• Introduction of measures aimed at increased efficiency of health care expenditure	Yes
• Cost-control measures in public pharmaceutical spending	Yes
Education	
1970s	
• Increase of education supply with the aim of curbing unemployment	Yes
• Extension of professional training	Yes
1980s, 1990s	
Measures to limit the 'academic' orientation of education system	Unclear

Note: The policy recommendations stem from the analysis of OECD country surveys (cf. Table 14.1). Details on the assessment are given in the text.

increasingly dependent on fixed-term contracts, with this type of labour relationship eventually amounting to over one third of all contracts by the end of
the 1980s. Temporary workers' continuous entrances to and exits from the
labour market were the main reason for the tremendous deficit incurred by the
National Institute for Employment at the beginning of the 1990s and the
restrictive reform of unemployment benefits enacted in 1992. The labour
market was made even more flexible in 1992–93 and again in 1996–97, the
latter changes including a reduction of redundancy payments. Moreover, since
the early 1990s, private employment agencies have been allowed to operate.
Social pacts on the reform of the labour market were reached in 1996 and
2001. Thus, general concordance with OECD recommendations may be again
discerned. There is one major exception: although attempts at addressing
labour mobility have been made, little advancement has taken place.

Pension

In line with OECD recommendations, retirement pensions were expanded in
the 1970s, and financing patterns were reformed (through the creation of the
Tesorería de la Seguridad Social and the linkage of social contributions to real
salaries). The reform of the pension system during the 1980s also conformed
with the most prominent guidelines expressed in OECD surveys; in 1985 a
restrictive reform was enacted which enlarged the minimum contributory
period necessary in order to have access to the system (from eight to 15 years),
and incorporated more salaried years into the formula to calculate the initial
pension (eight instead of two). An internal reorganisation of the system took
place, which tended to reduce special regimes. Still, not much attention was
paid to reducing employers' contributions (among the highest in Europe).
Private pension plans and funds have been allowed since 1987 and fostered
through fiscal exemptions. Once again, the 1990s witnessed several rationalisation measures which followed OECD recommendations. In 1994, pensions
were indexed to estimated upcoming inflation instead of adapted automatically to past inflation. The Toledo Pact – reached in 1995 by all political
parties with parliamentary representation and then corroborated by the unions,
employers' associations and the banking sector – set the lines of reform for the
future sustainability of the public pension sector. A new law was passed in
1997, increasing once more the number of salaried years used to calculate
initial pension amounts and ameliorating widows' and orphans' pensions.

Health Care

Health care in Spain followed a pattern of expanded public spending and
coverage during the 1970s, full universalisation of the health care system

during the 1980s, and a search for increased efficiency during the 1990s – policies totally in line with OECD recommendations, even ahead of them. A reform of primary care took place from 1984 onwards. The *Ley General de Sanidad* passed in 1986 established a National Health System by integrating all previously existing public health care networks. In 1989, a decree incorporated all previous beneficiaries of poor relief into the national health system (around 1 per cent of the population). In conjunction with this reform, the system was decentralised to several autonomous regions and was increasingly financed out of state revenues (100 per cent by 1999). Several cost-control and efficiency-seeking measures were incorporated during the 1990s, such as prospective funding, contract agreements, new managerial formulas, and free choice in general and specialist doctors.

Education

The reform of the education system in Spain is also a success story of expanded public provision and improved equity in terms of access. However, one of the repeated recommendations of the OECD – concerning the amelioration of professional training – has rendered little results to date despite several reforms pursued during recent decades.

THE OECD'S RECOMMENDATIONS IN THE PUBLIC DISCOURSE ON MAJOR SOCIAL POLICY REFORMS

As described in the last section, concordance between OECD recommendations and Spanish social policy reforms are the rule, with very few exceptions. Spain seems to be highly receptive to external advice (i.e. to recommendations from international organisations). This is true not only of the OECD but of other international institutions, most prominently the EU. One of the reasons for such behaviour on the part of Spain is that respect and admiration for more economically and/or socially 'advanced' countries and organisations fills the public discourse (government, opposition, interest groups, etc.), and there is a tradition of supporting the declarations of outsiders as more 'fashionable'. In fact, open and explicit disagreement between the Spanish government and the OECD has seldom occurred. However, this does not imply that being receptive is tantamount to actually putting into practice recommendations and/or specific advice.

If we go back to Table 14.2, we can observe that, first, concordance is reached sometimes only several years (or even a decade) after the recommendation has been formulated. In retrospect, it is easy to conclude that in those cases noted in Table 14.2 as 'postponed concordance', the recommendation was only followed when it was desirable/appropriate in domestic (political, electoral, economic) terms even though public authorities were receptive to it at the very time of its formulation.

Second, OECD recommendations sometimes bear a general or generic character. Any move in the general direction may, then, be classified as concordance with the recommendation. Such is the case of some efficiency-seeking measures introduced in the 1990s, in which the OECD recommendation had specified the result but not the precise means to achieve it.

Third, politicians and policy makers can and do use 'external' recommendations in their discourse either to reinforce the desirability of their own reform proposals or in the search for blame-avoidance strategies in case the reforms go against the vested interests or the opinion of the population.

Fourth and last, real political will to implement a recommendation can meet with severe difficulties. For example, given the extremely high levels of unemployment, it was very difficult in financial terms to introduce universal subsidies for young people in search of their first job during the 1980s, as the OECD advised, even if such a move would render electoral benefits. On the contrary, in Spain the search for efficiency in welfare services (especially with regard to health care and education) has been a delicate task. The reason for this is that the population is not ready to easily accept any reductions to the long-wished-for and only recently attained high levels of equity.

NOTE

1. The subsequent content analysis is based mainly on the following volumes and summarising sections of the *OECD Economic Surveys* on Spain: 1975, pp. 33–37; 1976, pp. 37–40; 1977, pp. 35–38; 1978, pp. 43–46; 1979, pp. 37–40; 1980, pp. 48–50; 1982, pp. 44–47; 1984, pp. 53–56; 1986, pp. 70–73; 1988, pp. 74–76; 1989, pp. 90–95; 1990, pp. 77–81; 1992, pp. 77–83; 1993, pp. 87–95; 1994, pp. 93–100; 1996, pp. 127–138; 1998, pp. 1–18; 2000, pp. 11–24; 2001, pp. 11–26.

REFERENCE

OECD [various years], *OECD Economic Survey, Spain*, Paris: Organisation for Economic Co-operation and Development.

15. Mutual admiration? OECD advice to the UK

Nick Manning

INSTITUTIONAL AND POLITICAL CONTEXT

The British welfare state took shape in two bursts of legislation, initially under the liberal government of 1906–11, and then under the post-war labour government between 1946 and 1948. Often characterised as exhibiting the 'Beveridge model', after William Beveridge's famous and at the time best-selling, 1942 report on *Social Insurance and Allied Services*, there were in fact rather mixed models buried within the overall system. The National Health Service (NHS) was central government provided, free at the point of consumption, of a classical 'command and control' type. Income security however was through compulsory national insurance – a mixture of graded contributions and relatively meagre flat rate benefits; while education was explicitly elitist, in which working-class children were channelled into inferior schools, and universities were reserved for a privileged elite. Insurance in the continental style was never a part of the system, which contained a mixture of socialist and elitist elements. In Esping-Andersen's (1990) terms the British case was mixed: education was conservative; health care was social democratic; and income security, while universal in coverage, was paid at very low rates – a kind of mean-spirited social democracy.

Since the 1950s, this mixed system has evolved, but yet again not in a uniform direction. Up until the 1973 oil crisis, state social expenditure grew slowly, and social democratic elements evolved further, particularly the reorganisation of schools into a less elitist system. However, state expenditure was never generous, and with the weak performance of the economy in the 1960s and 1970s, the funding of services for health and income security remained meagre. Nevertheless there was reasonable cross-party agreement on the general shape and size of the British welfare state, summed up in the famous phrase 'butskellism' invented to convey the social policy consensus between two successive conservative and labour politicians, Butler and Gaitskell. After the 1973 crisis however this consensus disappeared, and a deep ideological divide was opened up under the governments of Margaret Thatcher and her successors from 1979–97. Over this period the British welfare state became a battleground. Income security spending was further weakened, and in combination with the erosion of trade union strength and greater wage dispersion, Britain's poverty rate (especially for children) exploded to become one of the highest in Europe. However, health care remained largely state-financed, while the education system continued to reproduce in practice the elitism of the older system, but underneath a formal commitment to mass higher education. In structure and certainly in its effects the British welfare state moved more and more towards the neo-liberal model.

Table 15.1 summarises social policy advice to the UK government between 1975 and 2000. In the 1970s, OECD commentary on the UK economy was characterised by two overriding issues – inflation and slow growth[1]. These problems were of course well recognised in the UK, and had been accelerating since the impact of the oil price rise shock earlier in 1973. One consequence was that unemployment was growing inexorably, reaching 6 per cent by 1977 (OECD 1979, p. 12) and the stress of this combination of economic factors highlighted the well-known tendency of British industrial relations to move towards conflict, with both sides unwilling to compromise. This difficult situation began to erode the strength of the currency, resulting in a dramatic and highly symbolic moment in 1976, when the Chancellor of the Exchequer felt impelled to turn to the IMF for a substantial loan to support the currency. The Labour government sent a 'Letter of intent' to the IMF on 15 December 1976, promising public expenditure cuts, tax rises and a reduction of the Public Expenditure Borrowing Requirement by one third, from 9 per cent of GDP to 6 per cent of GDP. At its worst, inflation peaked at 27 per cent in 1975 (OECD 1979, p. 14), and despite the agreement secured by the government with the unions over wage restraint, 1978/79 heralded an industrial relations breakdown in the public sector resulting in the 'winter of discontent' with the accumulation of uncollected garbage on the streets. Perhaps not surprisingly Margaret Thatcher was elected in 1979 promising a radical programme of economic, industrial and social reform.

The 1980s saw the complete transformation of the relations between the government, industry and the trade unions. It also saw steady changes in social policy and the structure of the British welfare state, although not perhaps as far-reaching as one might have supposed from the rhetoric heard from the government and its advisors at the beginning of the decade. The government set about tackling inflation as a priority through an aggressive deflation of the economy. This was effective. By 1985 inflation had fallen to 4 per cent, and the accompanying growth in unemployment, to 13 per cent, was managed politically by attacking the power of the unions through legislation, and the high-profile defeat of the miners' strike in 1983. This marked a watershed in industrial relations, after which the government felt much freer to pursue the

Table 15.1 Social policy in OECD reports on the UK

Year	Problems	Criticisms	Recommendations
Employment/Labour market			
1977	Inflation and unemployment		Curb trade union power
1979	Slow growth	Poor industrial relations	
1986	Rising unemployment	Labour markets too rigid	Reduce regulation
1989	Long-term unemployment Return of high inflation		Reform housing market
1993	Low productivity	Poor education and skills	Reform education
1996	Poverty/unemployment traps	Benefit traps too sharp	Tax credits
1998		High marginal tax rates	Minimum wage
2000		Inefficient active labour market policies	Increase flexibility of housing market in rented and owned units Reform active labour market policies
Health care			
1994	High administrative costs Long queues	Weak competition Over-centralised Too much bureaucracy	Better evaluation of major reforms More doctors
2000	Poor cancer survival rates	Poor contracts culture for the 'internal market' Too much private practice Too many reforms	Invest in physical infrastructure Stable long-term finances Performance indicators Research on outcomes and waiting times

continued overleaf

Table 15.1 continued

Year	Problems	Criticisms	Recommendations
	Poverty		
1989	Poverty	Benefit tapers too sharp High marginal tax rates	Tax credits Minimum wage
1993	Social exclusion and low skills Child poverty	Low post-school participation rate Poor acquisition of skills by young people	Get welfare claimants into work Education reform Post-education reform
1998 2000	Work rich/poor households (98) Pay inequalities (2000)		
	Education		
1989, 1991	Low skills acquisition	Low post-school participation rate	Active labour market policies
1993, 1994	Poor articulation with labour market		Approve of 'welfare to work'
1996, 1998 2000		Post-school education is poor	Approves 'individual learning accounts'
	Old age		
1994	Little problem		

Source: OECD Economic Surveys on the UK from 1975 to 2000 (cf. note 1). The column 'Year' indicates the year of publication of the quoted surveys.

restructuring of the economy. From the mid-1980s the economy grew steadily, although unemployment remained high, with inflation relatively under control. By the end of the decade, unemployment was seen to be the big issue, with rigidities in the labour market the key cause. The government argued that workers were unwilling to be flexible about the kind of work they were prepared to take on, and that young people were unwilling to take up the kind of practical or industrially oriented training that would make them employable in the future.

The 1990s began with a sharp recession following the runaway, and unsustainable, expansion of the economy that had been allowed to develop in the late 1980s. The OECD's report for 1989 had raised the spectre of a return to the inflation levels of the 1970s. In the event the early 1990s did not suffer in this way. With the recovery from the recession, the key economic issue for the 1990s was the relatively lower productivity of British workers compared with their European, American and Japanese counterparts. This in turn resulted, in the OECD's view, in an unacceptably high rate of unemployment, particularly of the long-term unemployed, overwhelmingly likely to be of workers with a low level of education and skill.

In 1997, the long run of conservative government came to a dramatic end with the election of a labour government with an overwhelming parliamentary majority ('New Labour'). The 1998 OECD report commends the reform programme of the new government, particularly the 'welfare to work' strategy for the labour market. This laid an obligation on young people to take up job-related training after they left school, if they had no job; the Chancellor of the Exchequer, Gordon Brown, observed that staying unemployed was 'not an option'. The report (1998, pp. 9, 70–71) observed that the UK was one of the few countries in Europe to have implemented the OECD jobs strategy. Educational attainment was rising (though still with a way to go), the minimum wage was judged to be sensible, and income benefits through tax credits were applauded. Nevertheless, poverty and inequality were a cause for concern, which was the focus of a long special feature in the report. The 2000 report once again commends the macro-economic situation, and many social reforms and initiatives.

HAS THE OECD MADE AN IMPACT ON UK DOMESTIC POLICIES?

To what extent has the OECD made an impact on UK domestic policies? Table 15.2 lists the policy areas in which the OECD has made recommendations, and our assessment of the alignment between them and UK domestic policies.

Table 15.2 Concordance between UK policy development and OECD recommendations

Recommendations/Criticisms	Concordance
Employment	
Curb trade union power	Yes
Reduce regulation	Yes
Reform housing market	No
Reform education	No
Tax credits	Yes
Minimum work	Yes
Reform active labour market policies	Yes
Health	
Better intelligence about reforms	No
More doctors	Yes
Invest in physical infrastructure	Yes
Stable long-term finances	Yes
Performance indicators	Yes
Research on outcomes and waiting times	Yes
Poverty	
Tax credits	Yes
Minimum wage	Yes
'Welfare to work'	Yes
Education reform	No
Post-education reform	No
Education	
Education reform	No
Post-education reform	No
Active labour market policies	Yes
Approve 'welfare to work'	Yes
Approve 'individual learning accounts'	Yes

Note: The policy recommendations stem from the analysis of OECD country surveys (cf. Table 15.1). Details on the assessment are given in the text. Some items appear in more than one category where the same policy recommendation has been proposed separately to deal with different problems.

Employment (and the Labour Market)

At the time of the 1976 currency crisis, the OECD's advice mirrored that of the IMF: tight monetary and fiscal policies, closer monitoring of pay settlements, higher profit targets for industry, and the focus of North Sea oil revenues on investment rather than consumption. This amounted to a major change in the relations between the state and the trade unions – a development that was in the event to take a highly dramatic turn under the new Thatcher government of the 1980s.

Commentary and advice from the OECD from the middle of the 1980s reflected strong approval over the way the Thatcher government had tackled the major economic problems of inflation and growth, but increasing analysis and concern over the social consequences of this economic policy. The 1986 report had a special section devote to the labour market, the first time such a special focus had been produced. The problem was posed as the rising rate of unemployment, and the cause was encapsulated in the phrase 'labour market rigidities'. The solutions suggested by the OECD special focus were: a less regulated labour market; employment and training schemes; special programmes for the long-term unemployed.

1988 heralded a marked change in the style of OECD advice, with a sustained series of commentaries from this year onwards concerning social policies, partly oriented to the underlying analysis of the British labour market as suffering rigidities, and in parallel a growing concern with the social consequences of the way in which the economic policies of the 1980s had resulted in growing inequality and poverty (see below).

The last three reports have carried extensive analyses of the labour market in the UK, beginning in 1996 with the application of the 1994 *OECD Jobs Study* to the UK, as a special focus. There is commendation for the labour market changes that the Conservative government had introduced since it first came to power in 1979 (1996, p. 112). These included: very low levels of regulation of the labour market; low levels of income benefits; low income replacement rates; and falling unemployment rates.

However, the OECD (1996, p. 82) nevertheless raised four concerns: inefficient use of active labour market policies; inadequate labour force skills and competencies; disincentives to employment from high marginal tax rate and means tests; and widening poverty and inequality. The solution from the OECD's point of view has been a growing concern with the British education system, and the relatively low level of skills of British workers. Seven of the last eight OECD reports have had substantial analysis and commentary on the education system, discussed in more detail below.

In the final report in 2000, while there is acknowledgement that the unemployment rate is low, the analysis touches on a number of factors in relation to the labour market which the OECD argues are as yet insufficiently resolved. They include a continuing concern with the productivity and skills gap between the UK and other OECD economies, high child poverty rates, weak employability and the need for housing benefit reform. All these may yet impact on the labour market, it is argued, in the future and therefore need attention.

Education (and the Labour Market)

The education system, particularly where it interfaces with the labour market, has received sustained attention in recent OECD reports. In the 1980s the initial efforts at loosening up the labour market focused on the trade unions in the UK. Once that aim had been achieved, however, high unemployment rates, especially, long-term rates, were felt to emanate from the poor educational achievements of young people, and the dislocation of education from the requirements of a modern economy. Initially this was seen through such indicators as mathematical skill acquisition. For example, scores in international maths tests for 1990 were: UK, 59; France, 64; Switzerland, 71 (OECD 1994, p. 86).

In the 1989 report attention focused on post-school educational experience, where UK rates of participation were well below those typical elsewhere in the OECD. In 1991, skills training and post-school participation rates were again criticised, and in 1993 and 1994 once again education was seen as under-performing. For example, the percentage of the workforce with vocational education/training in 1988 was: UK, 25 per cent; France, 40 per cent; Germany, 63 per cent.

By 1996, the training of young people in the 16–19 years group was felt to have improved, but still with a long way to go. Reiterated in 1998 and 2000, the reports observe that the skills gap in young people contributes towards the social exclusion that the reports discuss elsewhere, and that while 'individual learning accounts' are useful, they are too small and need targeting. All in all the OECD regards educational achievement as still a very mixed picture.

Poverty/Social Exclusion (and the Consequences of the Labour Market)

At the same time as celebrating the way in which UK governments have followed the OECD strategy for jobs by deregulating the labour market, there has been growing criticism of the poverty and inequality that have accompanied the new flexibility. This was first raised in the 1989 report (p. 100), in terms not of the overall rate of poverty, but the 'poverty trap' created by the interaction of the growing use of means or income tests before benefits could be obtained, combined with low wages at the unskilled end of the labour market. Means tests create very high marginal tax rates, as benefits are withdrawn on receipt of wages by the newly employed. Where those wages are low, then this marginal tax rate can rise to close to 100 per cent, removing almost any incentive to work, and 'trapping' people in poverty. Concern was reiterated in the 1993 report (p. 86) where the same effect was analysed under the notion of an 'unemployment trap'.

However, in the very next report for 1996, which contained a long special report of the OECD jobs strategy as it applied to the UK, the government is commended for the achievements of having low rates of benefit, and low income replacement ratios for benefits. This clearly signals a contradiction in OECD advice, which is only too apparent when the 1998 report returns to the theme of the poverty and inequality created by the 'success' of the UK in managing the most deregulated labour market in Europe. Here the contradiction is fully displayed in that there is a special section devoted to poverty and inequality (pp. 69–128), while at the same time a celebration of the implementation of the OECD jobs strategy (pp. 9, 70–71).

The report observes that the deregulation of the labour market which has reduced unemployment successfully has also resulted in a sharply growing polarity in British society, with the sharpest divide between 'work rich' and 'work poor' households, partly created by the benefit system which creates a particularly strong incentive for partners of unemployed people not to take up paid employment themselves. This inequality is compounded by the growing divide between rates of pay, with the lowest deciles steadily falling behind the growing income levels in the upper deciles. 'New Labour's' plans to deal with this situation by linking benefits to work through the use of American style tax credits, and the introduction of a minimum wage are welcomed cautiously in the 1998 report, written just after the new government was elected.

Two years later, with continued economic growth and ever lower rates of unemployment, there is little for the OECD to criticise in the labour market. Poverty is now referred to particularly in terms of its impact on children. By this time the UK had 'achieved' the highest rates of child poverty in Europe, and the Chancellor, Gordon Brown, made a high profile commitment to eliminate child poverty over the following 15 years – not a particularly onerous time scale. The OECD report (p. 17) suggests that the continuing skills gap amongst young people was reinforcing the social exclusion of poor households and perpetuating the circumstances that led to child poverty.

Health

The OECD reports have traditionally concerned themselves with economic performance, and particularly the contribution of domestic economic policies. Understandable, as far as labour market issues are concerned, the contribution of the education system to the efficiency of labour, and the more complex interaction between the labour market and poverty and inequality, have become the object of regular analysis, criticism and advice. However, the reason for the coverage of health care issues is not immediately obvious. Health activities do not, empirically, have a great impact on the supply or productivity of labour. Most health care expenditure per capita goes on those no longer working. Yet strangely, health is the only social policy to have been blessed with two special focus sections, contained in the 1994 and 2000 reports.

The attraction may have been the attempt by the government to break up the East European style organisation of the National Health Service. This was entirely of the 'command and control' variety, with the government raising the money, regulating the activity and supplying the service, altogether. The great advantage of this system was that, as both monopsony and monopoly, the government could keep costs strictly under control. The spiralling of medical costs has been the major difficulty for European and American health care systems, from which the UK does not suffer. As a result UK health care costs have always been lower as a proportion of GDP than almost any other OECD country. However, this has resulted in a highly charged and acrimonious politicisation of health care services in the UK, with the professions endlessly lobbying the government for more resources, and with some justification, since, while cheap, the delivery of health care services, and the standards of health of the UK population have tended drift down the OECD league tables.

In 1991 the government decided to de-politicise the NHS by radically separating the supply of health care from demand for it through the development of an 'internal' or quasi-market in health care services. The 1994 report reviews the success of this major reorganisation, and rightly observes that if it is to work the contractual arrangements between the different sides of the internal market, suppliers and consumers, need to be efficiently and effectively developed. The evidence such as it was at that time, was not encouraging. Not familiar with a contract-driven environment, most negotiators settled for routine contracts which reproduced existing patterns of referral and consumption. The cost of this administrative process was, however, heavy, and the employment of administrative staff mushroomed – just as it has done for private systems elsewhere in the world.

'New Labour' thus decided in the late 1990s to unravel the internal market, while retaining the purchaser/provider split. The 2000 report observes that the administrative costs of the 1991 reforms were unsustainably high (p. 19), and that queues for health care and in particular cancer survival rates were still poor by OECD country standards. The hoped for competition that the internal market was supposed to generate, thereby raising standards and putting pressure on under-performing units to improve, had not in fact materialised, particularly in primary care. At the top of the system centralisation has increased, and specialists were still benefiting from strong incentives towards private practice which further compromised standards in the national service. In 2000, the OECD observed, managers were suffering from reform fatigue. OECD recommendations included:

- more focused and prioritised reforms;
- more doctors, particularly specialists;
- investment in physical infrastructure;
- stable long-term financial commitments;
- more performance indicators;
- more research on health outcomes and waiting times, which were relatively poor by international standards.

In 2001, a new and arguably the biggest yet reform of the NHS has been undertaken, which places the commissioning responsibility for 75 per cent of health care (in cost terms) at the primary care level. Designed to place the patient's interests at the heart of the service, this has been followed in 2002 with a commitment to raise health care spending to the European average, a remarkable 50 per cent expansion.

Pensions

In contrast to a number of other OECD cases (for example Switzerland), there has been relatively little discussion of pensions, or other problems associated with older people. This area is really only mentioned briefly in the 1994 report, where the comment is made that there is no serious problem with the UK pensions policy. What this means is that the UK demographic future does not hold a particular problem in terms of the growth of the number of older people, and therefore the government will not face a funding crisis. However, the reason for this is that public pensions are very meagre in the UK, and getting worse. But the government has managed the politics of this so that most people, but far from all, now have private occupational pensions. The great unrecognised problem here is that the private financial interests involved have been poorly regulated, with bad pension deals being sold unscrupulously, and the growth of a significant rise in poverty amongst those old people unable to have built up a good contributions record in a private scheme.

EXPLICIT REFERENCES TO THE OECD IN NATIONAL DEBATES

References in national debates to the OECD can be quickly traced from the record of government debates and reports that are publicly available back to 1988 in an electronic form. This is a huge database including all the speeches in both houses of parliament (Lords and Commons) together with all the working ('select') committee discussions, and all the legislation and any special reports prepared in any of these places. The OECD gets mentioned on average about once a day from any of these sources, which might suggest a considerable influence over British affairs. Typically the OECD is used in three distinct ways in these debates. First, and most commonly, it is used as a source of legitimate data with which the UK can be compared with other OECD countries. All politicians across the parties regard this data source as reliable and authoritative, and use it extensively. Second the OECD's various reports are used where they support the government of the day's policies and achievements. Here they are once again taken to be an authoritative judgement. Third, the OECD reports are used in a parallel manner by opposition speakers who wish to look for criticism or shortcomings in the policies and achievements of the incumbent government. However, there is never any suggestion in these references to any direct or indirect moulding of policies to meet the demands of the OECD.

As can be seen from Table 15.2, there is considerable concordance between the recommendations made in the OECD reports, and the social policy developments undertaken by the UK government. However, while the contents of these reports are often quoted in political debate over policy alternatives, it has not been possible to identify a single instance where OECD recommended policies have been influential over the UK domestic debate in any substantial way. More often the converse is the case. The OECD has for the most part made many approving comments about the domestic policies of both the Thatcher government, its successor conservative government in the 1990s, and the new policies of the Labour government from 1997.

There have been vigorous attempts to transform the UK *labour market* over the last 25 years. Many of the policies have been effective in the terms they set themselves, and much of the thrust of these reforms have been approved strongly in successive OECD reports. However, it is not true to say that the OECD reports appear to have had much influence over the domestic policy debates. Rather they have been for the most part applauding the UK government's efforts.

Health policy is a relatively recent area for the OECD to have tackled, and interest was kindled probably by the attempt to set up a quasi, or 'internal', market in health care in the UK in the 1990s. Criticism offered by the OECD was already well rehearsed in the UK, not least by the Labour Party in opposition before it came to power in 1997, and set about 'reforming the health reforms'.

The OECD has been more critical of UK governments in the area of *poverty and social exclusion*. It expressed concerns from the early 1990s that the successful deregulation of the labour market, and the dramatic reversal of high inflation and high unemployment rates, were being bought at too high a cost in terms of inequality, poverty and social exclusion, especially as it impacted on children. 'New Labour' have been expressly committed to dealing with these issues in the last few years, and the OECD has been commending this change strongly.

Education, again, is an area in which the OECD has continually criticised the UK government. Indeed it has been the most frequently discussed area, apart from the normal regular comment on the labour market. While all UK governments have made continual reforms in the education system, these are regarded as having had a very mixed success, and improvements in the skill and participation rates of young people are still poor by OECD averages. Nevertheless even here it has not been clear whether OECD reports or comments have in any way influenced the UK debate on these issues.

Old age has not really been regarded as a problem area by the OECD.

CONCLUSION

The overwhelming impression from this review is the general concordance between UK government policies and the recommendations from the OECD. During the years of the Thatcher governments it seems likely that the UK was helping, along with the USA, to set the OECD agenda. The neo-liberal labour market revolution in the UK in the 1980s was echoed by, rather than led by, the OECD. However, after Thatcher's ousting in the early 1990s, criticisms began to grow: education policy was regularly blamed by the OECD for the low level of UK skills acquisition, and the growth of poverty and social exclusion brought condemnation of a type unseen for any other OECD country. However, since these were concerns already voiced by the opposition parties, there is still no evidence that the OECD was setting the agenda. With the new government in 1997, there has been a further round of policy approval voiced by the OECD – albeit for different policies at this stage, as the government began to get to grips with the consequences of 18 years of liberal policies.

NOTE

1. The subsequent content analysis is based mainly on the following volumes and summarising

sections of the *OECD Economic Surveys* on the UK: 1975, pp. 24–29; 1976, pp. 31–36; 1977, pp. 41–43; 1978, pp. 39–42; 1979, pp. 38–43; 1980, pp. 43–48; 1981, pp. 48–50; 1983, pp. 51–53; 1984, pp. 46–48; 1985, pp. 49–51; 1986, pp. 47–51; 1987, pp. 63–66; 1988, pp. 81–85; 1989, pp. 97–101; 1991, pp. 89–93; 1993, pp. 82–87; 1994, pp. 101–107; 1996, pp. 107–114; 1998, pp. 1–14; 2000, pp. 9–21.

REFERENCES

Beveridge, W. (1942), *Social Insurance and Allied Services*, London: HMSO.
Esping-Andersen, G. (1990), *The Three Worlds of Welfare Capitalism*, Cambridge: Polity Press.
OECD [various years], *OECD Economic Survey, United Kingdom*, Organisation for Economic Co-operation and Development: Paris.

16. Ireland: disinterested commentary, but how effective?

Séamus Ó Cinnéide and Paul Ryan

INSTITUTIONAL AND POLITICAL CONTEXT

Ireland is a small (population 3.9 million) unitary state with a highly centralised administration. Over the past decade it has experienced a dramatic and unexpected economic boom which is at variance with its experience since becoming independent in 1922. Before independence Ireland shared with the rest of the United Kingdom the social policy provisions that provided the foundations of the welfare state in the two islands: a Poor Law system, including limited health services, universal primary education, means-tested old age pensions and a rudimentary social insurance system for low-income workers. The development of the Irish welfare state was delayed and has been slow. The resulting welfare state defies classification (O'Donnell 1999 reviews the vain efforts); for those who insist on 'three worlds' it can be said that Ireland combines some of the features of the 'liberal' and 'corporatist' regimes and accords least with the 'social democratic' regime.

During the 1930s and 1940s various contingency-specific national income-maintenance schemes were added to the British heritage, social insurance schemes for manual workers and other low-paid employees, and means-tested schemes for those not so covered. In 1944 universal Children's Allowances (now Child Benefit) were introduced for families of three or more children, but Ireland had not the resources to emulate the British welfare state innovations of the post-war years. In 1952 the government consolidated social insurance legislation and administration, but retained flat-rate contributions and benefits. However, contributory old-age pensions were only introduced in 1961; it was not until 1974 that the income limit for the insurance of non-manual workers was abolished; social insurance was extended to the self-employed in 1988 and to part-time workers in 1991. Even now only 60 per cent of state pensioners have (flat-rate) *contributory* pensions. Some of them have private/occupational pensions as well, but less than half of all people at work are covered for such pensions. Significant additional supports are available on a universal basis to certain welfare recipients, especially old age pensioners, such as free public travel, free electricity and free telephone rental.

In 1967 free second-level education was introduced, building on a network of mainly church-run secondary schools and public vocational schools. Since the 1960s Ireland has a largely undifferentiated five to six-year second-level education system, with a national curriculum and examinations; it provides a general education, with less emphasis on technical subjects. Most schools are independently managed on a confessional basis, and there is some negative selection to the fewer public schools. University fees for undergraduates were abolished in 1995; nearly 40 per cent of third-level students get maintenance grants.

Eligibility for health services is complex. Since 1991 everyone is entitled to free public hospital and outpatient services, and to free medication above a certain excess limit. One third of the population (means-tested, except for those aged 70 and over) are also entitled to free primary health care, including dentistry and medicines. About 40 per cent of the population have private health insurance cover, which gives them more immediate access to hospital and other specialist services, and a choice of more exclusive care. Long-term residential care in old age is increasingly dominated by private providers, but with substantial public support.

The Irish welfare state has best been described as a 'pay-related' or 'three-tier' welfare state. Old-age pensions exemplify the three tiers: non-contributory means-tested pensions, contributory pensions and private or occupational pensions. The emphasis has been on achieving and reinforcing social solidarity – a feature of the social democratic regime – 'by maintaining a basic level of social citizenship rights on near-universal grounds', but there has been no corresponding commitment to reducing inequality. Those who are better off have an incentive to build on universal provisions from their own resources (O'Connell and Rottman 1992; O'Riain and O'Connell 2000).

The Irish welfare state has departed from the 'liberal regime' in two significant respects. First, for over 30 years, in good times and in bad, there has been an unrelenting commitment to increasing the value of social welfare payments (insurance and assistance; pensions and unemployment support) in real terms in defiance of the crisis of the welfare state. Second, the response to unemployment has emphasised active labour market policies and 'social inclusion', without an emphasis on penalties for 'welfare dependency'.

In attempts to explain the development of the welfare state in Ireland political mobilisation cannot be relied on. Although until recently the country was predominantly and devoutly Catholic there was no specific Catholic political party, and the church was critical of statism. The left was fragmented and never became a powerful political force.

Since the 1960s, when a certain momentum for change was achieved, three things have been important. First, the state itself has played a crucial role in all aspects of economic and social development; it was undoubtedly the driving force in the growth of the welfare state (O'Connell and Rottman 1992). Second, Ireland's membership of the EU since 1973 has influenced policy and in many different ways; for example EU equality legislation has had implications for women's participation in the labour force. Ireland contributed significantly to the EU discussion on poverty and social exclusion, and EU initiatives in these areas have highlighted the issue of poverty in Ireland and have thereby influenced social protection policies. The National Anti-Poverty Strategy in 1997 represented an Irish commitment to mainstreaming the issue of poverty in all aspects of government policy. Conversely, the public finance criteria for admission to the EMU influenced fiscal and budgetary policy.

Third, neo-corporatism, in the form of national agreements on wages and fiscal and social policies, has become an important feature of national planning, especially since 1987. Indeed Irish politicians and many commentators ascribe much of the credit for the Irish economic recovery of the past decade to this system. From the rediscovery of poverty in 1971 it was the trade unions that insisted on social welfare increases as part of national agreements. Alongside the pay moderation a commitment to social inclusion was institutionalised, even before that term had come into use.

Only ten years ago, experts confronted by stagnation, extremely high unemployment, and renewed emigration, were trying to explain why the Irish economy and Irish society had failed (Lee 1989; Mjøset 1992). But in its 1999 *Economic Survey* of Ireland the OECD reported a remarkable turn-around.

The Irish economy has notched up five straight years of stunning economic performance. No other OECD member country has been able to match its outstanding outcomes in a variety of dimensions. Output growth has averaged over 9 per cent per year on a GDP basis in the period 1994–98, bringing GDP per capita in purchasing power parity terms to a higher level than the European Union average.

That growth rate is only now (2002) declining. The unemployment rate has fallen to 4 per cent, the National Debt has been brought under control, and the prospects for the future are good. Analysis suggests that the Irish economic miracle is no flash in the pan, but the cumulative result of well considered and consistent policies over 40 years. Despite the economic success major problems remain, in particular serious and intractable social inequality, in relation to which Ireland compares very badly with its European neighbours (Nolan et al. 2000).

OECD IDEAS CONCERNING IRISH SOCIAL POLICIES

The OECD Economic Surveys on Ireland since 1970 have contained many

Table 16.1 Social policy in OECD reports on Ireland

Year	Problems	Criticisms	Recommendations
Employment/Labour market			
1970	Rise in wages increasing production costs and reducing competitiveness		Reduce consumer spending, re-negotiate the wage settlements
1972	Slow growth, rising unemployment and inflation		Decrease indirect taxation, public expenditure to stimulate investment; increase trial industrial (re)training
1973	Shortage of skilled workforce at various levels in the labour force		Expand training for women; promote light industry, in which Ireland may have a comparative advantage
1981, 1983	Fiscal crisis, sharp increase in unemployment (14% of the labour force)	Faster hourly wage increases than other OECD countries	Impose wage restraint and cut social services; cuts in health and education transfers now 'unavoidable'
1987	Personal taxation rates too high		Decreases rates of personal income tax; reform industrial policy; a residential property tax recommended
1995, 1997	Highest rate of long-term unemployment in OECD area	Little incentive for younger people to take low paid jobs	Abolish national wage agreements; make unemployment benefit conditional on efforts to seek work; rethink active labour market policies that are expensive and inefficient
Health care			
1983	Costs of public services, like health and education, too high		Curtail services; bring in/increase fees for existing services

Year	Issue	Recommendation
1997	Hospital administrations have remained overly bureaucratic	Improve management of hospital budgets and devolve financial authority; rely less on junior doctors.

Education

Year	Issue	Recommendation
1995–1999	Problems of early school leavers	Extend pre-primary education, directing scarce resources to specific areas of neglect; put more emphasis on science and foreign languages
	Structural problems in the Department of Education	Reintroduce university fees; extend school year; recognise the importance of adult learners

Poverty

Year	Issue	Recommendation
1987, 1999	Personal taxes too high	Introduce greater selectivity in social welfare tranfers; consider taxing benefits; abandon minimum wage which has a negative effect on labour supply
	Coverage of social welfare tranfers needs to be assessed	

Old age

Year	Issue	Recommendation
1999	Ageing population likely to become a financial burden in the next decade	Establish a reserve fund financed by a budget contribution of IR£250 million

Housing

Year	Issue	Recommendation
1997	The increase in the price of housing	Tighten the demand for credit, thus lessening the pressure on housing
1999	High housing costs affecting the attractiveness of Ireland to migrant labour	Local authorities should speed up planning procedures and increase housing densities

Source: OECD *Economic Surveys, Ireland* from 1970 to 2000 (cf. note 1). The column 'Year' indicates the year of publication of the quoted surveys.

references to social policy, which are summarised in Table 16.1. They have highlighted problems, registered criticisms and made recommendations.[1]

The majority of OECD references to Irish social policy in the 1970s and 1980s addressed the issue of unemployment and the measures the Irish government could take to alleviate the problem. The unemployment rate increased from under 10 per cent of the labour force in 1981 to almost 17 per cent in 1987. The OECD approach was twofold. Measures had to be taken that would reduce public expenditure and therefore personal taxation. Second, the labour force would have to be retrained to ensure the economy would be flexible enough to diversify into areas in which Ireland might have a comparative advantage, for example light industry (OECD 1972, p. 33; 1973, p. 41; 1978, p. 36). Another theme was the shortage of skilled workers: women should be encouraged back to work, to supplement the skilled labour force. Ireland's policies did respond in line with many of these OECD recommendations but there was no agreement about the extent to which cutbacks could be made in health and education budgets. By the 1980s the OECD saw the fiscal crisis in Ireland as being so grave that pay restraint was no longer sufficient without substantial cuts in public services (OECD 1981, p. 44). However, the government baulked at such a policy because of the political implications.

Fiscal policy was also an OECD concern in the 1980s, on the basis that high personal taxation was a disincentive to work and fuelled emigration. Irish policies responded to this concern and measures were taken to reduce the tax burden. The dramatic changes in the Irish labour market in the period under discussion are illustrated by OECD concern a decade later about the government's failure to facilitate foreign workers entering the state to fill labour shortages, whose difficulties were compounded by the high cost of housing (OECD 1999). Throughout the 1990s the OECD continued to address the high rates of taxation in Ireland, highlighting the discrepancy between personal and corporate rates.

Specific OECD recommendations about health, education and old age did not feature until the reports of the 1990s. Previous references to health (for example in OECD 1983) only addressed the high cost of the services to the exchequer, but the 1990s saw a shift towards an emphasis on the lower health status indicators in Ireland compared to other OECD countries. OECD references to education were critical of Irish policy, especially the neglect of funding directed towards early school leavers and the impact of this on the persistence of long-term unemployment, which was particularly high among this group. After the government had abolished third-level fees in 1995 the OECD suggested that they should reverse this and divert the resources saved towards early school-leavers (OECD 1999, p. 20).

Given the more favourable demographic structure in Ireland, as compared with other developed countries, the issue of old age has not featured extensively in the OECD reports. In the late 1990s the OECD did recommend the establishment of a reserve fund to finance welfare payments over the next 25 years (OECD 1999, p. 23), an idea that was taken up in 1999.

Recently too, the OECD addressed the social consequences of the dramatic economic recovery in the late 1990s. Irish policy on housing was criticised and the government warned of the negative economic consequences. Ineffective planning laws and low housing densities were highlighted as major causes of the crisis.

OECD RECOMMENDATIONS AND POLICY DEVELOPMENT

To what extent were Irish policy developments either in concordance or discordance with OECD recommendations? Table 16.2 summarises the recommendations and our assessment. In tracing Irish responses to OECD recommendations we have relied largely on statements in parliament (Dáil Éireann) by the Minister for Finance and other ministers, and on reviews of economic and social policy by the National Economic and Social Council (NESC). The NESC is a corporatist consultative body representing the government and the social partners. Since its establishment in 1973 it has periodically produced (every three years since 1986) comprehensive and critical surveys of national policy, together with recommendations for further policy developments. The work of other economic and social policy research bodies, notably the Economic and Social Research Institute, feeds into the NESC.

Employment

In the 1970s the OECD proposed tax reforms as the key to reducing unemployment by creating greater incentives to work. These reforms were hampered by the wage demands being made by Irish workers, reducing the competitiveness of the economy. The government concurred with OECD: the Minister for Finance referred to the demands as being 'selfish' but still refused to renegotiate the most recent wage agreement with the social partners as the OECD had recommended (Dáil Éireann 1970, p. 3). Similarly in 1981, when there was a sharp increase in unemployment and the government was faced with recommendations from OECD to cut spending in health and education, not only were there no cuts but social welfare spending actually increased by 25 per cent; the government hoped that £25 million pounds in savings could be achieved instead by a rationalisation of public services. The 1980s are also marked by periods of concordance with the OECD. The Irish government

Table 16.2 Concordance between Irish policy development and OECD recommendations

Recommendations/Criticisms	Concordance
Employment	
Consumer spending should be reduced by the re-negotiation of the wage settlements (70, 78)	No
The skilled labour force needs to be increased by the training of the female labour force (73)	Yes
Tackle the fiscal crisis and large-scale unemployment by having greater wage constraints and cuts in health and education transfers (81, 83)	No
Reduce high rates of personal taxation and initiate further tax reform (87)	Yes
A residential property tax is recommended (93)	No
Broadening the tax base to reduce the disparity between personal and corporate tax rates (93)	Unclear
Need to abolish minimum wage agreements as they affect the supply of low wage labour (95)	No
Need to reduce long-term unemployment and social welfare transfers (95)	Yes
Transfers must be conditional on efforts to seek work (95, 97, 99)	Yes
Labour market training schemes require rationalisation (95, 97, 99)	No
Old age	
Socio-economic consequences of the ageing population need to be addressed by established reserve fund to finance future welfare benefits (99)	Yes
Health	
Services need to be curtailed and fees introduced for existing services to curb the high cost of health services (83)	Yes (partial)
Improvements to be made to the management of hospital budgets (83)	Yes
The reliance on junior doctors needs to be reduced (97)	Yes (partial)
Devolution of authority to the regions (97)	Yes (partial)
Education	
Reducing class sizes on a generalised basis rather than a focus on schools in lower socio-economic areas (95, 99)	No
Extension of pre-primary education is also recommended along with curricular changes with a greater focus on science and language and a possible extension of the school year (95, 99)	Yes (partial)
Encourages a focus on adult learning in response to future demographic change (95, 99)	Yes
Further work needs to be done on the school curriculum including greater emphasis on science and foreign languages. The re-introduction of university fees should be considered. Also adult literacy needs to be tackled (95, 99)	No

Housing

Attempts need to be made to tighten the demand for credit thus lessening the pressure on housing (97, 99, 01)   Yes
Ineffective planning laws need to be reformed with high housing densities introduced (97, 99, 01)   Yes
Tax changes to reduce speculative investment   Yes

Poverty

The introduction of a property tax to redress the balance between personal and corporate taxation (87)   No
Greater selectivity required when granting social welfare transfers (87)   No
The introduction of the minimum wage should be reconsidered given its negative effect on the labour supply (99)   No

Note: The policy recommendations stem from the analysis of *OECD Economic Surveys* (cf. Table 16.1). Details of the assessment are given in the text.

enabled local authorities to introduce new charges for services, and to seek increases for existing services, and pressed ahead with further reform of tax measures that was impacting negatively on the labour market. However Ireland ignored OECD recommendations that a property tax abolished in 1987 be reintroduced.

Education

In the 1990s the OECD proposed that scarce educational resources should be directed towards specific areas of neglect, in particular that schools within lower socio-economic areas with a high percentage of early school leavers should be singled out for extra resources. The OECD identified measures for pre-primary education as a mechanism to reduce the disparities in the life chances of students. Ireland recognised the importance of pre-primary schooling with the publication of a White Paper on *Early Childhood Education* in concordance with the OECD. This concordance is also shown in relation to adult education. The OECD proposed in 1994 that the encouragement of adult learners could offset the reduction in student numbers due to future demographic change. In Ireland *Learning for Life: White Paper on Adult Education* was published in 2000, proposing policy developments very much in line with OECD recommendations.

Health

In the past 20 years there were two main OECD recommendations on health. During the Irish economic crisis of the mid-1980s it was proposed that services be curtailed and fees brought in for existing services. NESC (1986, p. 215) concurred with the recommendation that hospital beds be tightly controlled. There was some cost-cutting, including a reduction in the number of hospital beds, but not in the spirit of the more drastic OECD recommendation. The OECD also proposed improvements to the management of hospital budgets, to reduce reliance on junior doctors, and advocated devolution of authority to the regions (OECD 1997, p. 9). It is again unclear whether Ireland has acted in concordance with the OECD.

Old Age, Poverty and Housing

Ireland does not face the prospect of the negative economic and social effects of an *ageing population* to the same extent as most of its European neighbours. However, the OECD recommendation to establish a reserve fund to finance future welfare benefits was followed (OECD 1999, p. 23). Several measures have been introduced, including the Pensions (Amendment) Bill 2001, with a view to increasing the coverage of occupational and personal pensions from less than 50 per cent to over 70 per cent over the next 30 years.

The OECD recommended reducing spending on education, health and social welfare in the 1980s, but because of very high unemployment the welfare budget continued to be a large burden on the exchequer. The OECD saw *poverty* alleviation measures, like the introduction of the minimum wage, as having a negative effect on labour supply, but, in another instance of discordance, the National Minimum Wage Act became law in 2000 (OECD 1999, p. 22).

There is significant concordance between the OECD recommendations on *housing* and Irish public policy development. Since 1996 the OECD has warned against spiralling housing prices having an adverse effect on maintaining a labour force sufficient to maintain the economy. Tightening the demand for credit, reforming planning laws and increasing housing densities were some of the recommendations put forward. In 1998 the government commissioned reports by a consultant to examine house prices, and several policy changes were brought in to make more land available for housing and to facilitate house purchasers.

Major Social Policy Reforms and Explicit Reference to OECD

Employment

A number of major reforms to Ireland's labour market policies have taken place between 1970 and 2000. These reforms were driven by two factors. The modernisation of the Irish economy in the early 1970s exposed weaknesses in the supply of a skilled labour force. Successive Irish governments introduced new manpower policies to increase industrial training and the supply of skilled labour, and to make industry more adaptable to the changing economic climate. The desirability of encouraging more women into the labour market was identified by the OECD and supported by the NESC (1975, p. 18–20). In the early 1970s there had been incentives to change, an active women's movement and accession to the European Economic Community with the prospect of equality legislation. In 1973 significant changes were made to the income tax relief on a married woman's earnings and legislation was promised to remove statutory prohibitions affecting the employment of married women (Dáil Éireann 1973, p. 21).

The OECD has also been critical of the high rate of personal taxation in Ireland. This has been seen as a disincentive to work and Irish governments have sought to reduce this burden. In 1988 the government introduced measures that reduced the tax rate to the standard 35 per cent rate for 93 000 taxpayers hitherto paying tax at the highest rate of 48 per cent. While there is an obvious acceptance of OECD recommendations in this case, other fiscal measures proposed were not considered. A highly unpopular residential property tax was introduced in 1983 and abolished in 1987 and since then both the OECD and NESC have unsuccessfully called for its reintroduction (OECD 1990, p. 95).

With regard to labour market policy domestic political considerations are usually paramount. The Minister for Industry and Commerce, Desmond O'Malley, responding to questions from opposition deputies criticising the use of industrial development incentives, said 'I do not necessarily accept all of the views put forward by OECD in their recent published Economic Survey as appropriate to a small open economy such as Ireland' (Dáil Éireann, Volume 392-01 November, 1989).[2] Training schemes also came in for OECD criticism, that they were an inadequate means of tackling long-term unemployment, but they proved popular with governments under political pressure to reduce unemployment figures. In 1993, on the basis of OECD research, the NESC had alerted the government to the ineffectiveness of Irish active labour market policies (NESC 1993, pp. 85–89). Despite OECD reservations expressed in 1996, the government expanded schemes like the Vocational Training Opportunities Scheme. The OECD was also critical of the corporatist national wage agreements entered into by successive Irish governments, claiming that they reduced the supply of low wage labour (OECD 1994, p. 103). But the OECD criticisms were ignored and the agreements have since been seen as the cornerstone of industrial peace and economic development.

Education
OECD recommendations have made no great impact on Irish education policy: for example, proposals for giving foreign languages a greater emphasis in the schools have had limited success. The OECD also highlighted that the Irish school year is the shortest in the OECD countries, and recommended that at third level the reintroduction of college fees should be considered. There was no serious debate on policy changes in those two areas, though politicians used OECD reports in discussing other areas of education policy.[3]

Poverty
During the economic crisis of the 1980s, social welfare transfers were targeted as providing possible savings to the exchequer. The OECD suggested greater selectivity when granting welfare transfers (OECD 1987, p. 7), and although the government considered a number of these measures they considered them 'too harsh' to be implemented (Financial Statement, Budget 1987, p. 3). The NESC, while acknowledging that social welfare reform was necessary, dismissed speculation that there was a correlation between generous social welfare payments and induced unemployment (NESC 1986, p. 193). The NESC refers to an OECD (1979) report *The Role of the Public Sector* to support its claim.

Health

The extent of OECD influence on Irish health policy is disputable. The OECD's concern in the 1980s about the cost of the health budget in Ireland was well founded but the NESC could point to the growing costs of health provision across all OECD countries. Between 1960 and 1984 Ireland's health expenditure grew at an annual rate of 7.5 per cent, significantly higher than the OECD average (NESC 1990, p. 294). Both NESC and OECD recommended an overhaul of hospital management structures, and reforms undertaken had a strong domestic rationale.

CONCLUSION

The past 30 years have been years of great change in Ireland. For most of that period Ireland experienced serious problems in relation to economic development and employment. But analysts now conclude that the recent economic boom, and the social policy improvements that have been achieved, are the result of a whole range of positive political and policy decisions over the period which took time to bear fruit. On the face of it the effects of OECD surveillance and reports on Irish policy have been limited. Behind the scenes the discussions between the OECD survey report writers and policy makers at the national level may have allowed OECD ideas to seep into the Irish policy makers' consciousness, but we have not been able to test this. From time to time government ministers and opposition spokespersons refer to OECD recommendations, but usually only in passing or to reinforce a point, rather than as a weighty argument. When Ireland comes in for praise, as in the 1999 report, with its special focus on the origins of the economic boom, politicians and technical experts alike are gratified. OECD reports are certainly not the stuff of political polemics: although scholars, consultants and commentators refer to them they do not feature in the national media to any extent.

In Irish policy making the two more powerful influences than the OECD are the EU at the transnational level and the NESC at the national level. The Economic and Social Research Institute (ESRI), as the main national research agency producing original data, analysis, projections and recommendations must be considered in association with the NESC. The ESRI is essentially a research agency, but because the NESC is a corporatist organisation, linked to the institutional arrangements by which the three-yearly national agreements and policy plans or programmes are negotiated, its influence is direct and powerful. The five programmes since 1987 are evidence of this. As far as external influences are concerned, the EU is on a different plane from the OECD. Its influences are pervasive and operate at many different levels (political, administrative, technical) and through many different modalities (legislative, financial, regulatory, exhortatory). In the Irish case at least, Europeanisation has not been systematically studied and should, therefore, be the subject of another comparative study.

NOTES

1. The subsequent content analysis is based mainly on the following volumes and summarising sections of the *OECD Economic Surveys* on Ireland: 1970, pp. 34–38; 1971, pp. 41–44; 1972, pp. 32–36; 1973, pp. 41–44; 1974, pp. 34–38; 1975, pp. 28–29; 1978, pp. 33–36; 1981, pp. 41–46; 1982, pp. 45–48; 1984, pp. 44–46; 1985, pp. 51–52; 1988, pp. 77–82; 1989, pp. 77–82; 1991, pp. 71–97; 1993, pp. 98–105; 1995, pp. 100–107; 1997, pp. 1–10; 1999, pp. 9–24; 2001, pp. 9–21.
2. The Minister for Finance in a later government, Ruairi Quinn, also qualified the extent to which OECD recommendations should be accepted, stating that 'few countries will agree with everything the OECD might say. But commonsense indicates that we should listen hard to the disinterested commentary of experts (Seanad Éireann, Volume 144, 22 June 1995).
3. In 1996 opposition politicians used an OECD report on European literacy standards as a basis to seek further funding for literacy programmes (Dáil Éireann, Volume 469, 10 October 1996). Similarly arguments ensued over the publication of the OECD report, *Education at a Glance* (OECD 1992), that showed that out of all countries studied only Turkey had larger primary school classes than Ireland (Dáil Éireann, Volume 424, 22 October 1992).

REFERENCES

Dáil Éireann (1970), Volume 245, 22 April 1970, financial statement, budget.
Dáil Éireann (1973), Volume 265, 16 May 1973, financial statement, budget.
Dáil Éireann (1987), Volume 371, 31 March 1987, financial statement, budget.
Dáil Éireann (1992), Volume 424, 22 October 1992.
Lee, Joseph J. (1989), *Ireland: 1912–1985, Politics and Society*, Cambridge: Cambridge University Press.
Mjøset, Lars (1992), *The Irish Economy in Comparative Institutional Perspective*, Dublin: National Economic and Social Council.
NESC (1975), *Economy in 1975 and Prospects for 1976*, report no. 13, Dublin: National Economic and Social Council.
NESC (1986), *A Strategy for Development 1986–1990*, report no. 83, Dublin: National Economic and Social Council.
NESC (1990), *A Strategy for the Nineties: Economic Stability and Structural Change*, report no. 89, Dublin: National Economic and Social Council.
NESC (1993), *A Strategy for Competitiveness, Growth and Employment*, report no. 96, Dublin: National Economic and Social Council.
Nolan, Brian, Philip J. O'Connell and Christopher T. Whelan (eds) (2000), *Bust to Boom? The Irish Experience of Growth and Inequality*, Dublin: Institute of Public Administration.
O'Connell, Philip J. and David B. Rottman (1992), 'The Irish welfare state in comparative perspective', in John H. Goldthorpe and Christopher T. Whelan (eds), *The Development of Industrial Society in Ireland*, Oxford: Oxford University Press, pp. 205–239.
O'Donnell, Anne (1999), 'Comparing welfare states: considering the case of Ireland',

in Gabriel Kiely et al. (eds), *Irish Social Policy in Context*, Dublin: University College Dublin Press, pp. 70–89.

OECD [various years], *OECD Economic Survey, Ireland*, Paris: Organisation for Economic Co-operation and Development.

OECD (1979), *The Role of the Public Sector*, Paris: Organisation for Economic Co-operation and Development.

OECD (1992), *Education at a Glance*, Paris: Organisation for Economic Co-operation and Development.

O'Riain, Seán and Philip J. O'Connell (2000), 'The role of the state in growth and welfare', in Brian J. Nolan, Philip J. O'Connell and Christopher T. Whelan (eds), *Bust to Boom? The Irish Experience of Growth and Inequality*, Dublin: Institute of Public Administration, pp. 310–339.

17. OECD and national welfare state development

Klaus Armingeon

INTRODUCTION

Economic surveys are a key product of the Organisation for Economic Co-operation and Development (OECD) and its secretariat in Paris. The organisation analyses and assesses a wide range of policy areas that have the potential to improve economic performance. It evaluates national experience in the light of international best practice, and provides specific policy recommendations.[1] Economic surveys offer recommendations based on empirical analyses of a country's economy. After focusing on purely economic issues for a long time, in the 1990s the surveys increasingly considered questions of social policy with regard to their economic implications. One of the core tasks of the OECD is to spread 'best practice' information through these and related analyses. The OECD is convinced that national policy makers take into account its recommendations (Sullivan 1997, p. 62): proving the effectiveness of the surveys and their recommendations. A second claim concerns the consistency of its analyses and recommendations across time and for different countries. Since the OECD identifies 'best practices', neither the benchmarks for analysis nor the type of advice given should vary depending on the nation under study or the timeframe – at least in the short term.

If both claims of consistency and efficacy are justified, the OECD is a powerful international organisation. Its recommendations should have far-reaching implications on social and economic policy in fields like employment and unemployment benefits, pensions, health policy, education and the alleviation of poverty. By its own evaluation, the secretariat and its general secretary in Paris adhered to the Keynesian economic paradigm until the mid-1970s. This was replaced by supply-side theories in the 1980s. At the end of the 1990s the notion that economic growth must be a social process was added to this paradigm. Too much austerity, rapid budget cutting and a lack of attention to the needs of ordinary citizens can lead to a violent popular 'back-lash', the new secretary-general argued from1996 onwards (Sullivan 1997, pp. 55, 108). Given its theoretical orientation and its claims of consistency and efficacy, we have to conclude that from the mid-1970s until the end of the 1990s, the OECD exerted a unidirectional effect on national welfare states, supporting the idea of welfare state retrenchment and an increased onus on individuals and families to shoulder greater personal responsibility for their security in times of need. This political stance raised fervent criticism from some quarters of the left, who argued that the OECD represents those international organisations and global forces that destroy national welfare states. In reaction to the demands for the dismantling of job protection legislation and the reduction of unemployment benefits expressed in the Jobs Study (OECD 1994a; OECD 1994b), the OECD's cornerstone analysis of labour market problems, the journal *Le Monde Diplomatique* voiced the fear that thanks to unemployment, the OECD will 'finally be able to conquer the irreducible enemy: the Welfare State' (Sullivan 1997, p. 100).

Is that statement true? Did the OECD really play an important international role in welfare state retrenchment in the 1980s and 1990s by issuing consistent and effective recommendations for all member countries? This was the question our research project set out to answer, resulting in the 14 country studies presented in this volume. There were at least two serious reasons to doubt the double claim of consistency and efficacy. The first reason is the nature of the OECD as an international organisation and its decision-making processes, which rest on consensus between member states (Pagani 2002; Marcussen in this volume). A tenet of the neo-realist approach to international organisations states that under such conditions, national interest will prevail. Either the international organisation will not issue any recommendation or demand that goes beyond a 'lowest common denominator', or it will recommend to national governments what they want to hear. Hence the recommendations will tend to be either trivial or influenced by the interests of the respective national governments.

The claim to efficacy is also doubtful. Even if recommendations are consistent, it is far from clear that national political actors will adhere to the advice. In contrast to the European Union, the OECD cannot issue binding regulations, directives or decisions for the design of national economic and social policy. And it cannot reduce the room for manoeuvring in social policy by indirect effects caused by, for example, the criteria of the Maastricht Treaty or the implications of negative integration in the case of the single market (Leibfried and Pierson 2000). In contrast to the International Labour Organization (ILO), the OECD has no means to put its goals and advice directly on the agenda of national parliaments. The ILO conventions have to be submitted to parliaments, and once they are adopted, they are binding for the country (Senti 2001). However, the parliaments and governments of member states can choose to totally disregard OECD advice. Since national welfare states are firmly rooted in their societies, institutionally secured and backed up by strong political coalitions (Esping-Andersen 1990; Pierson 1994), it is unlikely that criticism and arguments presented by a remote international organisation will cause major change.

In bringing together the findings from the 14 country chapters, I will show that the efficacy of OECD recommendations is low. In contrast, the consistency of the recommendations is very high. I argue that the high consistency is a function of the low efficacy. This does not imply that the OECD has no impact on welfare state development. Rather, I suggest that the way it can influence national social policy decisions is by creating epistemic communities which can guide long-term policy orientations.

CONSISTENCY

Are OECD recommendations consistent across time and national borders? This question can be answered based on the sections on OECD ideas and the standard table 1 presented in the country chapters in this volume. Consistent supply-side OECD recommendations are to cut budgets, eliminate labour market rigidities, strengthen competition, free international trade, rationalise production, exploit all new technologies, refrain from demand management, strengthen the personal responsibility of individuals and families and reduce generous social security benefits. For the field of employment policy, the *OECD Jobs Study* (OECD 1994a; OECD 1994b) provides detailed benchmarks, such as non-inflationary macroeconomic policy; flexibility of working time, wages, and labour costs; employment security provisions enhancing the flexibility of firms; unemployment benefits which set strong incentives for recipients to accept new jobs; an active labour market policy; and the improvement of (vocational) education.

The result of this comparison of recommendations across time and nations is unequivocal. In the early 1970s, the major advice given by the OECD to national policy makers was not supply-side oriented; rather, the general idea was to apply macroeconomic demand management. This changed dramatically after the mid-1970s, when the organisation stopped recommending the active use of fiscal means to fine-tune the business cycle. Since 1980, proposals incompatible with supply-side recipes have vanished from the economic surveys, with the possible exception of introducing a minimum wage to the UK (1989) to alleviate poverty. In addition to suggestions concerning labour market policies and social security benefits, the OECD's general advice regarding health policy has been to allow for more competition. In education policy the principal suggestion is to improve education – particularly vocational training – and to better target higher education towards the labour market. Pension policy recommendations generally consist of a double strategy: increase the average age for retirement and add funded or private pension systems to public pay-as-you-go systems.

Another difference between the periods before and after the mid-1970s concerns the breadth and number of recommendations. Since our project focuses on the OECD's impact on the welfare state in broad terms, we are also interested in advice put forward in the fields of employment, education, health, old age and poverty. The sheer number of recommendations is to a large extent due to the difference in the number of economic surveys, which have been analysed in the years 1970–75 and 1975–2000, respectively. But this does not explain the change in breadth. Until the mid-1980s, when dealing with the welfare state, the OECD was concerned solely with employment issues; by the mid- to late 1980s, health, pension and education policy were included in all country surveys. Poverty is only discussed in the surveys for Ireland and the UK, and then only after the change of government in 1997. In the case of the UK, this might be due to the prominence the new government gave to the question of poverty in its official policy. Hence the OECD could not avoid addressing the issue. The newly added fields of education, old age and health policy are discussed with regard to their direct economic implications. Indirect effects, like the supportive contribution of a functioning welfare state for economic development, are not scrutinised. The same applies to non-economic effects, like the avoidance of poverty and of major social conflicts, or the contribution to the stability of democracy. Hence the welfare state is treated in standard liberal economics terms. It is conceived mainly as a burden for the economy, and this burden is due to non-market institutions and goals.

In addition to the general advice given, country-specific recommendations are added which conform to the standard framework of recommendations. Hence the OECD has a coherent ideational strategy, which resembles the general liberal advice to reduce state intervention in society and the economy and to free markets from public regulations as long as these are not indispensable for the functioning of the economic exchange. In order to systematise these findings, for the period after 1975 I started from a list of recommendations which are compatible with a supply-side approach and which appeared frequently in the surveys.[2] According to this list, the UK and Switzerland received the lowest number of such recommendations (four or five), while Finland, France and Germany lead the list with ten or 11 recommendations. These data should be interpreted cautiously, since results depend on the definition of categories of recommendations and difficult coding decisions by the authors. Having said that, the data support the view that there has been a set of standard recommendations or benchmarks which are applied consistently to most countries.

EFFICACY

Do these recommendations impact on the development of the national welfare state? This has been our second major question. Since we covered a large number of nations and a large time span, we were unable to trace the influence of OECD advice through in-depth qualitative analyses. Rather, we collected indications of a match between recommendations and policy development. Based on these data we are able to reject the hypothesis of a strong and direct impact. For the alternative hypothesis I can present only indirect evidence, though. This hypothesis states that the major impact consists of a change in national policy ideas in the long term. The principal actor behind these new ideas is an epistemic community. This community is influenced by the inter-action of national senior civil servants and researchers at the OECD.

Data on the subject of efficacy come from the country chapters, that is in the tables about concordance, as well as the analysis in the texts. The period under study is the years after the turn to the supply-side theories. It is under the regime of supply-side economics that we expect major restrictions and changes to the welfare state.

At first glance, if only the criterion of concordance is considered, the argument that the OECD lacks a direct and strong impact is not convincing. Judged by the standard list of recommendations (see above and note 2), Finland, France, Germany, Italy, Norway, Spain, Switzerland and the UK all adhered to more than half of the recommendations, while policy changes in Belgium, Netherlands, Denmark, Sweden, Greece and Ireland corresponded to OECD recommendations in 50 per cent or less of the time. Hence there is some support for the OECD's claim that most of its recommendations are followed by member countries that consider OECD policy ideas to be a blueprint for domestic strategies (Sullivan 1997). Some qualifications are in order, though.

If there is concordance this could be due to other supra- or international organisations pursuing similar ideas (cf. Bayne 1998). In particular, the chapters on Belgium, Greece, Italy and Spain point to the impact of the EU, which was felt much more strongly in the national discourse when reforms were in line both with OECD and EU suggestions. In Belgium, the raised retirement age for women is primarily a result of EU rules and in Italy the labour market reform of 1997, which increased flexibility, was similarly motivated by the country's position in the EU.

A second qualification is related to the domestic causes of reforms. For many policy makers, insights gleaned from OECD studies may not be the main reason they opt to make changes to the structure of the pension system. Rather, they are aware of the domestic problems of changing demographic structure and the ensuing difficulties of providing sound financing for pension schemes. They do not need any analytical help from the OECD, and may have reacted simply to a domestic challenge – not to a simultaneous warning from Paris. In our country chapters many examples are given of policy changes which have been under way long before they have been recommended by the OECD. One of the many examples provided is the German health care reform, which passed in parliament before the OECD published the relevant reform proposal in its survey.

Third, some policy changes may result not from new insights but rather from new constellations of domestic political power. If, for example, traditional trade unions in the secondary sector become weaker in terms of membership and political influence, and if the electoral basis of pro-welfare state parties like the social democrats and the Christian democrats is changing from blue-collar working class to white-collar tertiary sector employees, many options which in former times would have been risky in electoral terms now become very feasible, without any real threat to success at the ballot box. Finally, there has been a change in economic paradigms not only at the level of the OECD but also on the national level among politicians and policy advisors in the national administrations (Hall, 1986, 1989, 1993; Jobert 1994). Hence these cases of concordance of OECD policy recommendations and policy changes may not be directly and causally linked.

But even if it were only the OECD's ideas that led to domestic policy change, the extent of this concordance could be overrated due to two reasons. In particular, the chapter on France shows that it takes some time for ideas to be incorporated into policy making. In our country analyses we found a good deal of convergence, but with considerable time lags. There are many restrictions to short-term steering capacity, which the OECD claims it achieves by issuing recommendations at intervals of one year or 18 months. Another reason for a limited impact in case of concordance may be even more severe: we coded for concordance if a policy changed in the direction of the OECD recommendations. In many cases of concordance, changes may have been very small and incremental, falling short of the reform the OECD had in mind, for example the case of policy modifications to Norwegian public and social expenditure, which were much less drastic than proposed, or the flexibilisation of the Spanish labour market. A case in point is the reform of employment protection legislation, considered by the OECD to be clear proof of its effectiveness as an agency of social policy reform. In its job studies and its economic surveys, the OECD has proposed reductions to certain job securities so that employers have more incentives to hire additional employees, even if they cannot guarantee employment for these workers in the long run. In fact, in most countries correspondent reforms have been undertaken. However, this did not lead to a strong convergence. Rather, the relative position of the countries on the scale of employment protection legislation did not change dramatically. Reforms have been path dependent and limited in size.[3]

Table 17.1 *Recommendations which have been disregarded*

Recommendations	BEL	DEN	FIN	FRA	GER	GRE	IRE	ITA	NET	NOR	SPA	SWE	SWI	UK
Introduce greater wage differentials	x	x						x						
Decentralise/deregulate wage setting/flexibility of collective agreed wages	x	x	x		x	x		x	x					
Abolish wage indexation	x					x								
Offer less early retirements	x	x			x	x					x	x		
Encourage a more flexible labour market	x													
Cut back minimum wage				x			x		x					
Scale back social security benefits/duration of benefits										x		x		
Reduce government spending						x								
Tax the self-employed sector						x								
Renegotiate wage settlements for reducing consumer spending							x							
Introduce premiums/limits to overtime in respective collective agreements						x								
Tackle fiscal crisis and unemployment by having greater wage constraint and cuts to health and education transfers							x							
Introduce residential property taxes							x							
Require rationalisation for labour market training schemes							x							
Introduce wage moderation measures												x		
Put in place measures to reduce expenditures and inequalities								x						

Recommendations	BEL	DEN	FIN	FRA	GER	GRE	IRE	ITA	NET	NOR	SPA	SWE	SWI	UK
Reduce taxes												x		
Reform unemployment insurance/offer shorter duration of benefits												x		
Liberalise employment protection regulation												x		
Introduce various tax reforms													x	
Increase share of foreign labour													x	
Remove obstacles to part-time employment													x	
Raise participation of women and support family policies														
Introduce immediate pension reforms								x						
Introduce better linkages between contributions and benefits in the pension system														
Control social security tax evasion						x								
Increase the standard/effective age of retirement			x			x								
Increase funding rate of pension			x											
Reform the housing market (more labour mobility)														x
Reduce cost of public pension schemes by minimum pension										x				
Introduce estate charges to finance institutional care services			x											
Introduce more competition and market rules in health services				x					x					
Introduce active purchasing of health care					x									
Collect fees for training		x												

continued overleaf

Table 17.1 continued

Recommendations	Criticisms			Recommendations										
Problems	BEL	DEN	FIN	FRA	GER	GRE	IRE	ITA	NET	NOR	SPA	SWE	SWI	UK
Provide students with loans instead of grants		x												
Review structure of student loans and grants												x		
Cut grants available to students		x												
Reduce period during which students receive state support		x												
Offer performance-based financial incentives to vocational training			x											
Introduce a private apprenticeship system			x											
Improve labour qualifications				x										
Introduce fees in higher education					x									
Reduce central state influence in education, enforce stricter rules on promotion						x								
Introduce time limits for obtaining university degrees														
Introduce loans to student, require repayment through tax system													x	
Introduce various reforms to primary and secondary education													x	
Reform the educational system														x

A look at cases of discordance, rather than concordance, gives further insights into the preconditions of the OECD's impact on the national welfare state (cf. tables in the country chapters and Table 17.1). While one can belittle the significance of cases of concordance by assuming that national policy makers may have undertaken these changes regardless of the OECD's influence, discordance indicates resistance from politicians to advice from Paris. In general, discordance can be observed much less often than concordance. If it appears, it is in policy fields where recommendations could alter major domestic political institutions or when they are incompatible with the nation's political culture and the power distribution between political parties and interest groups. In Belgium it has been the corporatist system of labour relations, with its strong trade unions, which has been incompatible with the demands for deregulation, flexibilisation and the abolishment of wage indexation. In Denmark the proposed wage differentiation and the dismantling of generous public tertiary education has been at odds with the Scandinavian consensus regarding equality. In Finland the majority of the political elite has not accepted the increase in the age of retirement, the deregulation of labour relations and the privatisation and increased competition in vocational training. Having a statist tradition, France resisted the proposals for less state influence and more competition in health policy. In Sweden recommendations were only acceptable so long as they did not endanger the large and generous welfare state. In Switzerland, the OECD's demand for more foreign labour was rejected, due to fears of xenophobic reactions and due to patterns of too large a share of poorly qualified workers. These examples support an interpretation of the preconditions for the exertion of influence by international organisations, which starts from the idea of the primacy of central national institutions, power distributions and political cultures. Hence if there is concordance, it occurs in those areas where there is little ideological distance between the OECD and the national tradition (Börzel and Risse 2000). In a systematic manner, we can identify the most frequently occurring instances of discordance.

Decentralisation and flexibilisation of wage bargaining is most frequently opposed in countries with strong or centralised trade unions, a tradition of centralised wage bargaining or a tradition of providing broad coverage for employees through collective agreements (*Flächentarifvertrag*) (e.g. Belgium, Denmark, Germany, Finland, France, Greece, Italy, Netherlands, Sweden).

Retrenchment of policies which reduce inequalities in income or in educational opportunities is opposed in countries where equality is a broadly accepted societal norm (e.g. Denmark, Sweden, Norway).

Wage policies are opposed if they are not in accordance with settlements and procedures of institutionalised and successful co-operation between social partners and the government (e.g. Belgium, Netherlands, Ireland).

The abolishment of restrictive public regulations is opposed, if these regulations are broadly accepted to be one of the state's major tasks, as is the case with the public regulation of the health sector (France) or controlling the inflow of low-skilled foreign labour (Switzerland).

A third criterion for assessing the efficacy of OECD proposals is by studying the number of explicit references to the OECD in major public debates. If the OECD is an autonomous force of change, it should be referred to in these debates. In particular, this is to be expected if a consequential logic of action is assumed (March and Olsen 1998, p. 949). According to this logic, international organisations change relative domestic power positions: those domestic actors whose interests coincide with the proposals of the OECD are strengthened; those who hold different views lose in power. Most country studies included content analyses of major social policy debates. They show that the OECD is not referred to as an authority for a major policy change. Rather, the OECD is mentioned as a source of reliable data and descriptions, and sometimes politicians from both the left and the right use OECD-supported arguments if they fit their needs. This finding does not exclude the possibility that OECD ideas have played an important role in framing the analyses, goals and visions of politicians. However, once it comes to national debates, the OECD is not an authority which can give a policy position additional weight.

In summary, we do not find evidence to support the notion that the OECD produces blueprints for policy change which are then easily applied to a country's national political agenda. Rather, the organisation's impact is contingent and indirect. Policy proposals have a chance of being considered if they do not conflict with the power of major domestic actors (like major political parties and strong trade unions), or with the values and attitudes held by the overwhelming majority of the citizens (like the egalitarian values in Scandinavia). This effect is indirect and hard to distinguish from other influences: the role played by other international and supranational organisations; purely domestic analyses and learning processes; and the changing goals of political parties as they shift to accommodate the changing attitudes of the electorate.

THE TRADE-OFF BETWEEN EFFICACY AND CONSISTENCY

Why are *OECD Economic Surveys* highly consistent across countries and within larger time periods, yet at the same time not very effective? I will argue that low direct efficacy is a precondition of high consistency.

At first glance, our findings could be read as evidence incompatible with neo-realist perceptions of international organisations. In the neo-realist view international organisations reflect the interests of nation-states; hence, by opposing these interests international organisations risk their own existence. The decision-making process concerning the *OECD Economic Surveys* seems to be a worst-case scenario in this respect: by consensus, the representatives of national governments have to accept drafts of economic surveys – which often end up strongly criticising government policies due to the consistent application of common criteria for good economic and social policy. How can government representatives criticise their own governments without being replaced immediately? The answer can be found within the neo-realist framework, which states that criticism can take place as long as the recipient government does not feel hurt by it. Thus, the OECD and its surveys use various means, detailed below, to achieve this requirement of criticising without hurting interests.

First and foremost, the OECD has no severe sanctions at its disposal, except the practice of 'naming and shaming'. This is in stark contrast to the WTO or the EU, which can impose considerable fines if common rules are disobeyed. In addition, 'naming and shaming' works only if there is an audience paying attention to a finger-pointing OECD. This could be the political opposition or the media in member countries. However, the media and the opposition are most receptive to criticisms that are as unequivocal and general as possible.

The OECD does not provide that kind of feedback, and the abstention from devastating and unequivocal criticism and the avoidance of normative statements are another major explanation for the low usability of OECD criticisms for journalists and politicians. In their assessments and recommendations sections, economic surveys list achievements and shortcomings, and sometimes try to give structural reasons for failures.[4] They do not arrive at general and simplistic conclusions – although they do present rankings and unequivocal assessments for specific fields of economic policy making – nor do they challenge the self-perception widely held by a given nation. This explains why the PISA study on educational achievements – with a general and unequivocal ranking and a comparative bent (Allmendinger and Liebfried 2003) – has entered national debates, at least in the countries with lower ranks, while this has not been the case with *OECD Economic Surveys*.

A third reason that OECD discourse remains sheltered from interference by national governments is the organisation's lack of institutionalised access to member states' decision-making procedures. The OECD cannot force governments and parliaments to consider its criticisms or its proposals. This stands in contrast to the ILO. Conventions decided upon by the ILO have to be submitted to national parliaments (Senti 2001). Governments that want to avoid the OECD's shaming process simply have to remain silent about the reports.

A fourth factor in isolating OECD discourse from national political pressure is the lack of operational rules for successfully dealing with criticisms. This concerns time horizons and measurable information on targets, as detailed below. National policy is considered to be concordant with OECD recommendations as long as something – even if it is a very marginal effort – is done in the expected direction. And, in addition, usually no time spans are set within which the policy change should be brought about, even if implicitly there is a clear understanding that certain policies should be done immediately.

For the reasons mentioned, it is clear that *OECD Economic Surveys* can do little to hurt the interests of national governments in a substantial way. Hence, for governments, there is no urgent need to tightly control national representatives working on OECD surveys, or to try to stall processes that might lead to unwanted conclusions in a survey. Despite this, at various points in time governments have tried to persuade their peers to adopt a different tone or offer an alternative prescription (Sullivan 1997, p. 49). Yet the insignificance of the threat posed by economic surveys has allowed national governments to give civil servants working at different ministries much greater leeway to discuss and reach a consensus on the criticisms and prescriptions. A crucial precondition is that these experts share normative and causal beliefs, and notions of validity (Haas 1992, p. 3). There is evidence that the OECD meetings help create and sustain communities that share a common language, techniques and methods of causal reasoning (see Marcussen in this volume). These epistemic communities search for truth and tend to become dysfunctional if their work becomes intertwined with conflicting politics (Ikenberry 1992). In that regard, the lack of efficacy, in the sense of steering policy change, is a crucial precondition for consistency in policy proposals. Otherwise governments have too large an incentive to interfere with the work of the OECD experts.

CONCLUSIONS

The issue at the heart of this book is the consistency and efficacy of proposals put forth in *OECD Economic Surveys* in regard to the topic of welfare state policies. We found a large degree of consistency, although the surveys represent consensus decisions by representatives of governments which have very different leanings in economic and social policy. While consistency is much in evidence, little efficacy was revealed. OECD proposals do not lead directly to far-reaching policy change. The fears expressed in *Le Monde Diplomatique* – that the OECD successfully attacks the welfare state and thereby promotes neo-liberal policy convergence (cf. McBride and Williams 2001, p. 283) are not supported by the data presented in the country chapters. If the economic surveys have an impact, it is in cases where the proposals resonate well with national politics, institutions and broadly held values. Otherwise they are likely to meet strong institutional inertia and political opposition. Hence, the

OECD recommendations are likely to be best received if they are compatible with collectively shared understandings and meaning structures on the national level (Börzel and Risse 2000).

So what? Is the OECD an international organisation without much relevance for national politics? There are good reasons to question such a statement. First, one of the OECD's major products is comparable statistical data for socio-economic variables, which are widely used by national governments, as indicated by the frequency with which political debates refer to OECD data. Second, the OECD delivers ideas, analyses and descriptions, which can frame discussions on national policy developments. Third, the OECD fulfils tasks in many fields of economic and social policy making other than those covered by the economic surveys. Fourth, the OECD works closely together with other inter- and supranational organizations such as the EU. There might be some intermediation or reinforcement: OECD influences the EU, and the EU influences member states. Therefore, it is very hard to argue that the OECD is an organisation with little significance.

However, one still has to ask whether the meetings of the OECD's Economic and Development Review Committee, which produce the surveys, are merely inconsequential seminars of likeminded economists from various national governments who debate desirable policies in Paris and often disregard these findings and recommendations when they later serve their political masters at home? There are reasons to doubt such an assessment. As an epistemic community, the OECD helps to align, sustain and stabilise beliefs in proper economic and social policy. These may seep into member states' national political processes. Often ideas which have been elaborated on in OECD committees may resurge in national policy debates without indication of the original source. We cannot exclude that some of the limited policy concordances depicted in the country chapters are influenced by ideas and proposals published in the economic surveys.

NOTES

1. OECD www.oecd.org; country surveillance, logdate 2003-01-24.
2. These are (1) more active labour market policy; (2) more flexibility of working conditions; (3) more wage flexibility and less (non-wage) labour costs; (4) less employment protection; (5) less generous social security benefits and/or a better targeting of benefits to the needy; (6) less taxes; (7) raised retirement age; (8) introduction of private pensions, and/or a strengthening of occupational and/or funded pensions; (9) cuts to pension benefits; (10) introduction of more competition in health policy; (11) improvements to labour force skills through better (vocational) training.
3. The correlation between the indicator of employment protection legislation in the late 1980s and the one in the late 1990s is 0.95 (OECD 1999, p. 66).
4. Quotes from the 2003 surveys for Finland and Belgium and from the 2002 survey of Germany illustrate this point:

'The pension reform to that will be implemented as from 2005 includes a number of striking features that should enhance the sustainability of the system. . . . While the reform is an important step towards enhancing the sustainability of the system over the coming decades, more could have been achieved in this respect, particularly because some aspects of the reform appear overly generous. (*OECD Economic Survey Finland* 2003, p. 8)

'[Debt reduction] . . . is also necessary for substantially lowering the tax burden, which is one of the highest in the OECD. Taxation of labour incomes is particularly high, with adverse employment consequences for the low skilled. . . . It is to the government's credit that it has continued to make progress on all of these fronts despite a weakening international economy and a complex institutional framework. (*OECD Economic Survey Belgium* 2003, p. 6)

'Insufficient incentives to take up work and hire labour together with a high tax wedge driving up labour costs, in combination with adverse macroeconomic factors, contributed to weak job creation which bears on consumer demand. . . . The German government is committed to addressing these problems; it is putting forward a fiscal consolidation programme and has adopted the findings of a labour market reform commission with many proposals going in the right direction. Nevertheless, more will be needed. (*OECD Economic Survey Germany* 2002, p. 5)

REFERENCES

Allmendinger, Jutta and Stephan Leibfried (2003), 'Education and the welfare state. Germany's poverty and plenty and the many worlds of "competence distribution" in the EC and the OECD', *Journal of European Social Policy* **13** (1), 63–81.

Bayne, Nicholas (1998), 'International economic organizations: more policy making, less autonomy', in Bob Reinalda and Bertjan Verbeek (eds), *Autonomous Policy Making by International Organizations*, London: Routledge, pp. 195–210.

Börzel, Tanja A. and Thomas Risse (2000), 'When Europe hits home: European and domestic change', *European Integration online Papers*, (EIoP) **4**(15), <http://eiop.or.at/eiop/texte/2000-015a.htm>

Esping-Andersen, Gøsta (1990), *The Three Worlds of Welfare Capitalism*, Princeton, NJ: Princeton University Press.

Haas, Peter M. (1992), 'Introduction: epistemic communities and international policy coordination', *International Organization* **46** (1), 1–35.

Hall, Peter A. (1986), *Governing the Economy. The Politics of State Intervention in Britain and France*, New York and Oxford: Oxford University Press.

Hall, Peter A. (ed.) (1989), *The Political Power of Economic Ideas: Keynesianism across Nations*, Princeton, NJ: Princeton University Press.

Hall, Peter A. (1993), 'Policy paradigms, social learning and the state. The case of economic policymaking in Britain', *Comparative Politics* **25** (3), 275–296.

Ikenberry, G. John (1992), 'A world economy restored: expert consensus and the Anglo-American postwar settlement', *International Organization* **46** (1), 289–321.

Jobert, Bruno (ed.) (1994), *Le tournant néo-libéral en Europe*, Paris: L'Harmattan.

Leibfriend, Stephan and Paul Pierson (2000), 'Social policy: left to courts and markets?', in Helen Wallace and William W. Wallace (eds), *Policy-Making in the European Union*, Oxford: Oxford University Press, pp. 267–292.

March, James G. and Johann P. Olsen (1998), 'The institutional dynamics of international political orders', *International Organization* **52** (4), 943–969.

McBride, Stephan and Russell A. Williams (2001), 'Globalization, the restructuring of labour markets and policy convergence: the OECD jobs strategy', *Global Social Policy* **1** (3), 281–309.

OECD (1994a), *The OECD Jobs Study, Evidence and Explanations*, Part I, Paris: Organisation for Economic Co-oporation and Development.

OECD (1994b), *The OECD Jobs Study. Evidence and Explanations*, Part II, Paris: Organisation for Economic Co-operation and Development.

OECD (1999), *Employment Outlook*, June, Paris: Organisation for Economic Co-operation and Development.

OECD [various years], *OECD Economic Survey* [various countries], Paris: Organisation for Economic Co-operation and Development.

Pagani, Fabrizio (2002), *Peer Review: A Tool for Co-operation and Change. An Analysis of an OECD Working Method*, Paris: Organisation for Economic Co-operation and Development.

Pierson, Paul (1994), *Dismantling the Welfare State? Reagan, Thatcher, and the Politics of Retrenchment*, Cambridge: Cambridge University Press.

Senti, Martin (2000), *Internationale Regime und nationale Politik*, Bern: Paul Haupt.

Sullivan, Scott (1997), *From War to Wealth. 50 Years of Innovation*, Paris: Organisation for Economic Co-operation and Development.

Index

Printed and bound by CPI Group (UK) Ltd, Croydon, CR0 4YY

23/04/2025

14661004-0004